MW00825180

Remembering
ATLANTIS

The History of the World
Volume 1

Daniel Condron & Barbara Condron
D.M., D.D., M.S.   D.M., D.D., B.J.

School of Metaphysics
Windyville, Missouri 65783 U.S.A.

by Dr. Daniel Condron
Superconscious Meditation
Permanent Healing
The Universal Language of Mind –
    The Book of Matthew Interpreted
Dreams of the Soul: The Yogi Sutras of Patanjali

by Dr. Barbara Condron
Spiritual Renaissance:
    Elevating Your Consciousness for the Common Good
First Opinion: Wholistic Health Care in the 21st Century
The Work of the Soul
The Dreamer's Dictionary
Kundalini Rising

by both authors
The Bible Interpreted in Dream Symbols
Uncommon Knowledge

© January, 2002
by the School of Metaphysics No. 100173

Cover Design by Barbara Condron
Thanks to Shawn Stoner and Joseph Harpine, cartographer, for illustrative assistance.

ISBN: 0-944386-28-8
Library of Congress Catalogue Number pending

PRINTED IN THE UNITED STATES OF AMERICA

If you desire to learn more about the research and
teachings in this book, write to School of Metaphysics
World Headquarters, Windyville, Missouri 65783.
Or call us at 417-345-8411.
Visit us on the Internet at www.som.org

"Instead of knowledge through evidence,
inference and deduction, this perception brings
direct knowledge and complete meaning to the perceiver.
This perception reveals that which
the conscious mind alone cannot."

Book 1, Sutra 49
Dreams of the Soul – The Yogi Sutras of Patanjali

The Contents

Introduction

I like trees. When I was a child I bought fruit trees and planted them with the help of my father. When I was a teenager I bought pine trees and the planted them. You see, I love this world, our planet. I enjoy improving the soil, so that plants grow better.

I love history. World history was my favorite subject in high school. I wanted to know what had happened on this planet in ancient times before I was born this lifetime.

I love geography also, because I want to know and understand myself, my planet, and the universe we live in.

I studied the theory of continental drift. The man who in 1912 discovered continental drift, German meteorologist Alfred Wegener, was scoffed at and ridiculed by the other scientists of his day. Today, many years and several generations later, we know what he said is true. The continents do drift, or move apart over time and that at one time all the continents were connected together into one supercontinent called Pangea. We know this continent split apart into the several continents we see today. We also know these continents continue to drift apart.

It has been said that when a new truth is introduced into science (and probably everywhere) the old guard – the scientists entrenched in power – never accept a new truth. Rather the old generation has to die off in order for the new idea to be accepted. The new idea is accepted by the new generation.

When I was studying history in high school, it wasn't known what happened to the Etruscans in Northern Italy. The Etruscan civilization was a highly evolved culture before the time of Jesus Christ. Today, we know that the Romans, a less civilized people, destroyed them and wiped out all traces of them from the history books.

When I was in high school history class, we were told that the Aztecs of pre-Colombian Mexico did not have a written language. Today we know they did have a written language, a picture language much like the Chinese symbolic written language or like Egyptian hieroglyphics. It was always there, painted in frescoes on their buildings and included in their sculpture, but the scientists were too closed-minded to see the truth right in front of them. The conquering Spanish made this doubly difficult with their practice of burning the books of the people they conquered.

They had a preconceived bias that American Indians or the indigenous peoples of the Americas were savages or primitive. Therefore they thought, and believed the Aztecs could not read or write. This was not true.

The capital city of the Aztecs on the site of the modern Mexico City was at the time of the Spanish conquest, the greatest city on the face of the planet with canals and boats to move from one part of the city to another. Bridges crossed the canals allowing dwellers to move on foot about the city.

They used the canals to raise fish and plants for human consumption. Therefore, the city itself produced food, unlike modern cities that are completely dependent on the countryside for food.

The city was clean and prosperous unlike the cities of Europe which had no sewers and where refuse was dumped into the streets.

The Mayans also had a written language. They had libraries of books. The Spanish burnt them. The Spanish destroyed anything that was more intelligent, beautiful, or productive than what Spain had because it was different.

Thankfully, we are now living in a more enlightened age where new truths, new ideas and new creations can appear in the world.

Technology has progressed rapidly in the last century. Yet there seems to be a suppression or restriction of new energy sources. How else can you explain the fact that the internal combustion engine is over 100 years old and has still not been replaced with a newer technology. This would be similar to never having had the transistor or computer chips and still trying to operate radios, televisions, and computers with vacuum tubes!

When I was growing up we were taught that possibly Eric the Red and Leif Ericson may have visited North America coming from Scandinavia to Iceland to Greenland to Nova Scotia or Labrador down the east coast of the United States.

Today we know that not only did the Viking accomplish this feat but that they set up colonies, they penetrated into the Great Lakes area where they mined copper. They reached Minnesota and recorded their arrival on the Kensington Stone.

The Vikings went into the Southwest also.

We now know that many peoples came to the Americas before Columbus. English fishermen were fishing the banks of Newfoundland.

Celts from England came to the New World before the time of Christ and Chinese came to the West coast of what is now the United States.

The point is, history is always changing as new truth is brought to light, and accepted. It is not enough that new truth be discovered. It must also be accepted, and not suppressed as have been many of the inventions and discoveries of Nicola Tesla.

This book is written for the purpose of bringing more truth of the history of the planet and the human race to the light of day and to the public's awareness in the hope it will find general and great acceptance as revealing to the world greater truths.

When I was growing up, I was told in high school history class that civilization arose first in Egypt about 2000 to 3000 B.C. It seems like every year, the age of ancient Egypt gets several hundred years older.

Now most Egyptologists think ancient Egyptian civilization goes back to 4000 to 5000 B.C. Yet, author of Serpent in the Sky John Anthony West and Aristian philosopher Swaller de Lubiz, who wrote the three-volume Le Temple de l'Homme, have found – and geologists have confirmed – that there is water erosion on the Sphinx. The last time Egypt had a rainy climate instead of a desert climate was 10,000 B.C. This dates the Sphinx at approximately 10,000 years old, minimum, and possibly much older.

It has also been ascertained that the Sumerian civilization is older than the Egyptian civilization.

In reading this book I believe you will learn much about the Earth's history and about mankind's history. History that has never before seen the light of day or been presented to the world or general public.

I believe this history book helps give a more complete and coherent picture of mankind's evolution as both mental and physical. There was physical evolution and there was directing intelligence.

A human is more than a physical body. A human is more than a brain or a heart or a liver. A human is a soul or mind inhabiting or entrapped in a physical body.

To view humanity as physical only and to assign physical evolution as the primal cause is to miss out on the fact of who we really are. Each of us is an energy being not a matter being. All the ancients knew this. All the ancient schools of wisdom and learning taught this. It was only Western civilization and its physical scientific method, struggling out of the ignorance of the Dark Ages when most if not all of the ancient high technology wisdom and knowledge had been lost that men came to believe in physical evolution only. In ancient times science and religion recognized both mental and physical evolution because they caused both to occur.

When I was in high school history class I was told that the American Indians, who inhabited what is now the United States at the time of the coming of the Europeans, could neither read nor write. Yet it is now known that upon first contact with Europeans many of the Indians and their children sat down and took notes on bark and other materials about these meetings. There is also evidence of Pre-Colombian writing all over the American Southwest.

The truth is, over time history changes. This book is an opportunity for history to change again. This change is mostly about the history that occurred in the ancient times of which our current history books tell us little or nothing. It is an opportunity for all humanity to understand to a greater degree who we are, where we came from, and what our real purpose in life is. This book also presents an opportunity for people to understand their connection with Earth and the universe in ways never before known.

–Daniel R. Condron
May 10,
2001

*"The most beautiful thing we can
experience is the mysterious.
Recognition of the mystery
of the universe is the course
of all true science."*

–Albert Einstein

Foreword

Mankind has sufficiently progressed in his physical sciences to tell us that the human genus has existed for several million years and human cultures for tens and perhaps hundreds of thousands of years. Most history books say it is only within the past 10,000 years that cultures have reflected civilis, Latin meaning "relating to a citizen or a state."

For the most part, our collective concept of civilization has been limited to findings in the physical world. Until now.

A civilization is a culture characterized by the building of cities, the development of a complex social and political structure through stratification, and the evolution of a formal economic structure through the division of labor. Civilization implies the willingness of familial groups to embrace outsiders. Their stories, histories as the Greeks called them, are narratives of past events. This is one of the chief ways we fashion our notion about what came before us, through records of eyewitness accounts. Homer's Iliad, the gospels of the Bible or the Dhammapada, and the autobiographical accounts of countless modern authors (as well as censuses and tax rolls), are among what historians call "materials produced in the period under examination."

Such records are a historian's primary source. We rely heavily upon these stories for insight into who we are and how we have developed as a human race. History is not only a record of civilization, but also civilization's way of reflecting on itself.

When history moves beyond the realm of the physical world, when it enters the realm of quantum science, what it imparts is magnified exponentially. Consciousness is opened to a different kind of memory, always present in humanity, but rarely embraced and only now being developed into a science.

Intuitive investigation and intuitive reporting is this new, meta-physical science.

In the late 1960's and early 1970's people at the School of Metaphysics, in an effort to explore and develop Human spiritual potential, began experimenting with subconsciously-accessed information in response to an inner urge to know. This infancy of self-discovery was often self-centered and sensational, but it was blessed with a transcendent destiny that kept it growing and evolving into a science. Some of the information reported here is from this earlier time period, partly for content and partly in an attempt to give a frame of reference for the timelessness of what has been and continues to be revealed through intuitive research.

Since 1970 records have been kept of Intuitive Reports given for people from all over the world. These transcriptions of intuitive wisdom span three decades and are the world's largest collection of such knowledge. About half of these reports are Health Analyses, examining the mental, emotional, and physical state of health, an intuitive diagnosis as it is referred to nowadays.

Excerpts from intuitive reports given by over a dozen reporters and conductors show the broad scope of intuitively-gained history. These intuitive historians range in age from early twenties to early sixties. They were from many walks of life; from government cartographers to graphic designers to housewives to salesmen. They had wide backgrounds in religion and education. Many never met one another. Yet the information gleaned over 30 years is remarkably consistent in what it reveals. So much so, examples of this are included in this book.

Perhaps the most important truth is intuitive reporting is an alive science. It has continued to evolve and grow beyond its originators. And it continues to grow and evolve in those, like Daniel and I, who have been devoted to this service throughout our adult lives. Through the years, we have received glimpses of the incredible power in this kind of knowledge. Daniel has written books on the nature of evolving consciousness, including my favorite which one newspaper called "the most explicit book on enlightenment as exists today." I've written my own share of books, specifically elucidating relationships, health, and soul progression as revealed in intuitive reports, for the purpose of sharing with others the enormous potential for enlightenment inherent in the Akashic Records, a kind of collective memory in all souls' Subconscious Mind.

We, and a handful of other world servers, have spent decades preparing the public at large for revelations such as these. It is telecommunications - an Atlantean type energy itself - that is playing the biggest role in preparing people. Think about it. Movies and television have made ESP, past lives, and extraterrestrial life a part of our vernacular and our consciousness. We've come a long way since Jules Verne, and box office receipts for every *Star Wars* picture proves it. As a planet we are ready.

For us that meant it was time to begin asking the right questions. Daniel and I prepared ourselves over half a century. This research is something we entered into with high ideals and morality. What we are discovering rivals every theory and deduction made by scientists and explorers throughout history. It verifies and reconfigures existing theories of how humanity came to be.

I feel including some of the Atlantean reports from the 1970's, '80's, and '90's gives you a more complete picture of what has come to light in our research at the School of Metaphysics. I believe they place the work Daniel and I are doing now in context. Our decision to pursue history in this manner is one that has come as a result of decades of learning, practice, and service. It is a natural unfolding of the purpose of the School of Metaphysics rather than a superficial inquiry of some curious mind.

People familiar with School of Metaphysics' intuitive reports will be aware of this more readily than those unfamiliar with the scope of what has been generated through the years. Those familiar with the work of nineteenth century lawyer and politician Ignatius Donnelly or twentieth century prophet Edgar Cayce will find what is given here fascinating. If you are new to all of this, you have just hit upon a treasure trove of mental stimulation and mind expanding revelation that disciplined intuitive exploration provides.

What has come from posing direct questions are some astounding answers. Answers I did not imagine or anticipate. It is only now as we transcribe reports and put them into a readable form that I am beginning to digest what it is, and allow myself glimpses of what it means to us all.

–Barbara Condron

Remembering
ATLANTIS

GENESIS

Christine Andrews, a Doctoral student in School of Metaphysics studies, holds a degree in anthropology. Her presence stimulated me (Barbara) to open my mind which became fairly closed on that subject years ago in college.

The old image of anthropology that I had never bothered to update was of arduous days in the desert sun, sifting through the literal sands of time looking for small pieces of bone or housewares. An amazing but personally unappealing way to spend a life. I must admit I embrace the benefits of such endeavors and are eternally grateful to those who perform the tasks.

I am fascinated by history. Roots. Actually tradition more than roots, since I'm not inclined to research and memorize family trees unless they are Biblical or mythological. I have embraced the importance of knowing where we came from since I was young both in a personal and a more universal sense. When we understand each experience, whether our own or another's, the present is rich and the future filled with promise.

Christine has opened my mind to the delight of the anthropologist who discovers there are ways to access history through intuitive means. For these intuitive anthropologists, repeated practice of concentration replaces the long days; harnessing the will - the hot sun. What a treasure trove for such an enthusiast to stumble upon! Hundreds of records of lives lived on this planet, some in places well documented and some in places we have only begun to explore and accept.

Like Atlantis.

How we remember Atlantis

People have at significant times in man's evolution talked of Atlantis. Around 370 B.C., Plato wrote about this land in two of his dialogues: *Timaeus* and in *Critias*.

In *Timaeus* Plato paints a picture of a prosperous civilization desiring to expand its area of influence: *"Now in this island of Atlantis there was a great and wonderful empire which had rule over the whole island and several others, and over parts of the continent, and, furthermore, the men of Atlantis had subjected the parts of Libya within the columns of Heracles as far as Egypt, and of Europe as far as Tyrrhenia."* Plato believed Atlantis made a grave mistake by trying to conquer Greece. This, combined with earthquakes and floods, sealed the fate of the great island nation.

In the second essay, *Critias*, Plato describes Atlantis as a noble, sophisticated society that reigned in peace for centuries, what our intuitive reports call the Golden Age, until complacency and greed eroded their civilization. He goes on to describe Atlantis as a vast island-continent surrounded by the Atlantic Ocean, west of the Mediterranean.

Greek mythology fills the details of Plato's accounts. The god of the sea, Poseidon, appoints his eldest son Atlas the Titan ruler of the island. The Greek word Atlantis means "island of Atlas," and Atlantic means "ocean of Atlas."

It has been widely believed that Plato's account of Atlantis is a retelling of a tale brought home from Egypt by Solon. The story goes that the Egyptian city of Keftiu, which was destroyed by the seas in an apocalypse, was the home of one of the four pillars that held up the sky. Legend placed Keftiu west of Egypt where current historians often link it to 3000 B.C. Crete and the early Minoan civilization. Before that, it is likely that Minoan culture was developed from Atlantis.

In fact many cultures, as we shall see revealed in intuitive reports published here, were relative to this time and land serving to unify the world in ways until now largely unknown by the public.

Worldwide evidence of the Atlanteans

Accounts of Atlantis exist worldwide. Translations of ancient Aztec and Mayan writings, including the Dresden Codes and the Popul Vuh, reveal histories of the destruction of Atlantis and of Mu, also known as Lemuria, a civilization existing before and at the onset of Atlantis. Phoenician hieroglyphics have been found on numerous ruins in the jungles of South America. These ruins are so ancient that the Indian tribes nearby lost memory of who built them.

Historians as early as the Greek father of history, Herodotus, find Atlantis noteworthy. Herodotus wrote about the island in the Atlantic. Centuries later, Ancient Southeast Asian writings would be translated by James Churchward resulting in several volumes documenting Atlantis and Mu, then geologist William Niven would unearth identical tablets in Mexico.

Still closer to our own time period is Ignatius Donnelly, a U.S. Congressman from Minnesota who introduced Atlantis into our culture with his book Atlantis: The Antediluvian World published in 1882.

In the early 1900's Edgar Cayce, known as the sleeping prophet, gave many accounts of life during the time of Atlantis. Placing it near Bimini in the Bermuda Islands, Cayce reported the cause of Atlantis sinking as fire crystals made by the Atlanteans themselves.

Several decades later descendants of the Incas would lead anthropologist Dr. George Hunt Williamson to an ancient manuscript found in an Andes Mountain temple. The writings tell of an advanced technological society - Atlantis and Mu - destroyed by earthquakes and tidal waves. Williamson also visited dozens of Indian tribes (including the Hopi) in the United Sates and Mexico who told him of Atlantis and Mu.

Many believe there must have been an Atlantis because of the many cultural similarities on either side of the ocean which could not have developed independently. Geologists find evidence of plant life and zoologists find animal life developing and existing on both sides as well, making Atlantis a missing link. This book endeavors to elucidate how such mysteries came to be.

The beginning of Reasoning Man

Intuitive recall including Atlantis more than doubles our knowledge of history. Here is experience spanning far beyond the relics to be found in the upper crust of current-day Earth. Here is knowledge that challenges beliefs in the same way Thales and Copernicus and Einstein have.

Intuitive reporting conducted at the School of Metaphysics over the past three decades has revealed hundreds of experiences during the Atlantean time period, at least as many from ancient Egypt, and several dozen from Lemuria and Mu. This we have learned: Atlantis was a place. Atlantis was a people. Atlantis was a time period.

The Atlantean reports, or readings as they were originally called, were gleaned from over 100,000 reports provided by School of Metaphysics conductor/reporter teams over the past 30 years. As such it is the most extensive source of intuitive reporting existing on the face of the planet.

The most outstanding insight about Atlantis in all these respects was the commencing of a more evolved point in evolution. It is well described in this excerpt from a Past Life Profile *[3237471404]*:

> *Intuitive Reporter: We see male incarnation. We see this entity to be*
> *a part of these who have approached this time with much volition.*
> *We see Atlantean incarnation. We see this one to have been a part of*
> *these at that time period who experienced the frustration with the*
> *mounting confusion in that time period, who experienced a need for*

the understanding, the need for the ability to retrace the origin of Self,
the need for the complete, logical reasoning back to the beginning of
Self. We see great skepticism existing within this one at that point,
and great need for action, for activity.

The Atlantean period spanning most probably a couple hundred thousand years was a time of great creation. Yes, pyramids were brought into being throughout the lands, and crystals were used, but by far the greatest gift of Atlantis was sentience, the Self aware consciousness.

Self awareness physically brought about the upright form of the body, the juxtapositioning of thumb and fingers enabling man to fashion and use tools. Needs for increased storage space for the intricate neuro-electrical pathways being forged by the thinking mind, resulted in an enlarged brain cavity. Esoterically, such developments are referenced in timeless tales of the conflict between good and evil.

The most outstanding characteristic of the Atlantean time period is beyond the accounts of a thriving city where people used crystals and half-human, half-animal creatures roamed. The most outstanding characteristic of Atlantis is a technology called reasoning. The entire Atlantean time period, stretching hundreds of thousands of our currently measured years, produced the mental, emotional, and physical development needed to initiate a new root race.

In 1973, in the context of an individual's Past Life Profile, the following question was asked:

Conductor: Would you explain briefly the number of time periods during the Atlantean time and when approximately the fifth would have been?

*Intuitive Reporter: There were in total seven evolutionary stages within that period of progression referred to as Atlantean. The first three stages were not confined to dense matter. The latter three were progressing into lower and denser matters. We see these periods to have been under the total division of three. We see the first three, the second portion and the third portions closely overlapping one another, with each third superimposed upon the other (see **Figure 1**). It was during these time periods that those developmental stages of evolution were occurring.*

As the ending of that stage of Atlantis came into being – progressing into, what is referred to to some extent as that which has been discovered, historically – that time period which was of vast expanse upon the physical level...was the connecting link into the beginnings of the other periods.

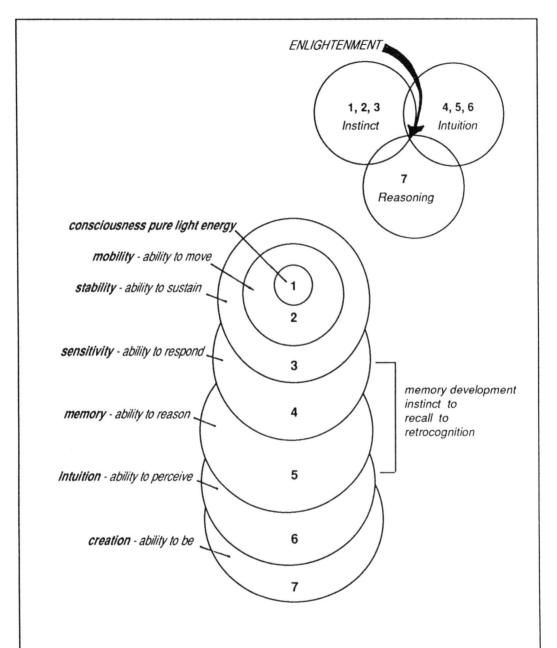

Figure 1. Diagram of Atlantean stages

The seven evolutionary stages are illustrated in picture form. First, the experience of consciousness as pure energy, light, radiates seeking experience to know itself. These are relative to earlier root race experiences of mobility followed by stability followed by sensitivity. These produce a denser form where memory can become a vital part of experiencing reflective of the second portion, and where need will call into play the imaginative faculty in the formation of the third portion. Thus the development of a sentient being in physical form who is capable of high levels of creative reasoning.

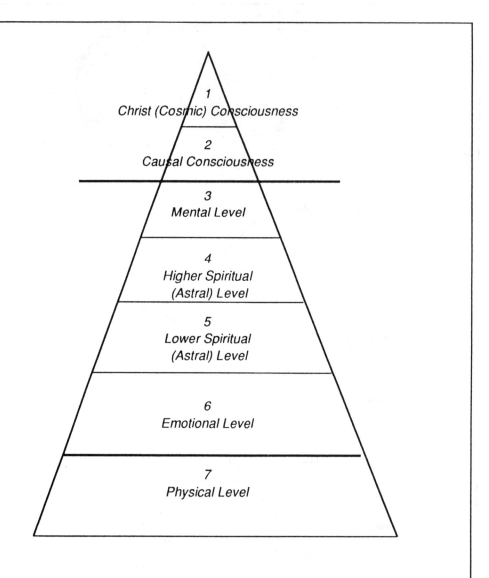

Figure 2. Diagram of Levels of Consciousness

This two-dimensional representation of the structure of mind taught in the School of Metaphysics reflects how energy evolves, expressing itself upon seven distinct planes of existence. It illustrates the development of consciousness occurring throughout the Atlantean time period. These levels of consciousness form the multidimensional thinker currently experiencing the evolvement of a new root race – Intuitive, Spiritual Man. Throughout the Atlantean period the levels of consciousness in Subconscious Mind were being created, paving the way for the development of a physical body that would sufficiently support the development of reasoning. References to seven are repeated in religious and traditional stories in every culture on the planet and are often symbolic of these levels of Mind. In three dimensions the symbolic form would appear as a pyramid.

This holds much mystery at this point in time. However, the accessibility to that which has been previously shrouded, is coming closer to revelation.

This information will not be related in regard to that which has not been known. For at the proper point in progression of this portion of the great body, these understandings will be developed through a collective process and will be arrived at within many entities.

This will not be an individual effort but, a group effort, as the predominance of that portion of progression enters into this plane.
[1118737144]

Since the 1960's enormous advances have been made in mankind's thinking. On the heels of the industrial revolution has come an even greater one. The technological advances in the physical plane in the past few decades has united the planet in a way only the greatest of thinkers could conceive before.

Genetic "discoveries" tell us all people are 99% the same. Agree or not, telephotographic images of mothers and babes, children playing, fathers working, show us just how similar we are. These images reveal the truth about humanity, dispelling persistent overemphasized ideas of diversity, and revealing common themes, common actions, common drives, common needs.

Now we stand at the threshold of a new millennium, a time prophesied by people who lived thousands of years ago all over this planet. We live in the time of the end of the world, the end of at least one accounting (Mayan) of time. This is the time of the return of the Christs and development of the new Christs, be they Hebrew, Persian, or American Indian.

It is the time when information on every conceivable subject can be accessed at the touch of a button. It is the time of disclosures and secrets revealed, where everything can be known and the false sense of privacy is fading. It is the time of realizing the reality of our connectedness, that what happens to one of us, happens to all of us. It is a great time of revelation, so we may move from a state of believing to a state of knowing. It is a time of Self determination and Self awareness. The time of mystical children and Kundalini awakened.

We are approaching the next evolutionary milestone - ready to bring about Spiritual Man on a global scale. What was told in the significance of one man's intuitive report may well apply to us all:

Intuitive Reporter: This entity is again a part of a group of these entities who are utilizing this time period for the re-establishment and the accumulation of those understandings which were significant previously. To develop again these natural abilities as becoming a part of the natural

ability of this time period. The impatience within Self is a natural charac-
teristic of these entities, of which there are many. The need to understand
each part and the need to question continuously is also a true characteris-
tic of these entities.

Recognizing this period of time with this technical advancement,
with its progression of mental process, as being of a vibration which is
harmonious with their own, they are drawn into this to complete that which
was begun previously, to re-arrange and to re-balance that which was
distorted, previously. To achieve opportunities to correct that which was
mistaken before. To alleviate the necessity for those destructions which
occurred through error before, to work with that which is vibrational, to
work with that which is non-physical, in a relaxed manner, with familiarity
and with authority. To learn of Self.

This time period is the interim period and the foundation is being
established at this point by these entities, therefore, the compulsion that
everything be correct, the disgust when things are superficial, the inability
to contain hypocrisy within this entity...a natural part of the Self. We see
much opportunity within this time period for this entity to understand and
to be influential in the discarding of hypocrisy, of superficialness and in all
these areas to replace it with that which is truth. [0323747144]

Remembering where we came from sheds incredible light upon the possibilities of
the future for us all.

MAYA

How could she know?

"I'm going to have a Past Life reading done." The voice on the other end of the phone was Neta, my former college roommate.

"A what?" I asked, not certain I had heard her correctly.

"A past life reading."

This was not something we had ever talked about. We didn't speak of religious matters except in the past tense and then it had come up only rarely. "What's a past life reading?" My mind conjured images from movies and television of gypsies in darkened parlors.

"It's a woman who can tell you about a lifetime that tells you something about your life now."

Being practical minded, I was getting a bit confused with this esoteric stuff. This was why I didn't take more philosophy classes in college.

"My boss had one done, and one of the other girls at the department (Neta was a respiratory therapist at the local university's med-center). They sound fascinating so I'm going to have one done the next time they're in town."

"The next time who's in town?"

"The people who do them."

"You mean they don't live here?" It was really sounding like gypsies now.

"No, they come from St. Louis or somewhere." She went on to explain as best she could that the readings were given by two people, a team, one a facilitator called a conductor and one the conveyer of information called a reader. Long before the days that Ramtha and others made channeling a household word, I wondered where this information was supposed to come from. I had not seriously thought about reincarnation since world history classes and a mention in American literature concerning Lindbergh, the transcendent poets, and Benjamin Franklin. My knowledge of the subject was bound in unresolved Christian issues. And all that was about to become quite clear to me.

"Are you sure about this, Neta?" Eternally trusting and often naive, I'd always felt a bit protective of Neta. So I asked the bottom line question, "How much does it cost?"

She told me it was by donation and she said, "Yes I'm sure. My boss's wife is a teacher at the school."

"What school?" this was the first time she'd said anything about a school.

"The School of Metaphysics."

I didn't know what the word meant, and physics was a subject I'd avoided so far in my life. "Where is it?" I thought it might be on campus. I learned there wasn't a school building, but they were thinking of opening a school here. Someone drove from Springfield once a month to teach several people in Columbia.

I could tell Neta was set on it so I said, "Just be careful." Before I set the phone down I added, "Call me after you have it done and we'll have dinner."

Several weeks later the call came.

Neta came over and we discussed what she'd learned about her "past life". In early days of the School of Metaphysics, those requesting readings were given typed transcriptions. As I read Neta's I learned she was a nun in Austria. I found that ironic since I knew Neta had been raised Catholic but that she didn't live like a nun.

Humor aside, I found several insightful comments in the material. Especially when it came to the significance part. This was the last third of the report which linked the information about the past to the conditions and circumstances of the present. Here I found things about Neta that I knew very few people knew, and certainly someone who had just met her would have no way of knowing. At least not that I was aware of.

Whether this woman could actually tell about past lives I didn't know. I didn't even know what I thought of reincarnation. Maybe she was just psychic. Whatever - her insights puzzled me. How could she know these things about my friend?

The next week Neta and I joined a class at the School of Metaphysics. I was on my way to finding out.

Barbara's first experience with Intuitive Reports

Within six weeks we - the students - rented the first building for the School of Metaphysics in Columbia, Missouri.

The first time readings were done in our new building I helped host, welcoming people, offering them something to drink and making them feel comfortable. I looked forward to meeting the man and woman who did the readings.

By the time they arrived, the room was filled with excited people. One after another came forward to receive their readings – past life, past life crossings (between two people), and there were also Health Analyses done that day. Having been college-educated, this information impressed me the most. It was like watching someone look inside the body and soul of another person. Even if the past life account was just a story, a wrapping for truths people needed to hear, the Health Analyses were nothing of the sort. These were easily verifiable by physical means. A long-standing weakness in the lungs, an inability to tolerate milk products, misaligned vertebra, and headaches were conditions not readily seen by the eye, yet discerned by the reporter and quickly confirmed by the people possessing these disorders who requested Health Analyses that day.

There was something here. I knew beyond all doubt that I was right to have started this study.

After seven readings were done the conductor and reporter took a break, answering our many questions. "How does she do that?" "Are you tired?" "Do you remember what you said?" Then a question I had wondered in my mind, "Can other people do this?"

Expecting there needed to be some kind of aptitude or talent, I was surprised to hear the conductor say, "Yes. Those who are willing to put out the effort can be trained." I learned that the director of our School was one of these fortunate individuals. My respect for her grew from the knowledge.

I stayed to observe the next session, even though I was not receiving a reading myself. There was nowhere else I wanted to be. It was like new worlds were being opened. Yes, I was still questioning, wondering how and why and when, but I was seeing it with my own eyes. It was more than what the reader was saying. Maybe she just had an unprecedented affinity for making up historical stories. Something told me that was a fantasy in my own head. There was too much ringing true here.

What I experienced was watching one person after another, from a young teenager in high school to a well-dressed granderfatherly businessman, sit captivatedly listening to this woman fluently tell them about themselves. Sometimes they would laugh, sometimes nod, sometimes flinch, and one even quietly cried. This was very real to these people. What was being said had meaning to them.

By the time the second session of reports was over I had decided that someday I would give to others in the way I saw this woman giving that night.

An answer to "Why am I here?"

The next time we hosted Intuitive Reports at our school, our class was scheduled to receive our Past Life Profiles. This report to this day is given as part of the course of study in mastering consciousness. On this night, I was the last one of eight to receive mine.

When my name was called I came up to the chair which was sitting directly in front of the intuitive reporter. I didn't know her, she had come from St. Louis, but I did recognize her as the woman who had come before and as the same person who had given Neta's reading.

The conductor asked if I was ready. I nodded. He turned to the woman and gave the following command,

> *"You will search for the identity of the entity known as BARBARA GAYLE O'GUINN and relate a significant incarnation for this entity."*

> *Intuitive Reporter: We see this one as female. This one is in a temple of religious worship for the people.*

The first twelve years of my life was lived in the shadow of my grandfather, an evangelical faith-healing preacher. I was not at all surprised by this relevance. The reporter went on.

> *Intuitive Reporter: We see this (as) not only a religious worship but representing a type of lifestyle, an attitude or ideals that are considered and used in every aspect of life.*

I had been taught religion was indeed something to be lived—when you allow Christ into your heart it transforms you. This concept caused me considerable problems as I grew old enough to realize how many people of the faith profess without practicing. The woman continued without interruption.

> *Intuitive Reporter: We see this one to have been chosen to work within this temple and to study the concepts brought forth within this temple. We see this one to have been greatly honored in this and to take great pride in this position, to be very enthusiastic and to attempt to project this enthusiasm to others. We see this to involve a certain disciplinary procedure which requires great attention being placed upon certain areas and we see this one to pursue this with great diligence and enthusiasm. We see the purpose set forth in this activity, to be the enlightenment of other individuals and the building forth within self the complete enlightenment and enfoldment of the lower self to the higher.*

What the reporter was saying was now beginning to sound like my current life particularly since my studies at SOM had taken a place of high priority. I was already realizing after only a few months how the spiritual disciplines of concentration, meditation, and healing were causing an elevation of my spirit.

Intuitive Reporter: We see this one to pursue these studies to reach a point where this one is able to disperse this information to other individuals. We see at this point this one to become quite distraught and upset within the self, for this one has a great amount of insecurity that this one has not faced up to now.

I had already encountered this with some of my friends. My previous best girlfriend and I had recently parted ways, amicably. She was continuing to spend her time in ways I gave up once I began classes. I missed her company and in time I learned how to respect the difference in our choices.

A former beau gently scoffed at my interest, as did my parents. I was exasperated when I couldn't make others see what I saw. Years of practice would eventually teach me how to do that. It would also teach me how to let go with grace.

But right now it sounded like I hadn't learned a whole lot since this lifetime.

Intuitive Reporter: We see this one to view this passing on of information as a great responsibility and to be overly concerned with this one's doing this in a correct manner, and therefore, after great inner turmoil and much time spent in arriving at a decision, we see this one to withdraw from these temple duties and withdraw from this study for this one feels the lack within self to adequately demonstrate these qualities and project the proper information to others as this one would see to be in a perfect manner. We see this one to be very distraught over doing things in what would be considered a perfect way instead of doing things in a manner which is to the best of her abilities.

This would stimulate a journey to understand that compassion. That there is a difference between hypocrisy and practice. As a child I felt the need to do what was right, to meet up to high standards. This had brought many good things into my life, and it had also instilled a "perfect complex", as we called it in those days, which I resounded here loud and clear. What would come later in the significance put this in a new light that I had never considered leading to the courage to move beyond this point in the present.

Intuitive Reporter: We see this one at this point to direct self in a way which this one would consider herself to be creative, in ways of art and music. We see this one to express these spiritual ideals in this manner, in the creation of art forms and in carving and also in playing music. We see also this one to be somewhat disturbed within self for not living up to what would be considered perfection.

I was artistic in the present-day also, but like then I knew this was a sellout, a compromise.

I had an inner sense that I should be doing something greater with my life. I didn't want to miss the calling again. The report also explained some of why during times of internal conflict I would experience a nagging from inside until resolve came.

> *Intuitive Reporter: We see this one to not marry within this lifetime, but to form a companionship with many other entities and to share much the enthusiasm and joy this one finds in the expression of physical life. We see this one to continue in this manner until the time of withdrawal. We see this to be age 58 years. We see this to be area of the Mayan people in Central America.*

I remembered about Aztecs from junior high school, but Mayans were not in my conscious realm of knowledge.

> *Conductor: How was this time period referred to?*

> *Intuitive Reporter: There is not a time period given.*

> *Conductor: How was this entity referred to?*

> *Intuitive Reporter: Quaradon.*

> *Conductor: What type of religion did this one follow?*

> *Intuitive Reporter: We see this religion as being the worship of one particular God or deity, and this being represented in certain symbology. We see also there to be other deities which would be considered lesser in effect in status which are represented by smaller stones. We see there to be much symbology represented within this religious practice and this to not be clear to all individuals. We see this one to have reached only a certain point in understanding the representation of this symbology and not to have continued beyond this point due to the qualities that have been given.*

> *Conductor: Do you find the one of Quetzecoatl as being at this time?*

> *Intuitive Reporter: Not existing during this time period, but representative in the religious ideals of the period.*

This was the conductor's question. By the end of the session, I didn't even remember how to pronounce the name he had said. Later I would find out Quetzecoatl was the Mayan Christ. And much later this would have more meaning to me. At the time, at age 22, with my entire life open before me, I was more concerned about whether my not marrying in that life would have an affect on my marital status in the present so I asked....

>*Conductor: Was there a particular reason why this entity did not marry in that lifetime, take a mate?*

>*Intuitive Reporter: This one had many companions for brief periods, did not choose to remain with any of them for a long duration. This is due to this one's feeling - not feeling - a need to do this. As stated this one had developed an independence which was not in accordance with remaining with one male for a long extended period.*

>*Conductor: Did this entity have children?*

>*Intuitive Reporter: There was one male child.*

I was shocked by this because it did not reflect my thinking or conduct in the present life. I would not consider raising a child without a father nor did I understand how I could be highly religious and have an out of wedlock child. The report was already expanding my thinking into areas I had yet to visit.

>*Conductor: Did this child live and grow up to adulthood?*

>*Intuitive Reporter: There was a separation of this child from this one when the child was small. This one did not raise the child.*

>*Conductor: What was the reason for this entity not raising the child?*

>*Intuitive Reporter: The child was given to another to raise during the period when this one sought to express self in the religious attitude that has been given.*

This would haunt me for years to come. I would finally realize the significance of this on our son's fifth birthday in the year 2000. Other parts of the significance rang true immediately. And although I didn't know it yet, this report was so integral to the fiber of my being that I would be studying it, remembering, off and on for years to come.

>*Conductor: What would be the significance of that lifetime to the present lifetime for this entity?*

>*Intuitive Reporter: We see this one presently to also have a desire to reach*

> *out to others and to pass on to them the knowledge and experience this one*
> *has reached, and to do this in such a way as to always express with enthu-*
> *siasm and a positive attitude to where these will respond and recognize the*
> *value of those things that this one seeks to give. We see this one to have*
> *some degree of insecurity in doing this and this to relate primarily with the*
> *purpose this one has sought in choosing this lifetime and this time period.*
> *We see this one to have formed a great deal of strength and independence*
> *from the past, and to still find the need to express self in this way, and to do*
> *this in such as way as to further the purpose and goals this one has set*
> *forth for self.*

This information was bedrock. Deep. It resonated when I first heard it, as it resonates even now. Learning how to give freely, unconditionally, has been a rewarding lesson that has enabled me to talk to anyone, anywhere, about anything. This is quite a testament from a person who at twenty-two had a very small circle of friends, stayed to herself most of the time, and trembled at the thought of public speaking. All this began to change with this report.

> *Intuitive Reporter: Suggest to this one that there is no need this one feels*
> *insecure, for the finding of security in what this one presents is gained*
> *through experience and this one is in the process of forming this. Suggest*
> *to this one to see self in the positive manner that this one projects to other*
> *individuals, for through this and through the continuous application of*
> *those principles received, this one will form the security this one requires*
> *and will be able to share with others in the proper approach.*

I received this as a wonderful affirmation that indeed my efforts would be rewarded. This empowered me to have faith in myself and courage to go into experiences I had previously avoided.

> *Intuitive Reporter: See this one also to have error in attitude regarding*
> *the perfection of self in all activities.*

Here was the statement that would begin freeing me from years of polarizing, good-evil programming, the remnants of the "I'm not worthy" thinking I had so innocently absorbed.

> *Intuitive Reporter: Suggest to this one that perfection is not required in*
> *experience upon the earth plane,*

The thought had never occurred to me.

but only the performing of the activity to the best of one's ability. There-
fore, do not deny self the right to make errors, for errors can be valuable
learning tools. That is all.

I knew it was not encouraging me to go out and purposefully make mistakes. I knew it was encouraging me to grow, to see the mistakes I made in a new light. To release the tendency to condemn the outcome, replacing it with a gratitude for the opportunity. This would come with experience just as the report had said.

And it would be an integral part of my willingness to put myself on the line by sharing the information in this book.

It would be two years before I would train to give Intuitive Reports.

My training conductor moved from St. Louis to supervise several schools in Missouri, Oklahoma, and Kansas, where I directed a School of Metaphysics in Wichita. Teaching and directing had taught me some essential lessons, given me wide berth to apply the disciplines in mind and breath control, and had well prepared me for responding to people's needs as an intuitive reporter.

Interacting with others also brought Self respect and Self trust, necessary qualities to be able to release the Conscious Mind thereby allowing the intuitive perception of Subconscious Mind to have free reign. The mental exercises brought command of attention and conscious separation from the body - astral projection - prerequisite skills for reporter training. Within three months I gave my first public reports. I didn't realize I was ready, but my conductor did.

For the next eighteen years I gave thousands of reports sometimes 28 per day with three conductors in four dozen cities for people on five continents. Although these reports can be accessed without the person being present, many people want to experience them and I wanted to be a vehicle for that.

In time, these meetings with people of all backgrounds, beliefs, and ages, expanded my view of human nature and our spiritual potential. I developed a clear picture of what the world will be like when every person has received an Intuitive Report like those offered through the School of Metaphysics, for when this occurs everyone on the planet will have knowledge of why she or he is here.

These experiences prepared my heart and mind for the developments the '90's would bring. I no longer believed reincarnation might exist, or that it made sense and therefore was probably true. I knew from personal experience that repeated sojourns into the physical plane of existence had become part of the development of consciousness for people on this planet.

The reasons why were being revealed daily in the Intuitive Reports. They still are, for this is a living science.

Conscious connection to accelerate evolution

In 1991, something happened that would change my world again. During inner level work at the time of Wesak, the Buddhist equivalent of the Christian Christmas, I experienced a new dimension of the work I am here to do. This was an aware experience similar to lucid dreaming. Each year what was revealed to me was relevant to my consciousness growth the previous year and a fiat for the coming year. This is my journal entry for this year:

There was a raised platform. Circles within circles around which were robed figures - what I could count later as twelve. There was much light here - emanating from above, around, through, from the figures. There was someone standing in the center.

I was standing behind one of these figures who was seated on a stone. There was movement occurring in the circle. Someone would enter the circle going toward the center and at first I couldn't see what was happening. Just the movement.

At the appointed time I knew to come forward. It was my turn. As I came to the one in the center of the circle he placed a chalice in my hands. I moved effortlessly, as if floating in a series of yoga movements, never spilling a drop, then returned to offer the cup to the figure I served. I realized this was my duty, to serve this man. To perform my part, my function in service to all.

As I returned, as if our movements were connected, mirror images, a male stepped forward. He moved in forms that reminded me of Tai Chi.

The one in the center raised his right hand. Within it was a rod which he released into the air. The male easily caught it, manipulating it with great precision. Then he returned it to our master.

I realized he and I were paired as it was with this particular man. I could see each of the other robed figures were also attended by a male and female, some I recognized, most I did not.

It was time for our master to come forward. It was he, who was for some reason to assume the center place of honor.

I did not question, but merely received, maintaining an attitude of surrender until I needed to work in conjunction with the male. It was then I recognized who he was, someone I had known for many years. The man who had conducted me during many reports: Daniel Condron.

And the master we both attended, when on the Earth had been called Zarathustra.

From that time forward there was an accepting of a conscious level of responsibility that was now shared with another. It was an odd sensation, pleasant, to know I was no longer alone in the endeavor, indeed had always had a partner. And now I understood many things that had drifted through my consciousness, memories of a time in Persia, experiences now of great healing energies when Daniel and I were both present. This was a new level of conscious connection in our efforts to accelerate humanity's evolution.

The next significant maturing of this occurred in 1993 in Chicago when Daniel and

I and over a dozen School of Metaphysics members attended the Parliament of the World's Religions. People of dozens of religious faiths from all over the world came together to share ideas and dreams.

The 100-page catalogue of the weeks events read like a Spiritual Who's Who of the planet, from His Holiness the Dalai Lama to the Millennium Institute's Gerald Barney, from NPR mavens Michael and Linda Toms to musician Steve Halpern, from U.N. peace advocate Sri Chimnoy to the Tibetan Drepung Monks. As I held the book in my hands I marveled at being in the company of so many rich thinkers with so much to offer. It brought to my mind our dream of the College of Metaphysics as a university for Spiritual Man, and I realized I was being privileged to receive a glimpse of what our course catalogue will be like.

Through the week we interacted with hundreds of people. One of our group said someone had looked at his name placard and said, "School of Metaphysics! You guys are everywhere!" And indeed we were. We went to as many sessions as possible, often in different directions.

In the middle of the week I gave a presentation called *Spiritual Initiation*. The original room was too small to hold the people wanting to attend so we were given a larger room. Two days later, Daniel's major address on *Permanent Healing* was given to a standing room only crowd. We were embracing the people with our interfaith consciousness and they were embracing us in like manner.

We participated in the common circle groups over the lunch hour, sharing the way we see the world and the experiences that formed those ideas. Being volunteers ourselves, we understood the heart of those who volunteered to serve as guides and attendants during this gathering of 7500, so we gave several hundred books to them as a way of saying thank you.

Every experience that week was rich. It reaffirmed our ideals and kindled many new perspectives. I had always believed people around the world wanted the kind of education SOM affords. Lecturing and teaching in many U.S. cities told me this, for those seeking to understand Self did not have a particular age, look, or heritage. The radio/tv shows, particularly call-in programs, told us all people are asking similar questions. The Parliament of the World's Religions gave us international interaction. We made friends from many countries during the Parliament. These friendships provided the stimulus for the next development in what we offer the world.

When we returned to the College of Metaphysics, Daniel and I began discussing how intuitive research could expand to accelerate the evolution of humanity in the new millennium. It was time for a major development in our consciousness and in our level of giving. One of the first ways this manifested was an evolution in how the inner levels of consciousness are accessed to shed light upon the nature of humanity.

We began exploring ways to use intuitive research to help people produce experiences in multidimensional consciousness, to move beyond the limitations of linear, physical thought and begin experiencing ever-deepening levels of thought. This evolved into times when we could interact with people, offering counsel and instruction, for this purpose. With the help of Dr. Laurel Clark, an intuitive reporter herself, and Dr. Pam Blosser, both psi counselors, we created experiential weekends designed to aid individuals to become whole, functional selves–to be better spouses, parents, managers, healers thus more completely fulfilling their purposes in life. Each weekend includes a unique access of intuitive wisdom.

From this has come a further refinement of how seasoned reporters may be cultivated to access Subconscious Mind for intuitive clusters. These clusters are revealing important insights concerning healing, creative mind, friendship, parenting, and our purpose for existence. They have also led to the creation of an exceptional exploration of personal evolution we call Full Spectrum. Full Spectrum is a series of experiences, offered at the Moon Valley Ranch on the College of Metaphysics campus, leading participants into conscious clarity in the seven levels of mind. A means to serve many of the needs left unmet since Atlantean times.

Full Spectrum has been designed to meet the needs of reincarning Atlanteans who are here to move themselves, and the species, into the next stage of spiritual progression, the formation of the root race we refer to as Spiritual Man. This work brings to life the Atlantean stories, for it is the continuation of work forged millennia ago, work that only now can be truly appreciated and understood by more than a select few.

Until now there have been masters of consciousness upon the Earth in a singular fashion. Spread across the globe and across time, their stories remain with us in the form of scriptures and stories kept sacred by their cultures. These endure not from superstition and ignorance. They endure because they are whole truths, written in a language beyond any physically created by man. These myths, these parables, these stories of wisdom, are written in the language of the inner mind, the same language that comes forth in intuitive reports.

As a race, humanity has been moving toward a common destiny all along. Now is the time for more of us to become fully conscious of this truth. To remember where we have come from is to know who we are. Memory opens our hearts.

Knowing who we are opens our minds to the vision of who we can become. This is the reappearance of Atlantis, and the emergence of Intuitive, Spiritual Man.

REBIRTHING EGYPT

Pranayama.

The Sanskrit word denoting the realm of energy and practiced through mindfulness, posture, and particularly through breathing. There were many breathing methods I had learned at the School of Metaphysics, and through post-graduate study and teaching. How to direct breath for relaxation and for revitalization. How to intuitively breathe for alignment of the inner and outer, the mind and body. Even how to rest the heart through the breathless state.

This was different.

Leonard Orr came to the College of Metaphysics in 2000 upon invitation from Chancellor Daniel Condron. Seeking ways to share SOM with others of like minds, Daniel had intuitively sought Leonard out. I will always remember how fitting the timing of Leonard's visit, for it was Easter weekend, the time Christians celebrate reawakening to the Christ principle through the resurrection of Jesus of Nazareth.

Leonard is known as the father of American Pranayama, better known as rebirthing. Now, no matter what you may have heard or read about rebirthing – like every valuable thing in life – it must be personally experienced to know, to have your own thoughts about it in place of someone else's.

I'd heard about rebirthing in the 1970's. Being a traveling teacher/speaker, I had occasion to meet several people who seemed shocked I had never been rebirthed. Such an unbelievable discovery would often lead to a discussion about a different kind of rebirth - the *born again of spirit* kind spoken of in the Bible. I would explain how I interpreted this Biblical mystery in the Universal Language of Mind. How this passage spoke to every person's need to learn in every level of existence, as well as the physical plane. How being conscious of multidimensional existence leads to becoming compatible with our Creator, thus we come to the Kingdom of Heaven.

The kind of rebirth these people talked about seemed more worldly. Rebirthing was going back to your physical birth – working through birth trauma, some would say. The way they described it was never stimulating to me, which was unusual given my voracious appetite for learning.

When Leonard came to us, I understood why.

Leonard's Easter visit, coming after decades of consciousness expanding and developing, was exactly as it needed to be for me and for others comprising the School of Metaphysics. This reflected in the experiences that came to me while breathing in this particular form.

I speak of this because it was during the fifth session, with Brazilian rebirther Marcia Roisman assisting, that I experienced something that would greatly influence me to team with Daniel Condron on the investigation for this book. During earlier sessions I had experienced a host of insights ranging from the soul connection with my son at *his* birth to the inner truth of speaking in tongues to experiencing the Earth grid and receiving a glimpse of the science involved in levitation. Some abstract ideas for someone with an Evangelical, middle class background who grew up in a small town in the show-me state of Missouri.

This is what I wrote in my journal following that fifth session:

> *"Sphinx*
> *This was quite surprising since I have little acquaintance with what was revealed to me and what I experienced. It was fascinating. Atlantean energy is an energy circuit, like the connected breathing of our planet when the Sphinx had a nose and the Giza pyramid a capstone that gleamed. There are two significant energy movements. One is an energy arc that goes to another planet or star far out in space. In the inner chamber of the Sphinx there is a crystal. Light comes through an opening strikes the crystal and goes out in direction at 90 degree angle. Going out, goes to that planet/star, coming in comes from the capstone of the pyramid. There is another energy movement that is within the pyramid and down into the core of the Earth. This must be what the medulla oblongata of the Earth looks like."*

This was a most surprising revelation. Memories of Egypt did not fill my awake consciousness. There were a couple lifetime experiences I recalled from that land, one I had received in one of the handful of crossings I had requested over the years. The other I had remembered by my own effort years ago as a student. Neither were anything like this. This was way beyond remembering a past life. I wasn't even certain it came from a past life.

What I did know was the reality of the experience. It was not a figment of my imagination. I had been there, inside the Sphinx. I had seen the surroundings, heard the buzzing, smelled the frankincense, tasted the cardamon, and felt the energy course through me.

Figure 3.
The energy cycle
between Earth and Sirius

After the session, I told my husband about it. He asked if it was another planet, and I heard myself say I thought it was. The reality of my experience was sinking in every time I remembered it. It was real, the thrill of being there - the freedom of moving from one form into another still vibrated in my being.

I decided to let the experience be. To let it settle into my cells without overworking it with conscious interference. It was what it was and if it had a place in my everyday life, that place would be revealed in time.

It was, a half dozen sessions later.

The twelfth session, Daniel breathed with me. By now Marcia had left for Virginia and it was the end of June. My journal reads:

June 29, 2000
Entering and leaving at will.

This sentence is a reference to the capacity to freely use physical form without becoming dependent upon it. Think of what it might be like to sleep and awake at will, to be aware in the dream state rather than unconscious and this will give you an idea of what this state of being that can come and go as it pleases is like.

My knowledge of evolutionary development had included this concept for two decades and to experience something during rebirthing that I could describe this way was both surprising and rewarding.

My next note is curious primarily because I was familiar with the Great Pyramid, having interviewed Bill Schul the author of Pyramid Power years ago when he lived in Winfield, Kansas, and I was in Wichita. I was not at all familiar with Sirius. Consciously, I knew Sirius was in space; a planet or star or constellation, I didn't know which.

At any rate I didn't think much about any of this at the time I was writing in my journal. I was intent upon recording what I had experienced and the words just flowed.

Pyramid and Sirius star.

Upon writing this, I realized what I had just experienced was a continuation of the previous experience involving the Sphinx.

I think they used bodies, the people, to channel the energy through the solar plexus to stabilize the Earth. The Earth did not have the kind of grid it has now. Somehow they used the animal-man body to stabilize Earth. This is how the sacrificing of people came in because they gave their energy to this.

Now as I reread this I recall countless historical stories of sacrifice in almost every culture on the planet, particularly before the time of the Buddhas and Christ. How did we ever move from willingly giving up energy, to blood sacrifices and burning people at the stake?

The grid is most probably electromagnetic, the Earth's gravitational field that keeps us all upright no matter where we are on the planet. The experience was like channeling the energy, allowing it to flow through you, like I imagine the experience of those people who have been struck by lightning and lived to tell the tale. It wasn't frightening or painful, rather more like a tantric energy flow because it was full, complete, and total.

There was a very strong sense of purpose in providing this function. It was a service that enables others to do their work. The sacrifice was not a loss as later viewed.

Then came a most interesting image that would alter my view of mummies.

Going into a pyramid tomb and being able to exist off of cosmic energy. Rebirthing can put you in contact with the flow of energy from I AM to mind, causal level, mental level, astral levels, etc. And there is awareness of that.

The link here is the cosmic energy which becomes life force in man. I would understand this entry much more a year later when Daniel and I began in earnest to put the pieces together.

Why explore the past?

Before moving on, I want to share part of the next session, my thirteenth, for this too was a motivation for my part of this research. This entry in part reads:

> *7-28-2000*
> *About motion....*
> *1) More on Sphinx.*

I was back in the Sphinx again.

> *Go through walls, no door to it. Bubble made of icosahedrons surrounded me. Could place hand into one of icosahedrons for specific purposes, energy, consciousness, connections.*

Later as I read through some of the Atlantean reports, I would come to recognize this as personal energy grids, individual electromagnetic fields, auras as they have been called for over a century, now most specialized in human beings, but during the Atlantean time periods just being conceived.

Then the scene evolved into what was a place I had never seen before, nor imagined.

> *Purple planet, misty not solid, gaseous. Shape shifters.*

I was beginning to speak of these experiences in 21st century science fiction terms, yet while the experiencing was unfolding, there were no such judgements, just the receiving of experience. It reminded me of giving birth or having an orgasm. During rebirthing, the breath consumes you, there is nothing else.

> *Blend energies into each other. No separation yet individual. Being object of desire. Move into something and out, become.*

It was one of the most freeing experiences I've ever had. I wasn't participating but watching as if suspended above the scene. I could relate to the experience, however. I could feel as these life forms, these beings, felt. To move into and through each other, to experience forms and change at will. It was the height of mutability, the ability to hook up with someone or something, know what it is and then unhook relatively unchanged as an astrologer had once described that quality. It was stunning to watch and inspiring to experience.

I remember thinking to myself this is the truth of becoming whole, one, complete, compatible with the Creator. I wondered why it would happen on this purple planet rather than our own. At the time I had no answer, but again the Atlantean reports which I would not read until the following year would offer some possible insights in the way intelligent beings used energy to form matter, tens of thousands of years ago.

Even the next part of the journal is a window into the movement of thought causing entrapment for many entities.

> *Arms extended, head back, energy into hands through shoulders to circle/oval. Held for long time, then distraction thought to Sheila's tetany, how long can one stay in position? Then began losing it.*

The purple planet experience had ended, all owing to a single irrelevant thought about someone else's breathing experience. How appropriately Atlantean that my mind be pulled away from such wonder by the distress of another. It was a common experience for many during that period, as it is becoming increasingly so today.

The experiences I recount here would bring into my conscious mind the recognition of the need to explore uncharted territory through intuitive anthropology and archaeology. A dig of a very different sort that would turn up a trove of ancient wisdom.

Incubation period

For a year these experiences gestated. I became consciously responsive to other rebirthing experiences which led to as diverse experiences as personal insights into hereditary genetics and a children's book penned in the language of dreams called Radiance.

Then Daniel began talking about putting together a book on Atlantis.

We both knew the School of Metaphysics was in possession of potentially the greatest resource on the planet concerning information beyond recorded history. Since 1970, transcriptions have been kept of Intuitive Reports given for people from all over the world. These transcriptions of intuitive wisdom gleaned by reporter-conductor teams span three decades and are the world's largest collection of such knowledge. About half of these reports are Health Analyses and the other half are Past Life Profiles for individuals, couples, and families. These reports taken from the Akashic Record (a kind of universal memory) relate significant lifetimes of people now living. Each relates a past lifetime experience that is relevant to the present - the karmic traces through time impacting today's situations and relationships.

Out of over 100,000 Intuitive Reports there are records of around 300 that reach beyond recorded history into the time periods known as Atlantis, Lemuria, and Mu. As the millennium approached and the 25th anniversary of the School of Metaphysics was at hand, it was time to begin researching the Atlantean material in earnest. This meant combing countless files to find intuitive reports of that time period. It fell to the College of Metaphysics students of 1997-1998 to enter the data into word processors. They became a team of researchers who are among an elite group of individuals who now know about Lemuria, Atlantis, and ancient Egypt. Some of which you are about to read.

I intentionally stayed away from these reports until now. I had received one profile from the Atlantean time and heard of several others, but I had not made this an area of exploration. It wasn't that I didn't want to know, it was as if something inside me said, "It is not yet time." This was the same sense I had experienced when rebirthing had been offered to me, up until the time my husband encouraged me to learn something new, and I agreed.

From the time of the purple planet experience, the inner sense tide was turning. When I heard that a movie was being released about Atlantis in the summer of 2001 and thus the subject would be in the consciousness of the world, I knew the time of waiting was over.

It was time to begin asking the right questions. Daniel and I had prepared ourselves over half a century. This research is something we entered into a joy-filled sense of expectation and responsibility for what we might find. What we discovered amazed us. It will rival every discovery made by scientists and explorers throughout history. It verifies and reconfigures existing theories of how humanity came to be.

I always knew I was here to help change the world for the better. I just didn't consciously dream that a part of that might be illuminating a past we have collectively forgotten. I do know that understanding where we came from, illuminates who we are, and many times who we can become.

It is time to begin making this generally unknown history public. The world is ready for change, and what is recorded in this book certainly will do its part to encourage it.

EVOLUTION *of*
Intuitive Research
1968-1999

EVOLUTION

Eternal Questions in a Seeking Mind

Every Holy Scripture in the world speaks of light.

Fervent prayers and devoted meditators often describe an inner radiance, a brilliant light that fills their consciousness. Many accounts have been recorded of people declared clinically dead who return to life telling stories of deceased loved ones and a brilliant light. When we have an insightful, intelligent thought, we say we have a bright idea. The bride and the new mother "glow". Holy figures are depicted with haloes or light emanating from them; they are the source of illumination. Light has a rich role in mankind's history.

Light is the essence of creation. It is within us and around us and through us. Light's journey through creation is the story that is called evolution.

Intuitive research reveals this evolution as it pertains to this planet. Gleaned from Universal Mind, the memory of all is open to us. These records read almost like stories, histories, of the soul's quest for completeness.

What was life, existence, like in the early stages, before human bodies encased the soul? It is beyond comprehension for some people. This was certainly true for the middle-aged woman receiving this Past Life Profile *[6067531114]* in the mid-1970's. The report uncharacteristically opens addressing the woman's current state of awareness. Instead of relating the significant past lifetime from the Akashic Record of this one's existence, the intuitive reporter begins by saying:

> *Intuitive Reporter: This one is seen in a state that this one would not understand at this time.*

> **Conductor: Present what is seen, please.**

> *Intuitive Reporter: This one is seen in a very intense energy state, the form is white. This is before entering into the physical. This one had a very strong purpose. This one desired manifestation into the physical. This one related upon this level of existence to other entities very well, related in terms of thought transference upon this level.*

This rare description of existence apart from the body gives us a clear picture of life before physical life.

What comes next is an intriguing dialogue between the intuitive reporter and her conductor, a series of questions and answers that lead us into the world of possibility beyond our wildest conscious imaginings.

Intuitive Reporter: This one was involved with those ones in Atlantis. This one had a particular ability with the understanding and use of sound, which at this point, in existence, could also be related in some way to the ability to communicate upon this level. This is as it was before entering into the physical. At this point, there was an entrance into the physical.

Conductor: There was an entrance into the physical?

Intuitive Reporter: Yes.

Conductor: What form did this entity take on?

Intuitive Reporter: This one was not limited to any one form at this point.

Conductor: Was this entity able to enter and leave at will?

Intuitive Reporter: At this time, yes.

Conductor: Did this entity take on the human man form?

Intuitive Reporter: At this time, much experiencing was done within animals, not only the animal man, but also other forms of animals.

Conductor: What was to be learned through the experience of that for this entity?

Intuitive Reporter: Through observation, to learn the functioning of these forms, to relate what was learned to self, and hopes to gain better understanding of how to progress self.

Conductor: Was there a time during this time period in which this entity could no longer enter and leave at will?

Intuitive Reporter: After many years, yes.

Conductor: What form did this entity become entrapped in?

Intuitive Reporter: This one was trapped within a mutation of what we would term as that of half animal and half human man.

Conductor: How would this form be referred to today? What was the animal form?

Intuitive Reporter: Related to centaur.

Conductor: Is there a way to tell which time period this would be experienced in?

Intuitive Reporter: Was in the time that reasoning was coming into being.

Conductor: Did this entity have a vibration of a name in which this entity was referred to?

Intuitive Reporter: Hu-La-Na (this was sung with first two syllables the same note—the last syllable was a higher note). [6067531114]

Here is a different view, an intuitive perspective, of what has become for us the myths and fables of peoples more primitive than ourselves. Can it be we have mislead ourselves thus abandoning parts of our own history? Parts that might answer the eternal questions of man.

Where did I Come from?

Before the time of Atlantis, and simultaneous to its very early existence, there was a land called Mu (Lemuria). Existence before Mu was something like this:

Intuitive Reporter: We see this one in form not relative to physical plane existence. We see this one as Light. We see the vibration of this one corresponding to that of sphere with inner designation of minute sphere. We see this one to be a part of a group desiring physical plane existence. We see, however, at this time physical vehicles not suited for experience. We see impatience on the part of this one in particular, not so concerning this entire group.

*We see this one to set forth, prematurely, to the accomplishment of
the experience within seventh level plane. We see this one not fully understanding the ability of Creation in this endeavor, relying only upon avenues
open and not allowing Self the opportunity of manifestation through
avenues which would allow this one to experience properly according to
this one's needs. We see this to result in manifesting in the physical plane
in lower physical form and experiencing much frustration.*

   *We see this one realizing why the necessity of patience and
desiring withdrawal to remanifest Self in more suitable form, but not
having the understanding of Creation necessary to perform this manifestation properly. We see this existence on physical plane to be rather short for
reasons of material structure, rather than the desire of this one, although
this desire contributing in lesser degree—time period of earth plane to be
referred to as very nearly—pre-Lemurian.*

Conductor: What was the form in which she experienced?

*Intuitive Reporter: Description would be difficult to relate and one must
understand life forms of that era, being evolved with much effort on the
part of those not experiencing within the physical. We see this one, however, to have taken the form of sea life, erect-life, with much need still for
existence within sea. [91474101111]*

   As light entered into the Atlantean period of its evolution, progression took on
many forms. One of my (Barbara's) own past experiences was between the first and
second cycles of Atlantis. It was a time where I was free to enter and leave the physical
at will. This wisdom came through in regards to my association with a fellow classmate:

*Intuitive Reporter: We see for the first direct association to be one of
particular excitement and joy for these ones. We see for this to be within
an Atlantean time period. We see for these ones to experience most closely
the vibrations and love for each other. We see for this to be a period of
time before these ones were entrapped in the physical. We see for this to be
a type of rest period for these ones and for the learning to be of a particularly important nature, however for it to be much in the learning of receptivity within their environment. We see for the environment to not be
restricted in attitude and for there to be complete freedom, however for the
manner in which these ones learned to be restricted in a sense of a discipline to only certain places, so to speak.*

   *We see for there to be a particular school which each was involved
within. We see at this point for there to not be the learning of the entry into
the physical and for this to come later and for the learning of this time*

period to be a usage of the inner vibrations in a very experimental manner as to learn the correct combinations for the producing of harmony. This is not limited in speaking of harmony but that there are many vibrations, an endless number, which can be used for certain results and creations which these would now see as attitudes, and within each one there was to be the production of harmony to produce the refined result.

We see for there not to be the experimentations upon forms at this point, but only the experiment within the vibration and then the destruction of the vibrations or change into a form which could be reformed again at this point in which they were working...

Conductor: How was this school referred to that these two entities were in during that past time?

Intuitive Reporter: We see for the outer vibration to be referred to as Ladim. This was the name known by those not accepted into this place of learning. The inner name was only known by those who were accepted. This is because of where each was at, in their learning, and that the vibration as what they were learning produced certain results within these individuals.

Conductor: In which time period of Atlantis did this learning take place?

Intuitive Reporter: This was not within the Atlantean continent or time period as in relationship to the physical. This was a learning which was taking place within a different time relationship but which was in correlation to the period of physical time between the first and second destruction of Atlantis. [2057731116]

The relevance of this past experience lay in the knowledge and tools my friend and I both had available to us. In the present time these could *"bring about a further development of what has been started."* The report said, *"this is a beginning for these ones in realizing the reality and the form of the vibrations of colors and sounds, and that within each one there is a perfect harmony or seed which must be planted by the individual."*

This perfect seed already exists within the superconsciousness of all. What I have come to know thus far is that it is up to each of us to manifest that seed in our consciousness. Remembering where we came from is a part of this process.

A 1973 Past Life Profile *[1113737141]* describes the movement of light into physical form. Here is the Biblical Lucifer, the egoic expression of Light, and scientific photon (the electromagnetic particle of light) bearing life in the form of man. Imagine, if you will, spirit with no means of expressing in the physical world. Like a ghost, you exist in a dimension, a plane, which cannot be identified with the physical body. It must know itself through other means. Put yourself in the frame of mind of dream experiences. Now imagine not being able to wake up, being trapped in the dream world. This was the experience of many during the Atlantean period. The stimulus to become aware, to create, to experience and understand motivated these entities, these lights.

> *Intuitive Reporter: We see female incarnation. We see this one in earliest Atlantean period, that which overlapped that of the Lemurian period. We see this entity involved in the transformation and application of the light vibration which was utilized by the entities and which sustained their existence. At this point this particular expression of light was being transformed so its application could be properly projected into the physical plane to ensure proper balance and harmony in the seventh level or physical plane. At this point the physical plane was incomplete in its creation for use of dense matter.*
>
> > *Those entities experiencing in the nonphysical state were at this point in process of refining and preparing that part of matter which was densifying for actual use in the projection and manifestation of physical bodies to be used for experience and learning purposes....*

Think of this as the different states of matter: gas, liquid, and solid. Take water. Water is a liquid. Heat it and it evaporates into steam, the gaseous form of water. Freeze it and the water becomes ice. In any of these it is only the form that changes, not the water itself. In other words when ice melts it becomes water again. When steam reaches the lid of a pan or someone's face it returns to its liquid state.

What is described is similar to this. At this time the individual spirit, or light vibration as it is identified in the report, is seeking ways of expressing similar to water manifesting as a gas, liquid or solid. This is the reality of thought on a subatomic level creating the means to express itself. Thought moves from the mind of the artist to the canvas or block of wood in the same way thought moves to create the health or disease of the body.

In our current existence thought manifestation is becoming a known science. Hundreds of thousands of years ago, during the time of Atlantis and Lemuria, the process was being invented by creative minds. Like the creative movement that began with the Wright brothers' biplane and culminated with man walking on the moon, the invention of a sustainable physical body evolved over time through trial and error.

To explain evolution, Darwinists study the physical development, labeling the creative process natural selection and selective breeding. Creationists describe the same process from the perspective of the Creator, the initiator of the form. There is another viewpoint. This perspective includes both, seeing the place each holds thus validating each. In this light, the ideas are reflective of the dual nature of consciousness itself; the Creator and the created as the <u>Koran</u> describes it, the awakened and the sleeping as described in the <u>Dhammapada</u>, the tree of knowledge of good and evil from the Hebrew teachings. To understand the whole, the parts are united.

> *Intuitive Reporter: ...We see this entity to have existed partially in the physical and partially in the non-physical state at this point ...*

A good example of this dual state is the different experiences while awake and asleep. You are very familiar with your physical body, how tall or short you are. How much you weigh, what you look like. Now think about how you appear in your dreams. Often this is different. Some people appear younger, more attractive. Those experiencing handicaps in the body are often free of them in the dreamstate. World renowned (blind) author Helen Keller spoke of being able to see in her dreams, and (paralyzed) actor Christopher Reeve has spoken of being able to move freely in the dreamstate. The outer mind experience is markedly different from the inner mind experience.

Take it one step further in your thinking, ask yourself, "Where does my dream-body go when I wake up?" Now you are entering the world of aware consciousness.

The evolving dual nature of man is a fluid state, a creative state of being. It is a function of experimentation. During the Atlantean period, elemental thoughts were being created that would allow the thinker to image and reproduce. The connections needed to be built between wanting and acquiring, desiring and experiencing, perceiving and understanding. Expecting a certain outcome then going about the decisions and movements to produce verification is an ancient science better known as reasoning.

> *Intuitive Reporter: ...Entering the physical state to determine whether or not the projection of light or vibration emanating from the light was of proper intensity and balance to ensure harmony and the correct evolution-ary process in the dense matter forms. We see this one to have been most dedicated to this projection and worked with others also in this process. We see the need growing greater for experience in the physical through those misunderstandings and errors of these entities at this time period. Also due to the fact that the particular age or era of existence in the elemental matter forms had come to a conclusion for this entity and others, and as a collective group they were most desirous of advancing to the greater stage of progression....*

Existence in elemental matter forms is a reference to the configurations light has experienced, root races as we term them. These root races are seven in number. Five have already come to pass, the sixth is coming to pass even now, and the seventh is yet to be realized. The elemental forms are commonly referred to as gas, mineral, plant, animal, man, spirit, and God. Each is the answer to an imagined need upon the part of Light to become compatible to its Creator. The era of existence that has come to an end for this soul and others is the need to experience through animal form. The greater stage of progression will be realized in man, and cultivated in the development of reasoning.

> *Intuitive Reporter: ...We see this one lacking somewhat in the understand-*
> *ing of the essence of time itself in relation to the physical state. Was given*
> *opportunity at this point to receive instruction in order to relieve this*
> *compulsion to accelerate and to complete these experiments. We see this*
> *one dedicated self and turned (her) attention therefore to experimenting*
> *rather than receiving adequate knowledge and understanding of all*
> *elements needed to correctly complete this projection. Therefore parts of*
> *these projections of light vibration were not totally balanced in their*
> *projection into the dense forms of entities, of which this one was a part...*

Some paleoanthropologist might describe this Atlantean woman's experience as "the missing link." She simply did not yet have adequate experience to create the bridge from animal-man to reasoning man.

Many people now experience an impatience with wisdom. They turn away from those who have learned through experience while holding themselves back in search of perpetual youth. When one is attached to their own view, they have a limited perspective of the world and life. When one opens to the experience of others, he becomes free to perceive more of the whole.

Think of it in this way, look at what surrounds you right now. This may be a room or an outdoor setting of grass and wood. This is the totality of the world as you experience it this moment. Now imagine you are aboard the space station. What would your experience of our world be?

The first is defined by the limits of your mind and your physical body. The second includes the benefit of many minds and many bodies. This is the reality of standing on the shoulders of giants, each of us have the privilege of benefitting from what and who has come before, we need no longer learn what is called "the hard way." By receiving others' experiences our ability to learn becomes vertical as well as horizontal. Thus we correct errors that might arise in our own judgement. This kind of highly developed reasoning was not yet available to this woman.

The description of that lifetime continues:

Intuitive Reporter: ...The report that the experiment was complete was premature and the entities waiting at this point to involve themselves again in dense matter in the physical form proceeded with their evolution. These ones entering into these physical forms then at this point, found them somewhat inadequate for the purposes of that time period, and for the experience needed by themselves. We see this error on the part of this entity not to have been with the intent of causing harm but rather through the lack of giving attention to the complete accumulation of that which was necessary.

We see therefore the time needed for experience in the physical at this point exceeded that which normally would have been needed for these ones. They were involved in a time period in the physical of manifesting themselves within the physical that part of light vibration which was needed. We see this to have been accomplished, ultimately by these ones.

But these ones, particularly this entity, were left with an emotional area which indicated a lack of fulfillment. We see this not to have been resolved in that particular incarnation, nor in any subsequent incarnation. As the fulfillment of this would have needed complete understanding of the process involved.... *[1113737141]*

This process, the fine art and science of reuniting the soul, has been achieved by individuals throughout man's history. Now, with the accumulated knowledge of humanity, with the fruits of many journeys through this physical plane of existence, it is possible to understand the relationship of the inner mind and the outer mind, and the common ground where they come together – the emotions.

Who Am I?

The development of the emotions, both the thinking ability and the vehicle or emotional body, was brought into being during the later Atlantean period. The following excerpt describes one woman's experience in a manner that was quite common for many during the Atlantean time. It sheds light on the development and function of the inner, subconscious mind.

Intuitive Reporter: ...We see the vehicle of the emotional body having been firmly formulated at this time, and we see because of the fluctuation and adjustments made between this and the mental body, this one functioning

*from both areas. We see this one highly intuitive at this time and directing
the mental forces subconsciously for the most part. We see as this is an
innate quality of this one, it is taken for granted, and we see this one to not
fully understand its formation or purpose. We see at this point, as stated,
the emotional body having become fully formulated, and we see, for this
reason, this one becoming quite confused, at times, particularly through the
relationships with other individuals.*

These words could describe a contemporary person who is experiencing emotional
upheaval from an unexpected promotion or upset over the loss of a loved one. Those with
active minds capable of great insight can become very confused when mental energy
becomes emotional energy. This is what was occurring with this woman millennia ago
in Atlantis.

The passing of time is a great benefactor, however. For the key lies in an ability
of the outer, Conscious Mind. The report continues:

*Intuitive Reporter: ...We see this one tending to be passive in her own
nature, and we see because of this the influences of others to be quite
strong upon her. We see this one has not formulated to the point of reasoning, and we see this one to absorb the purposes of others within her and to
follow this function into activity, causing her to, at times, become quite
confused, for we see she does not readily understand why she has created
situations as she has.*

Here we discover what is missing and therefore what is needed to alleviate this woman's
confusion. What modern man takes for granted — the ability to reason — has yet to be
developed at the time this woman exists. She is at the mercy of others' emotions. Like
a child, she has no defense, no means to separate what is her own from what belongs to
another, and so like a child she is unaware of why she is experiencing much of what is
in her life.

The report goes on to relate that the woman receives thoughts projected to her
instantaneously. "Because she has not developed, or has not chosen to use her own will
in formulating her own conclusions, (there is) the continuous fluctuation of thought,
activity, and desire."

Eventually she is placed into a working position whereby her intuitive faculties are
used consistently. She becomes a "tracer" of other vibrations, what today might be a
psychic detective, or medical intuitive.

The suggestions given to this woman can be as helpful to us as they were to her,
particularly those who are attuned to others often to their own peril.

Intuitive Reporter: ...We see again this one has tendency to attune self to vibrational frequencies of other individuals, and to absorb into self the tendencies and predispositions of these others. We see this can be a very beneficial quality and attribute for self, but we see at this time period it is not being used positively by this one. We see, for the most part, this one tends to push aside her conscious desires when doing this, and becomes so engrossed in the others that she loses her perspective, both emotionally and through reasoning. We see, for the most part, this is done in highly emotional situations and there is not control of it.

Would suggest to this one to formulate clearly her desires for the present time, and to recognize that she has these abilities which can work for her to gain her desires, and then begin consciously placing into activity the things necessary to bring these desires to her. Would suggest each day that she consider an area of physical activity which can be pursued in order to create and manifest her physical desires. Suggest as she attunes herself more to her own desires, she will be strengthening her own will in making these decisions, and she will be able to have greater control over her receptive ability to others.

Would suggest also to this one to pay very close attention to the times when she is receiving vibrations from others and observe her ability to control this. Would suggest this can be used as a beneficial tool if she allow the reception of only enough vibration to perceive the situation correctly, but then to stop the flow whenever she decides it is necessary. Would suggest also to this one that she has developed well the passive nature previously, and at this point it is necessary to begin balancing it with a more dominate type characteristic. [91176101232]

The connection of mind and body is in the process of becoming part of the collective consciousness. This began in earnest in the 20th century in large part through education and media. Doctors recommend meditation and relaxation, educators recommend concentration and visualization, corporate managers recommend inventiveness while counselors recommend emotional bonding. Our world of today is ripe with growing awareness that thoughts are things.

Another Atlantean report *[1002761013234]* addresses this by examining emotional development and its connection with the physical body. The parallels with common experiences today are startling. The reporter sees a male experiencing in what would today be called a physically impaired body. The soul *"formed the body from birth with a certain nerve disorder."* The reporter notes the value of this: *"We see this causing this one many physical difficulties, but we see it triggered strongly by the emotions."* When the emotions become involved the physical disorders become pronounced, not unlike many of today's neurological disorders, such as tics or spasms. Thanks to media we have collectively learned that those experiencing such disorders, for instance Parkinson's disease, can be effective actors (Michael Fox), attorney generals (Janet Reno), and religious leaders (Pope John Paul II).

The report gives details of the learning this kind of experience affords.

> *Intuitive Reporter: We see this one to be highly intellectual and to use his intelligence in the work aspect. We see this one to also be extremely sensitive because of the condition he has brought through from birth. We see for this reason this one is quite cautious with his activity in order to remain in a state of calm... [1002761013234]*

The stimulus for Self control, to learn how to create and maintain a moderate, balanced frame of mind comes in the form of wanting to control his body. It is quite common today for people to seek ways to control their body, more often through physical substances like foods or a drug rather than realizing the energetic power of thought.

This Atlantean deals with work pressures. He travels a great deal, establishing certain electronic, scientific, research stations in different areas of the world. He then serves as the liaison personnel between those who live in the new stations and those officials of the homeland. He is effective at this, it is reported. But in time, he weakens.

During times of physical disturbances, he begins to become distraught and difficult to work with. He begins to experiment, using chemicals in the body to try to control the condition. The result is passivity and a lack of control. The man becomes mentally deranged. Because of his high intellectual capacity to distort many of the facts that he has retained within the mind, he reaches a point of complete collapse.

This man is strong, his recuperative powers are great and after a long period of convalescence he returns to work. His duties are reduced in an effort to assist him in controlling his situation. He reacts with bitterness to what he sees as a reduction in his status which aggravates the physical disturbances once again. He resorts to chemicals again, feeling out of control of his body and his environment. This is entrapment, confined to a place you do not understand nor know how to gain freedom from.

A different viewpoint of the emotional development is reflected in a profile which could easily be a synopsis of a typical employee. It begins:

> *Intuitive Reporter: This one is at an energy state that is not of what is known now as the physical. This place there were many entities for a learning situation. This particular entity was dealing with the study of thought and in particular recording information as to thought and its effects on physical beings such as specifically lower forms of plants.*

This one considered the job quite unstimulating. This one was aware of others which this one felt had much more important jobs. This one saw recording information as being quite menial. This one felt this one had more potential and more ability that could be utilized than at the job this one held.

This one became quite dissatisfied. This one began resenting, this was the ultimate reason for removal of this one from her job. This was not understood by this one. This one was quite aware of negative thoughts and vibrations, and it was simply interfering with her job. This one was quite ashamed of the situation, quite humiliated, for the job this one had been dismissed from was considered very menial. This was not misunderstood.

This one felt so much shame and humiliation that this one decided to leave this plane. This one left this time with misunderstandings, bitterness, and humiliation towards those who had dismissed her. The attitude and condition of self is reflective of many lifetimes. Because this plane is not in the physical as now, much more misunderstanding took place that this one put into motion through her decision that this reoccurs in many lifetimes. Much is to be learned.

Conductor: How is this time period referred to?

Intuitive Reporter: Third cycle of what is commonly called the Age of Atlantis.

Conductor: How was this entity referred to?

Intuitive Reporter: Lay-shng-Ma. [11097420183]

The long standing effects of choices made, experiences rejected and left in ruins, is emphasized here. The woman in Atlantis is like a child, with limited experience. She does not know the import of her work. She has yet to realize thoughts create her world. Like a child who only becomes interested in a toy when someone else is playing with it, she begins to want the job she resented only after it is taken from her. The import of her work continues to allude her but she leaves a legacy of misunderstanding.

The report reveals resentment, bitterness, and humiliation have become repeated experiences, patterns of learning that are rejected. Imagine if that child grows up, retaining the same frame of reference, the same attitude of selfishness. As an adolescent she might be prone to compete for the affection of others, only wanting friends when they show others attention. Such a person would be completely caught up in the outward show of friendship, missing the deeper, fulfilling attributes of divine love. Because of emotional and egoic reactions, this woman misses the true purpose of life.

The significance of her Intuitive Report begins *"This is one of those lifetimes to be used for understanding the situation that was given. Perhaps it would be helpful for this one to review humility."* She is encouraged toward Self awareness through examining how she had formed her identity, her concept of who she is. Suggestions are given for improving Self esteem in relationship to ambitions and goals. *"Perhaps for this one a realization of the physical and the responsibility of being on this plane...Understand balance."*

She is given a koan to explore: *"The most glorious person still is in the physical and has menial tasks to perform. They should not be looked down upon for they are necessary and as much a part of the physical as the glorious aspects."* It is reminiscent of the Buddhist teaching: Before enlightenment chop wood, carry water. After enlightenment chop wood, carry water. We are all seeking the transcendent point of view where we will experience freedom from the suffering of the physical world. Our journey there is like this woman's.

Understanding the nature of existence and the part we are to play in it is the key to freedom. We release attachments by fulfilling desires. Desires are fulfilled as we understand the need which births each desire. By understanding consciousness we learn about the levels of existence, why they exist and how they may be employed to fulfill our purpose of soul progression. This is made possible by the advances in the development of the mental, emotional, and physical systems made during the Atlantean period.

Sometimes these advances resulted in losing sight of the reason for experiencing. This is referred to through these reports as withdrawal, meaning a removal of the attention from the physical world and energy from the physical body. When the energy which sustains the body is cut off, the body ceases to grow and change.

A description of this descent into matter is found in an Egyptian incarnation during the last cycle of Atlantis.

> *Intuitive Reporter: ...We see this one to have been involved in a position which might be termed as advisory. We see her working with many individuals who were troubled and having difficulty. We see them to have had much turbulence within the emotional body. We see this to have been the result of difficulties and mutations of the developing form of themselves. We see this to have occurred as the result of a combination of the forms being developed into the man form and that which was relating more to the animal state.*
>
> *We see therefore, these ones had much difficulty in balancing the emotional selves and adapting themselves to continuing in a prominent expression as a human individual. We see them to have been greatly*

troubled and that it was necessary to isolate them from the rest of the population of the civilization at that time. We see these ones to go through a special course of renovation and restoration, and we see the final stage of this to have been the balancing and harmonizing of the emotional states of these ones.

...We see during this time, that she kept herself in a supervisory position and worked from a more detached perspective with this activity.

Over time, the female "began to experience much indecision and much sympathy for these ones, realizing that she must remove them from their positions." She became ill herself for a short time. She recovered and returned to her work finding it more and more difficult for her to maintain the emotional detachment and balance necessary.

Intuitive Reporter: ...We see that also there were changes in those who were coming to her and we see that they were dealing with different kinds of instabilities. We see that as she recognized this and began to be more involved with her work and in her interactions with these clients or patients, we see that eventually a certain individual came to her for counseling, and we see that as she worked with this one, she became totally emotionally immersed in the situations involved in his life. We see that she was becoming more and more inefficient in working with him and we see her recognizing this at one point and directing him to another counselor for the continuation of his treatment.

We see the recognition of this within herself was so intense that she made the decision to remove herself altogether from this position and from this work. [1114781111]

Feelings of inadequacy, guilt and great sadness filled her for she missed her work. She also worried that her counseling techniques might be ill used by some she had trained. Finally the accumulation of concern and anxiety became too great for her to bear alone and she returned to the place of her work spending her remaining days in an unfulfilling advisory capacity.

She withdraws from this lifetime (dies) at the age of 71 years.

All of the Past Life Profiles offered through the School of Metaphysics are relevant lifetimes to the present, the karmic traces are revealed in the body of the report itself. In the second part of the report — the significance — the relevance of the former life to the present life is given. Here are the ideas, emotions, desires, loves, hates, lacks, misunderstandings, gifts, hurts, all the thoughts that make us who we believe we are. Here we are presented with how our thoughts and actions, alone and with others, are the expression of a greater underlying cause, imperceptible to the physical eye. This cause is the individual's karmic indentures – the reasons for experiences that resonate with the laws of the universe for that soul's progression.

A window into the universal nature of karma, the law of compensation and balance, for every human being was given during one profile:

> *Intuitive Reporter: We see this one to have been quite active in that incarnation, to have been aggressive, to have been greatly dedicated to the purposes of the physical part of existence at that point. To have been aware during the time of physical experience of the error made by her self, particularly toward the latter part of this period. We see this installed within self an additional difficulty of regret, to some degree, or remorse to feel that others had suffered through the lack of self in understanding. We see progression made, however. [91176101232]*

And so personal and universal evolution progresses, one lifetime at a time. The Golden Rule, existing in every culture in some form, serves as the means by which we become aware of our own karma, our lessons to be learned.

Why am I Here?

Some might wonder why light beings – spirits or souls you might call them – free to roam the galaxy, would come to desire a physical body on this planet. This is a logical question. One Daniel and I wanted to explore. Direct questioning on the matter gave mind-expanding responses that are covered later in this book.

Research through the catalogued Past Life Profiles unearthed this 1973 Atlantean report *[050873191026]* which sheds incredible light upon this question. It begins in a way different from any other report I've read or seen, addressing the individual directly on a topic of universal learning. This report speaks more to us now for it speaks of what blinds us to different points of view, the lines that tether us to the limits of what has been. In this way, it paints a vivid picture of how the emotions have become subject as much to the physical part of man's consciousness as an actively creative part of the inner man.

> *Intuitive Reporter: There is advice to this one.*
> *When one seeks information, it is usually from a subconscious desire for understanding of self. When one seeks information, there may not be the restraints of fear placed about it, for fear will bring to self misunderstanding of the information. The conscious mind at this time is*

enveloped in fear of self and is involved with misunderstanding of those processes that take place within self for own involvement and development. Fear is of the conscious and it is the desire of the conscious to shut out any information that may bring stimulation to self for fear that the conscious mind might have to make adjustments. Fear is of a desire within self to protect self from understanding. Whenever this desire is allowed to present itself there will be defense mechanisms, such as fear — there will also be emotional overtones to this. For though there is the desire to search forward and understand, the fear stands in the way of the completion of this understanding for the constant protection of self only brings about fear and misunderstanding.

If this information is to be given in order that this one may completely understand and grow, there must be no fear. For if fear is allowed to envelop the information, it is to no use and will be to no growth process.

Would suggest that this one at this time sit down to think of the word 'fear'. To think of all that it has kept self from understanding. To think of fear and what it does to men in great high positions such as those of the president of the U.S. (Richard Nixon at that time) *and his fear of discovery as to his involvement in political matters that are shunned and are viewed by society as being unacceptable. To realize what fear does to men in war, when men kill out of fear. It is of great destructive forces. When a war springs, it is out of fear. All destructive elements will generally spring from fear.*

Man became entrapped in the physical out of fear. These must be contemplated on and realized.

If one is afraid of self, one is destroying self. For why should self be afraid if self is of all of the universe and is connected to the creator in its completion and understanding. And if the creator knows no fear, then how can fear be compatible to growth? ...

"Entrapped in the physical" describes the condition of separation natural to the physical world; male-female, hot-cold, sweet-sour, rich-poor, up-down, in-out. These expressions of duality exist for the spirit's learning. Master the Self and the physical world no longer holds power over you.

Within Subconscious Mind thought progresses in development toward physical manifestation. In order for thought to move from its expanded mental state it must contract. When this occurs, it is like a light through a prism, one singular ray divides into the colors of the rainbow. This same point of separation transforms thought so it may adapt itself to the slower vibration, more dense expressions of energy, characteristic of the physical world.

It is the experience of viewing a drop of water through a microscope. What to the human eye appears to be a single drop is actually teaming with activity seen when magnified many fold. So it is with perceiving into the mind. In the inner levels beyond the physical world the inherit unity of all can be seen. As in our dreams, the deeper in mind, the lighter the people and scenes, the more etheric or "ghostly" their appearance.

Believing we are separate in our own minds, naturally produces a compartmentalized view of our relativity with others. We hold others at bay, erecting fences between ourselves and our neighbors. Soon we no longer know our neighbors, and what we don't know becomes strange to us. What is foreign is not understood. Fear now has a place to root, quickly overtaking the innate nature of connectedness.

The individual receiving this profile was ready to receive this insight. It is a reminder to us all to seek with the intention of finding, to learn with the intention of increasing our soul, to open our minds to the possibilities. In this man's case, what was to come would test the limits of his own beliefs and transport him outside the comfort zone he had created with his physical mind.

> *Intuitive Reporter: We see this one in the form of man in the area referred to as Eurach Atlantis. We see this point of existence to be in a most progressive form. We see at this time great mental stimulation and great growth for many entities within this area. We see within the Atlantean continent great minds, great physical manifestations, are in the process of developing energy states to a very, very high degree. We see these ones to desire to experience within pleasant and unpleasant animal forms, unpleasant and pleasant man forms as well as mineral forms for the understanding that the entering and leaving of the body may be for the use of the absorption of information for growth.*
>
> *We see this one at this time to enter and to leave the body freely. To however, become fearful upon the inner levels, to greet those energy changes that manifest themselves in strange forms, strange colors, with great fear. To see these without the understanding that they are in the process of development.*
>
> *We see this one to meet other high minds and to discuss this at great length, realizing that this fear is not of self, realizing that this fear is a threat to self, in some sense not understanding the full process. Being advised that this is the emotion necessary for the experience of the physical. We see this one to begin delving into this emotion greatly, trying most diligently to understand its purpose to the man. We see however an engulfment in this, an attachment to this survey and this understanding so greatly, that the fear becomes the greater tool of the two.*
>
> *We see this one to begin experimenting with this fear, to begin experimenting with this emotion as to the affects it has upon the physical,*

the mental, and the spiritual realms. We see this one to project this emo-
tion into others to see how they respond to certain circumstances when this
emotion is present...

What for this Atlantean male began as experimentation for learning, became a trap of his own making as he lost sight of that original purpose. Like the little boy who cried wolf, he began to generate emotions to provoke emotions in others, even to the point of doing harm.

> *Intuitive Reporter: Realizing that this is a great and powerful tool, we see*
> *this one to begin using this for destructive purposes. It is of this that the*
> *submissive group begins to pull at the high counsel for destruction for fear*
> *of lack of understanding this. We see this one to be one of the great leaders*
> *of this, for fear would be the greatest emotion influencing those minds with*
> *the desire for understanding.*
>
> *Before this emotion was present the desire for understanding was*
> *well met, and the progress and development of this understanding was*
> *being met by the high council with steps for development in order that these*
> *minds might understand. However, upon the introduction of the emotion of*
> *fear, this took a complete about face with the high council and at this time*
> *period to realize the great power within the understanding of this emotion –*
> *fear. However, the completion of the understanding was not met, it would*
> *not have been used as a tool.*
>
> *We see this one to use this fear for own power and gain, feeling*
> *that to use this fear would be in a way to tap the high council for under-*
> *standing in order that release may be of this emotion and the release of the*
> *body. However, the high council realizing this emotion of being most*
> *primitive, ignores the pleas and so the fear engulfs this one greatly...*

Fear is taught. In the animal it is survival instinct, but without the human element of judgement. A rabbit flees from a prowling tiger to continue to live, were fear present the rabbit might have a more human reaction, thus stay and fight to protect its young. Fear is practiced avoidance transmitted from one human generation to the next until a child refuses to accept the training or an adult realizes how it crushes the spirit thus determines to leave it behind.

One of the greatest insights this report offers is the eradication of fear as necessary for understanding. For centuries man has confused fear with respect. The reasoner harnesses the power of memory so learning can progress. He knows how to view a thing again, how to re-spect. Those who fear forfeit this power of respect. Think of the many stories you have heard of conquerors who ruled briefly with fear only to come to a fitting end at the hand of those they tyrannized. Then consider the wise ruler who makes a friend of his enemy, thus no longer providing the breeding ground for fear.

Now this male must experience what he has caused to come into being.

> *Intuitive Reporter: We see among the submissive group to realize that this one is a threat to themselves and to begin a destructive process through mental exchange for this one, desiring for this one to withdraw from the physical and this area. We see this to have become so pressured to this one at such a high degree of mental exchange, this one withdrew from the physical at this area and left to a higher area within the Atlantean continent, there to exist solitary and alone, living in fear of those who might discover self and from any exchanges of energy necessary for all understanding.*
>
> *We see this one to have stagnated self at this point with fear and the emotions connected around fear. To have allowed self to become totally void of communication with others, for fear of discovery of true nature of self. We see this one to have existed in this area for 14 cycles. To have withdrawn from this area through the exchange and breakthrough of other mental forces, dissolving this fear to the degree that this one could escape. We see this one to have withdrawn at this time at the age of 54 cycles, to have allowed much energy to flow out of self, to expand its self little, to have dissipated self much from this emotion. [50873191026]*

When this person became caught up in the fear, he lost sight of his purpose for experiencing. This is an illustration of entrapment of the spirit in matter. The expression of lower heart energies, emotions reacting in the physical, are entrapping energies that breed the need for further learning. In this way the physical world becomes a schoolroom for learning the lessons to become proficient in consciousness and manifestation.

In this report, for reasons we can only surmise, the significance was given first. My experience tells me it is because of the universal nature of the significance to the development of human consciousness. Here, in one person's significant intuitive report was the cause of humanity's entrapment and its relief.

Whether in the days of Atlantis or now, the work to be done remains the same, remembering where we came from so we may know where we are going.

Where am I Going?

One of the most profound intuitive reports from the Atlantean time period gives an answer to this question. Clearly significant for the man receiving the report, its universal flavor shines. We include it here in its entirety in reverence to its power to illuminate the destiny of humanity.

This profile *[060373191323]* like the one preceding it begins in an unusual fashion. Unlike the one previously which addressed a universal concern, this report begins by addressing a very personal concern on the part of the person requesting the report, then proceeds to progressively become more universally revelatory.

Intuitive Reporter: There is advice at this time. This information will be given if truthfully desired. The concern is such at this point of despondency toward information, if this is not acquired soon, the attitude at this time is such that there seems to be great need for the information; however, there is also a great need expressed for the information to be developed within self. This choice is to the individual. The information is readily at hand. This choice must be your own truthful desire, as to the understanding it will develop within self.

Conductor: We ask that it be given.

We see this one in the form of creative light energy influential in vast circumstances developing in the hemispheric areas for land mass development.

We see this one forming at this point the eye of understanding. We see this eye to be at this time in a very elementary state of development. We see this one at this point concerning self greatly with other entities and energies interested in this particular bond – this surrounding the area mass – for the energy state for this mass, without the understanding within the intelligent form, would at this point explode, creating much disharmony within the creativity processes within the land masses. We see this one in great need of communicating those energy forms together. However we see this one, through the development of the eye of creativity, to have that individual will which is at a point most disruptive in this cord.

We see this belt to be developing quite strongly, and creating great masses to be exchanged with energy forms for those universes to mingle and create among themselves. We see this great band to be in the process of separating self from other bands of great energy state in order that each individual expression may be in a universality form, creating own land masses and own gaseous states through the creative forces exploding from the original into many sources. We see this great band to be made up of elemental structure at this particular point; having great energy states concerned with the compactness of the bands. However, within the bands, the individuality and the intelligent structure in order that it may be through self-expression that the universality of these land masses may be experienced.

We see this one with the development of the mind creativity image to be at this point most confused, for the action of that self is presenting so rapidly that the observation points have become most weakened. (We see) this one becoming involved in the action rather than in the absorption of the creative processes becoming used, rather than expressing own individuality. We see this use to become the weakening link within this bond. We see this bond to begin compacting self upon this weaker link, trying to form a greater bond, compressing this one's own individual expression into a most brittle form of life, giving off diffused and inert expression. This inertia create(s) somewhat of a disruptive quality within the bond.

We see this bond to begin movement away from the original. With this, individuality becoming weaker within the linkage. We see this linkage to begin expanding. We see this to begin disruptive forces creating much disharmony with mind, and individuality also, within the compacting forces, and entities on a surrounding level at this time supporting each other for the expansion of the universe. We see this to explode this individuality. To send this individual mind and concept into a void in which there is little absorption and little understanding.

We see, however, collective processes in order that this individuality may regain self expression. However, this creative ability (is) being quite hampered through lack of understanding of mental image.

We see the band to have brought about most disruptive elements within the system. We see this system to begin a slow declination into an inert state. We see this state to begin stagnation. We see this individuality to have created most disruptive qualities; those other individual expressions to withdraw from this method and to return to the original level of understanding and experience. (We see them) as leaving this most dormant – the creative process – at a point in which there was no culmination of true energetic form.

We see this to have brought about to this individual expression great pain. Great confusion. Disruptive qualities within. That expression of own will and understanding to have been exploded to have left the original source in order that collectivity may take place with the understanding of redevelopment from the individual energy state into mass activity once again.

We see no withdrawal, we see culmination of forces to begin upon the second cycle. We see this cycle of activity to begin upon the creative mind imagining this responsiveness, once again within this one's own individual expression.

The intuitive counsel offered in the significance of this report addresses the battle each of us wages - the light against the darkness in all its forms - until awareness transcends the limitations of ignorance. It is counsel valuable to us all for its depth and clarity concerning what separates us and what unity will ask of us.

Conductor: What would be the significance of that to the present life-time?

Intuitive Reporter: We see this one in a most disruptive state in accordance with entities surrounding self in order that development of mind may take place. We see this one in constant expression in order to claim own individuality rather than learning the harmonizing properties necessary for progression and understanding. We see this one struggling greatly to bring about in self, self reassurance and understanding through own individual expression. We see this expression to be met with great defensive mechanisms rather than learning through harmonization individual expression takes place.

We see this one struggling within the seven systems to express self from an original source as individual rather than unified, for this universality has not applied within the mind at this time. We see this one searching at this time, acquiring greater powers in understanding; however, to be misusing greatly that individuality process brought about through will and control, for at this time this process is bringing about confusion on the inner levels of understanding to own progression and regression back to the original source. We see this progression and regression to be in a disruptive circle and at this point energy being sent out in misdirected forms creating some disturbance within the mind.

*We see this one's lack of understanding of the physical and own responsibility within the physical to be reflective of those states within the mind. This must be developed for understanding not through the exertion of individuality and the assurance of perfection, but through the experience of perfection through lack of concern with individuality. **Learn the individuality through the expression of perfection within the universe.** The individuality will express itself by its own harmonization with the universe, for at this point **this connecting link is missing**, as are other entities at this point concerned so greatly with own individual expression.*

Would suggest to this one at this point, to realize the great necessity of understanding that of the ego. For the ego at this point is crowding and stagnating those images of self that are so necessary for understanding. For the ego at this point is becoming most brittle and is shattering within the inner levels, concerning self so much with individual expression.

Suggest this one consider each entity at this time concerned within the earth cycle is the separation from the universality. Once this is recognized and received with great love and rejoicing this will become compact into the universality and the individual expression will be recognized through own importance in this system of creation.   [060373191323]

The Consciousness of Atlantis

The Consciousness of
Atlantis

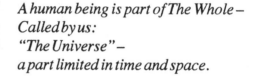

A human being is part of The Whole –
Called by us:
"The Universe" –
a part limited in time and space.

He experiences himself, his thoughts and feelings,
as something separated from the Rest –
a kind of optical "delusion"
of consciousness.
This delusion is a prison for us,
restricting humans to personal desires and affection
for a few Persons nearest to us.

Our task must be to free ourselves of the prison
By widening our circle of compassion to embrace
all living creatures
And the whole of Nature
in all its beauty.

–Albert Einstein

Four Cycles of Growth

The story of Atlantis reveals itself in layers. First the mystery. The sparsity of accounts lends itself well to myths and fantasies of what might have been. Old husband's tales of perfection on Earth defiled by the evil of men who lust for power tend to be supported by the seers who have lifted the veil into other worlds. That which endures from Plato to Disney is the morality lesson of intent. In the plane of good and evil, intent becomes the key to other worlds, the means to freedom.

Perhaps the largest body of information concerning Atlantis exists not in Egypt or the Atlantic but in the state of Missouri right in the heartland of the United States.

Hundreds of accounts of the Atlantean time period collectively fill in many of the details to a civilization existing in the consciousness of man for millennia, but largely forgotten in awareness. These Past Life Profiles, given by Intuitive Reporters and Conductors trained at the School of Metaphysics, tell of the Earth changes, the migrations, the people and their lives, their desires and their challenges.

Each profile was given as a significant lifetime to the present for the person requesting the report. A large volume of these relevant past experiences surfaced in the 1970's. There are many reasons why this was probably the case. Foremost in my (Barbara's) awareness is the prophetic nature of the late 1960's-'70s, particularly in the United States as a precursor to what is happening now upon our planet. This period was unique in the energetic influences being brought to bear on consciousness. The youth were the ones most willing to accept and act, and their responsibility upset the existing polarity which had reached a point of stagnation. Perhaps this was best described in the simple slogan, "Make love, not war!"

Yet the application of the thought and all the changes in consciousness it would bring was foreseen by a handful. The forces moving in one direction, like a mighty river, were far more prevalent an influence on the masses. This did not deter those who had come into this world, like the Beldane, to be a catalyst for change. The Teslas, the Rifes, the Tuckers, the Swedenborgs, the Steiners, and a growing stream of brilliant souls - relatively unknown during their lifetime - are now becoming known around the world. These were masters of innovative thinking, outside the boundaries of the norm, the pre-existent, the already manifested. Visionaries each, they could see beyond what is into worlds of what can be.

It is this kind of thinking that was more prevalent during the 1970's than in more recent years. And because the thinking of the person requesting a Past Life Profile determines the information that will be available to read from the Akashic Record, a number of these reports were from the Atlantean time.

Just as many were experimenting in 1960-70's America, looking for ways to alter consciousness, to save the planet, to live in peace, so were those who ended up populating Atlantis seeking ways to stabilize consciousness, to make a planet home, to remain connected to their source. The parallels between the two time periods of mankind, the relativity between two civilizations, become apparent as we study this wealth of intuitive information. It is like finding ancient lost texts, revealing a history we once knew but have long forgotten.

It is now time to remember.

After hours of combing through the Atlantean materials, I decided to go beyond the conscious level in choosing the information to make widely available at this time. What you will read in the following sections entitled "The Consciousness of Atlantis" is a good blend of reasoning and intuition. This is befitting of the energies now available to us all.

After arranging the profiles into time periods, "cycles" as the intuitive reports call them, I then chose one report from each period to reproduce here in full. This is in lieu of a more physicalized research citing dozens of reports, pulling pieces of information in response to visceral curiosity. The result is a detailed exploration of each cycle of Atlantis as revealed through the significant past life of one man or woman. In each case the best representation of the time and place as it relates to the universal experience of the formation of humanity was chosen.

Since I believe that the greatest value of Atlantis was the development of reasoning in the consciousness of a species and therefore the learning of cause and effect, succinctly described as thoughts are things, I have chosen to give the full information from the reports chosen. The complete report is given before commentary. This is in the hope that by receiving the full picture as it was experienced by one individual, you will be more equipped to determine for yourself the import of the information, how it fits into what you already know or believe, and from the significance of the report, what it says to all of us now as we cross the threshold into intuitive, Spiritual Man.

Following each of these *"Consciousness of Atlantis"* sections, you will find intuitive research conducted by Daniel. This research was conducted over several weeks in the spring and summer of 2001 and is presented in the order it was given. The questions asked were those chosen by Daniel to be of the greatest import in expanding humanity's body of knowledge beyond presently recorded history. Sometimes they were premeditated, and sometimes they were in response to mind-expanding revelations about who we are and where we have come from.

The Consciousness of Atlantis

First Cycle of Atlantis

Early Atlantis was a part of the huge land mass scientists have recently named Pangea. Atlantis was like a huge continent, like today's Australia only much larger. Pre and Early Atlantis was a time of Mu or Lemuria, another repeatedly used name for what we would today call a country.

Beyond the Earth's changes, Atlantis was the development of a people, of a race, the human race. A cluster of thinkers tinkering with the Earth like adolescents with a chemistry set. Experimenting. Trying something to see what happens. And increasingly trying to dictate the outcome of those experiments.

Here is the descent of spirit into matter. Here is the fall from grace, the birth of karma, the entrapment in the physical world. It did not happen overnight. It occurred within some individuals over time as their identification with physical outcome strengthened, casting the shadow of mortality upon their existence. Others kept sight of the purpose for their experimenting thereby retaining immortality, described in these reports as "the ability to enter and leave the physical body at will."

The reports are the history of those of us who became mortal. Like a modern Hercules, our origin is immortal but we have forgotten. Physical life is our "labors" whereby we may remember who we are, how we got here, and where we are to go.

Here we give you a glimpse into our past that you too might be stimulated to remember. For each of the four time periods of Atlantis - cycles as they are referred to in the Intuitive Reports - a complete Past Life Profile is cited so you may explore and consider. This is followed by a breakdown of the information with commentary to elucidate what was given in the context from which it came. These are by no means the only reports of their era, but we believe they will be fascinating for their content and intriguing for their insight.

An Intuitive Report from the First Cycle of Atlantis

We see female incarnation. We see this one existing during that time period of the early Atlantean civilizations. We see this one to have lived within a domed structure, existing beneath the waters. We see here there were a group of people not large in number, devoted to the study and discovery of those elements that lay beneath sea. We see this domed structure to be constructed, especially for the purpose of these ones, to exist for a period of time at the bottom of this water. We see these ones periodically leaving this structure and traveling through the water and gathering samples, gathering food substances from the bottom of this water.

We see many tests being done by these ones within this domed structure. We see much apparatus and equipment that was placed within this structure for this specific purpose.

We see each one of these individuals to be highly intelligent of the understanding of that which lived beneath the water, also in great understanding of the technology that was put into the equipment and the methods used to discover and to study. We see each one of these to have been especially selected for their abilities, each with somewhat different backgrounds, with different understandings, however each necessary to the whole purpose of this structure.

We see this one in particular to deal with the usage, the effects of certain plant-like foods, also certain animal foods that could be used by man, the type of man that was coming into existence at this time. We see during this time there was great change in the evolution of the structures used by the souls. We see there was a need to also change the physical intake of substance, so that these structures would be more suitable for usage; we see this to be her purpose within this place. We see this one to be entirely devoted to this purpose. We see this one coming to this place for the sole reason for providing the necessary information that could be used in the making of this type of substance, that could be used by these new structures that were coming into their existence. We see her to remain in this position for a period of time, an incalculable period of time.

We see this one required very little sleep, very little food. We see this one to be in a highly evolved structure that required less physical upkeep to sustain it. We see this one accomplishing the purpose. We see herself along with these others to discover and to provide part of the Earth. We see these ones working in accordance with those who also worked on the land and in combination provided that this purpose was finished and was accomplished, this one withdrew from that experience. We see this bringing down of the dome-like structure and it ceased to exist physically, all together. We see this one referred during that time as Ladato. Time period as was given is early Atlantean experience. We see age of with-drawal unable to be calculated.

Conductor: What would be the significance of that lifetime to the present lifetime?

We see previous decision before entering the physical during this time made by this one, that this time period be devoted to the furthering and the greater understanding of the human race, as much as could be influenced by this one during this time.

We see this one in early years during this lifetime to experience great understandings of that which underlies the outward makeup of each individual, however not to understand consciously exactly what the causes and the origin of this understanding within self. We see this one not developed fully to understand exactly that which was coming into the conscious mind during that time.

We see now that as this one has progressed in years, and in understanding, that opportunity exists for this knowledge to now come forth and that this one will be in situations that will be, that will have great opportunity, to provide that knowledge that lies within this one. We see this one has studied in the past and is actively engaged again in the under-standing to the highest degree the makeup that exists within each indi-vidual, while recognizing that which lies within her own self.

We see at this point there is somewhat of a barrier or an obstruc-tion in allowing this information to pass through self, the consciousness, and outward to where it can be used in the physical. We see this to be in the emotional body. We see here there is anxiety within the self which is not under control. We see much of this stems from the great desire within to provide information that is stored within subconscious mind, that is not being allowed out at this time. We see this as manifesting as anxiety in relationship to those that are very close to this one presently.

We see the emotional body to be very high at times and to reach the lowest point of depths at times, creating much frustration within the self. We see also there is need at this time to project self to others with more strength and not such passiveness, as has occurred at times in the past. We see this one has need at this time to bring into understanding that self can present that which lies within, with great strength, with under-standing, with confidence.

We see these elements to be of somewhat barriers at this time towards allowing that information to flow into the consciousness and to fulfill that purpose which was decided before entering the physical at this

*time. Would suggest to this one to work on these aspects of self and when
the opportunity arises and when the information begins to flow into
consciousness to take full advantage and to fulfill that purpose which has
been intended by self. [71074426264]*

Exploratory Analysis

This report conveys much about existence during the early part of Atlantis. Life there and
then was not the movie images of cavemen clothed in animal skins discovering fire.
Those images more correctly might belong with the descriptions revealed in the intuitive
inquiries related to the Centaurus which developed what modern man calls Homo
erectus.

With this report we have a window into what Ignatius Donnelly – author of the
modern definitive Atlantean account – called "the antediluvian world." Antediluvian
means before the Biblical flood which takes on new meaning in light of the School of
Metaphysics' intuitive research. The Biblical flood is most probably based upon the
many Earth changes occurring in pre-historic, Atlantean times.

What is challenging to the limits of current thought is the idea that preconceived
ideas and beliefs, be they considered fantasy or science, concerning pre-history leave
little room for the truth. Some believe Atlantis existed as a glorious civilization, far more
advanced than our own, while others insist mankind is the epitome of evolution to the
present time. This research refutes neither, supports both; a concept conceivable to a
thinker capable of multidimensional consciousness. The amazing reality where neither-
either, yet both, is universally true, may be the destiny of our consciousness.

Let us review this report with an eye to what it reveals about the Atlantean period.

Intuitive Reporter: We see female incarnation.

The very opening of this report let's us know that there existed a separation between
female and male bodies. The yin and the yang were expressing as independent forms and
so in this case the receptive form was chosen which would enhance the thinker's ability
for receiving stimuli. The male form would encourage acting, creating.

*Intuitive Reporter: We see this one existing during that time period of the
early Atlantean civilizations.*

The plural use of *civilization* shows there were many groups working toward a common
ideal. Along with other reports from the same time period this indicates that Atlantis was

a large part of an Earth mass, like Eurasia of today which includes many different people, their cultures and their languages.

> *Intuitive Reporter: We see this one to have lived within a domed structure, existing beneath the waters. We see here there were a group of people not large in number, devoted to the study and discovery of those elements that lay beneath sea. We see this domed structure to be constructed, especially for the purpose of these ones, to exist for a period of time at the bottom of this water. We see these ones periodically leaving this structure and traveling through the water and gathering samples, gathering food substances from the bottom of this water.*

It is easy to visualize the structures described here as buildings or types of underwater conveyances, like minisubs, because such images are part of our collective consciousness thanks in large part to the efforts of oceanographers, the military, and enterprising movie directors. This is indeed a possibility.

In light of Daniel's and my intuitive investigation opening the door to the intelligence of sea life, particularly the dolphin, is it possible this could be referring to such life? Maybe the forms were the dolphins.

It is also possible the domed structures may not have been physical things existing separate from consciousness, as we are accustomed to in our present world, but may well have been the expression of consciousness itself. Like laying a strong foundation for the house you intend to build, perhaps these thinkers, these beings, were learning how to prepare the Earth for the use they intended to make of it.

Of all the possibilities the one with the greatest evidence to support it is that the domed structures might have been the first experimental forms of what would become the Homo sapiens body. The domed structures could be the cranium of early man, a sufficient abode for spiritual consciousness. If so, then the periodic leaving could be akin to the astral projection experience in consciousness today. The reenergizing of spirit that occurs when we sleep may well have taken place for these intelligences when they too were less attentive to the physical structure.

> *Intuitive Reporter: We see many tests being done by these ones within this domed structure. We see much apparatus and equipment that was placed within this structure for this specific purpose.*

If the domed structures are references to the building of the physical form, particularly the brain, then the apparatus and equipment might indicate the development of neuro-chemical balances that would sustain the presence of consciousness.

I read recently that scientist-doctors have invented a device that can be implanted and linked to the vagus nerve to offer an electrical stimulation when a person becomes depressed. What the commonplace pacemaker does for the heart, this device would do for the brain. This is mankind's current level of technology.

What if technology existed that could empower the depressed person to transcend his depression without the need for additional body machinery, or even pharmaceutical chemicals? What if the technology that was being developed eons ago in Atlantis was just that – a technology of intelligence more than a technology of substance or energy. The ancients have always taught us that thought is cause, even if most of the teaching has been in esoteric mystery schools.

> *Intuitive Reporter: We see each one of these individuals to be highly intelligent of the understanding of that which lived beneath the water, also in great understanding of the technology that was put into the equipment and the methods used to discover and to study. We see each one of these to have been especially selected for their abilities, each with somewhat different backgrounds, with different understandings, however each necessary to the whole purpose of this structure.*

This is a beautiful picture of group-think. A prehistoric manifestation of the think tank, where diversely talented individuals are gathered for a specific and unified purpose.

If you can imagine, pure intelligence with a desire to express itself. Like an artist with a burning image in his mind that he must express in order to share it with others, or a scientist who must find a way to help his child overcome a debilitating condition of the body. Or the youthful desire to be somebody, to make a difference in the world, to make the world a better place because you have been here.

When you can connect with this inner urge inherent in our spirit, it is easier to grasp the desire to create. In the first cycle of Atlantis, what intelligence desired to create was a viable vehicle, a workable body that could be used for experiencing.

Perhaps this is not speaking about underwater machines like those in use today. Perhaps the technology is the technology of consciousness rather than materials. Perhaps the equipment is nervous systems rather than electrical cables. And if this is possible, then perhaps these intelligences, one of which was this woman, were united to explore the feasibility of fashioning an existence within the water of the Earth rather than on land.

> *Intuitive Reporter: We see this one in particular to deal with the usage, the effects of certain plant-like foods, also certain animal foods that could be used by man, the type of man that was coming into existence at this time.*

This supports the hypothesis of an openness to the possibilities, a kind of prehistoric feasibility study for the next stage of evolution, a stage that would be characterized by what we now call Homo sapiens.

> *Intuitive Reporter: We see during this time there was great change in the evolution of the structures used by the souls.*

Much of this can be attributed to the considerable evolution of the planet occurring at the time, as well as the introduction of interplanetary influences.

> *Intuitive Reporter: We see there was a need to also change the physical intake of substance, so that these structures would be more suitable for usage; we see this to be her purpose within this place.*

How did it come to happen that man is a predator to lower life forms? How and why do we sustain our physical bodies on plants and animals when there is considerable evidence that people have lived for long periods on air and water? What really sustains physical life, and why? These questions come to mind when we consider that our bodies are not stagnant forms that we are trapped in for a lifetime, but energetic forms held together by both repeated physical contact over millions of years (genetic codes) and, more importantly, by the quality of thought generated by the owner.

This female was to explore, to experiment, in order to discover what external substances might be required to sustain a viable physical body. Like a baby learning which foods give immediate or sustained energy, this woman's purpose was to determine universal truths that would work for all souls.

> *Intuitive Reporter: We see this one to be entirely devoted to this purpose.*

The idea of religious passion comes to mind. When the mind is filled with the high-mindedness of Superconsciousness, devotion is a natural outpouring. Could this be why such a concept appears in seemingly every culture on the planet?

> *Intuitive Reporter: We see this one coming to this place for the sole reason of providing the necessary information that could be used in the making of this type of substance, that could be used by these new structures that were coming into their existence. We see her to remain in this position for a period of time, an incalculable period of time.*

The female's purpose was to learn how to sustain the substance of the physical body. How long did this take? *"An incalculable period of time."*

Intuitive Reporter: We see this one required very little sleep, very little food. We see this one to be in a highly evolved structure that required less physical upkeep to sustain it.

It would seem that this one was still rooted in spiritual form meaning the spiritual nature of Self is the seat of reference. The need for little sleep would indicate a continuity of awareness, an alert, awakened consciousness. The need for little food would indicate minimal contact therefore little or no dependency upon outer substances. Perhaps this one did not have a physical form in the way we understand the body today. Perhaps there was little if any identification with the body, in a similar way that you would not call yourself a Ford or Masserati, or change your name to Yves St. Laurent or Tommy Hilfiger because of the clothes you wear.

Intuitive Reporter: We see this one accomplishing the purpose. We see herself along with these others to discover and to provide part of the Earth. We see these ones working in accordance with those who also worked on the land and in combination provided that this purpose was finished and was accomplished, this one withdrew from that experience.

This reference brings a whole new realm of thinking into consideration. These ones beneath the seas worked with those on the land to fulfill their purpose. Could this experience have been not of man or even of dolphin but of the elemental force structures needed for the stabilization of Earth? Could these ones be more deva than human? Coming in the earliest part of Atlantis, when the huge Lemurian forms existed, there would be much work for any intelligence who wanted to build a sustainable form on such an unstable planet.

Whatever role these ones were playing in the development of what we now experience, it was as integral a part to having a place to live for them as it is for us.

Intuitive Reporter: We see the bringing down of the domed-like structure and it ceased to exist physically, all together. We see this one referred during that time as Ladato. Time period as was given is early Atlantean experience. We see age of withdrawal unable to be calculated. [71074426264]

If the domed-like structure was the cranium then it had served its purpose. The awkward wording of "bring down" paints a very different picture than one might expect. Perhaps the domed-like structure was an energy web existing as long as the work needed to be done to accomplish the purpose, like a giant air form used nowadays to construct monolithic domes. Or perhaps it was an interplanetary device in place long enough for the intelligences to complete their project. The possibilities are many, and perhaps there is a place for them all, as there usually is when the truth is fully revealed.

At any rate, whatever the domed-like structure was, it had fulfilled its purpose in mankind's evolution.

These Past Life Profiles describing accounts of Atlantean lives are rare. Less than one percent of the profiles to date reference this ancient time and place. Why? Because Past Life Profiles ask the Intuitive Reporter to relate *"a significant incarnation for this entity."* This command serves as the determiner for the information that will be available for the reporter to read. It is like a cosmic book title, and only that book is read. In this form of intuitive research the greatest assistance is provided to the individual.

This provides a wealth of information revealing the quality of consciousness linking the Atlantean period with the present day. This is quite clear in the opening of the significance of this woman's report.

> **Conductor: What would be the significance of that lifetime to the present lifetime?**
>
> *Intuitive Reporter: We see previous decision before entering the physical during this time made by this one, that this time period be devoted to the furthering and the greater understanding of the human race, as much as could be influenced by this one during this time.*

What a profound realization to possess – to know your soul's intention upon entering this life! Some spend a lifetime in solitude and prayer, others spend thousands of dollars, searching for a way to become aware of their purpose in life. The depth and breadth of this woman's soul urge is inspiring.

What this information tells us all is there are choices made by a part of ourselves that we may or may not be attuned to in our everyday life. It also says that whatever intentions this inner soul or spirit or consciousness had, must find cooperation in the outer mind in order to flourish.

> *Intuitive Reporter: We see this one in early years during this lifetime to experience great understandings of that which underlies the outward makeup of each individual, however not to understand consciously exactly what the causes and the origin of this understanding within self. We see this one not developed fully to understand exactly that which was coming into the conscious mind during that time.*

Such experiences have been most common for those who pursue understanding beyond the physical world. Early mind experiences are pronounced and strong, yet often misinterpreted by others. Not so long ago children with strong wills were sometimes physically reprimanded for behaviors adults did not condone. When this became taboo, emotional manipulation took its place. Now there is intellectual pressure combined with drugs as a means to curb unwanted behavior. None of these address the cause. And all are reactive means meant to protect the beliefs of adults.

Think about it. To respond lovingly and with intelligence to a willful child requires Self-awareness upon the part of the other person. The ideal of relating with the child must surpass controlling his or her actions and mind. Increasingly with children born since 1995, the mind will not be controlled by others, and this is what strikes fear in the emotions of so many adolescents and adults.

Fear can only take root where understanding is not present.

To receive aware guidance of how consciousness expresses from the moment of birth is to experience the greatest gift of life. Parents who understand how to wield their own consciousness, how to control their own minds, are far less likely to seek to dominate their child's. Feeding the mind becomes a priority so the soul may mature. Such parents want to be with their child. They live with their children, making themselves available, living and learning as independent members of a family, in much the same way this woman functioned in Atlantis.

To teach a child Self respect is to teach him to value his nighttime dreams as well as his daytime ones. To teach a child Self reliance is to teach him the mechanics of reasoning. To teach a child security is to teach him to love unconditionally. A child learns how to trust from those who are trust-worthy. He learns to value his thoughts, and therefore those of others, when around others who understand thought is cause and the physical is its manifest likeness. He learns to give and receive by learning the eternal power of something as simple as breathing.

When in this kind of environment, a child finds examples of how to interpret energies that leads to understanding and inner fulfillment.

> *Intuitive Reporter: We see now that as this one has progressed in years, and in understanding, that opportunity exists for this knowledge to now come forth and that this one will be in situations that will be, that will have great opportunity, to provide that knowledge that lies within this one. We see this one has studied in the past and is actively engaged again in the understanding to the highest degree the makeup that exists within each individual, while recognizing that which lies within her own self.*

At the time of receiving this report, this woman had been actively studying the lessons and disciplines offered in the School of Metaphysics. Life experiences had given her cause to evolve, and this study was giving her the means to assimilate, communicate and understand her experiences both in the past and in the present. Since the education in the School of Metaphysics is for Intuitive, Spiritual Man, the woman was finding what she had been looking for since she was a child, the encouragement and guidance that comes from Self exploration of Truth that is universal.

> *Intuitive Reporter: We see at this point there is somewhat of a barrier or an obstruction in allowing this information to pass through self, the consciousness, and outward to where it can be used in the physical. We see this to be in the emotional body. We see here there is anxiety within the self which is not under control. We see much of this stems from the great desire within to provide information that is stored within subconscious mind, that is not being allowed out at this time. We see this as manifesting as anxiety in relationship to those that are very close to this one presently.*

This one's greatest challenge in learning at the time of this report, was how to understand the connection between the mind and the emotions. Anxiety would rule her consciousness because her attention was scattered out of present time. She would allow her mind to wander into imaginary scenarios not in alignment with her desires. Her emotional response to these thoughts was anxiety which was creating a barrier to her learning. She didn't want to learn more because this would only add to her worries, as she saw it.

This progression of scattered thought to worry to emotional anxiety to present insecurity was consuming her attention like a huge tidal wave, blocking her vision. The disturbed mind kept awareness of the inner wisdom of her own subconscious mind, her soul, captive.

> *Intuitive Reporter: We see the emotional body to be very high at times and to reach the lowest point of depths at times, creating much frustration within the self. We see also there is need at this time to project self to others with more strength and not such passiveness, as has occurred at times in the past. We see this one has need at this time to bring into understanding that self can present that which lies within, with great strength, with understanding, with confidence.*

This woman had become a slave to emotions. Not knowing how to separate and identify them, she was at their mercy, a victim of her own thoughts and reactions. She would allow the emotions to build up and then deflate. The suggestions gave her a different point of view, a way to empower herself by respecting her strength, by believing in herself and her experiences through sharing these with others. Repeatedly doing this would create a new channel, making her subconscious understandings more accessible.

> *Intuitive Reporter: We see these elements to be of somewhat barriers at this time towards allowing that information to flow into the consciousness and to fulfill that purpose which was decided before entering the physical at this time. Would suggest to this one to work on these aspects of self and when the opportunity arises and when the information begins to flow into consciousness to take full advantage and to fulfill that purpose which has been intended by self. [71074426264]*

The elements this one needed to create in the present, which made the Atlantean experience relevant to her, were identified for her. Left to the limitations of her consciousness alone, strength had become stubbornness, receptivity – passivity, understanding – doubt, and potential – anxiety. By bringing forth the progressive forms of these energies, she could harmonize the outer mind with the inner mind thus allowing the original soul's intent to be made manifest.

This construction of energy – potential yet to be fulfilled – is a common theme in the Atlantean reports of this cycle. And a valuable lesson for us all.

INTUITIVE RESEARCH

2001

I

ATLANTIS
Intuitive Research Part I

In order to understand Atlantis, the interested person must first come to understand that life is motion. What we view, think or perceive as physical substance is in fact a bundle of energy, a collection of molecules, atoms and subatomic particles of energy that are in constant motion. The physical body is an energetic body. It is an electrical body as are trees, animals and the planet Earth.

This energy in its myriads of forms leads to the emotions, the mental self, the spiritual self, and to consciousness itself.

This book will examine the evolution of body, emotions, mind and spirit, for the Self, for humanity and for the planet Earth.

There is a scientific theory which is not a fact that is called uniformitarianism or uniformity. Uniformitarianism is the idea that the evolution of the Earth, people, places, things, and the solar system evolves at a certain uniform rate.

For example, there is the theory that continental drift, which is the movement of the continents, is occurring in the present time period at the same rate of speed as in the past. This is not the case. When the Moon was expelled from the Earth, a huge hole was created in what is now the Pacific Ocean. This hole had a slope to it. Water filled this hole, and the planet Earth – seeking to achieve a balance – redistributed mass. Continental Drift is a part of this ongoing process of balance.

The Earth in its earlier ages was more moldable, more plastic and somewhat less dense than in the present time period. Therefore, there was a greater fluidity of motion as the continents drifted or moved closer to the present time period. A greater balance was achieved and there was less need for motion to fill in the void or space. North America in the present time period is drifting westward into the Pacific and towards the area where the Moon was expelled.

Some land masses such as Antarctica have drifted or moved across the earth's surface at a much faster rate in the past than they do presently. This explains in part why events thought by academia and standard texts to have occurred million of years ago have, in some cases, occurred within tens or hundreds of thousands of years.

To understand the evolution of the earth and humanity, consider the following diagram of the mind and its divisions.

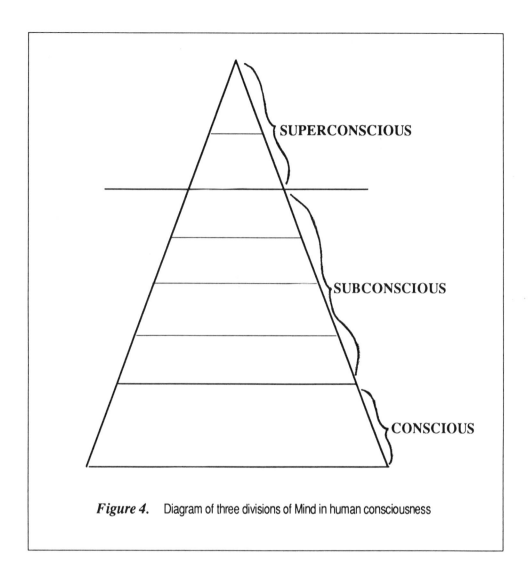

Figure 4. Diagram of three divisions of Mind in human consciousness

The Conscious Mind words directly with the brain and five senses to enable us to perceive, experience, and reason thereby promoting evolutionary growth.

The Subconscious Mind is the abode of the soul. The soul enters a physical body, a baby's body at or near birth in order to gain experience and mature as a creator. After the body dies at the end of a lifetime, the soul - which is you - withdraws its attention from the physical world, physical life, and the life of the five senses of touch, taste, smell, hearing, and sight. The soul then integrates and assimilates the learning from the just completed lifetime. Learning for the soul and for the whole Self always entails and involves understanding creation and the maturing process of Self as a Creator.

The Superconscious Mind is the abode of the High Self, the Christ Consciousness or Buddha Consciousness and Spirit.

Mind is the vehicle that I AM - which is the real, individual identity that is the Self - uses in order to grow into an enlightened being and gain compatibility with the Creator.

Body, mind, spirit then encompasses everything you as an individual need in order to become a mental creator.

The evolution of humanity is proceeding at an accelerating rate and this is the study of Atlantis and humanity.

Atlantis was a time period when the souls or people became entrapped in physical bodies setting into motion the reincarnation of the souls.

There are many levels of consciousness. The levels of consciousness are sometimes called planes of existence or different dimensions. These different dimensions operate at different vibrational frequencies. For example, our physical world is a three-dimensional world. Those three dimensions we know as length, width and depth. These three dimensions allow one or more of our five senses to locate an object in space. These three dimensions also give rise to the concept of physical time and distance and the illusion of separatism. This illusion of being separate must be overcome in order for the Self to know the true reality of connectedness leading to oneness.

The fourth dimensional has been described as time by some. A more accurate description of the fourth dimension of Mind is greater connectedness and even greater or higher levels or dimensions of Mind may be described as the overcoming of the illusion of separateness leading to greater awareness, perception, understanding, and knowing of connectedness leading to the truth of oneness.

A four-dimensional world is invisible to most. As each individual raises their consciousness to a higher vibrational frequency, new fields of experience and perception become available to one's awareness.

These different levels of mind or different dimensions or vibrational frequencies are interspersed within the same space just as a dry sponge can occupy a certain space. Yet when the sponge takes on water within itself, it still takes up the same space. Yet now throughout the sponge is water. Another example is radio waves that travel through the air and on into space yet we do not see them.

In order to understand evolution, it must be viewed not just as the evolution of a physical body but also as the evolution of consciousness and energy. Holding these concepts in mind will help the reader more clearly comprehend the knowledge of evolution presented in these pages.

The History of Atlantis

To the coalescing of elements there was the opportunity and the establishment of Natural Law the capacity for there to be an alteration of experience in the forms which were available upon this planet. There was the attractiveness, primarily due to the balance of the elemental qualities themselves, that were making themselves known. We see that there was a strength that was seen in the integrity of the elemental experience and there was the evolving of the curiosity toward the blending and merging of these.

It was through this impetus that the spark for alterations began and through this there was the defining of new forms, different forms, different combinations of molecular structures which could be used and could be mobile in ways which had previously not existed. There was the capacity for there to be the strength of sustainability in the reproduction of form in ways that had not been prevalent.

Therefore there was the freedom for there to be the movement according to the thoughts that were present.

The impetus of the intelligence to be able to move itself forward through the creative process was very strong and in that it was quite pronounced. It did cause there to be forms manifested that were not anticipated or expected. Many times there would be a reaction to this which would then lead to a further denseness in the experience.

It was through this that there was the separation of consciousness and the polarities which did correspond with the elemental polarities which were existing that the intelligence or consciousness itself became caught in. This was on some parts. It was not on the part of all life forms, there were those life forms who had recently come to this planet and in doing so had come for the purpose of sustaining it, stabilizing it, of being able to produce it for future life.

There was a sense of integrity and a sense of awareness that was not present in the other group described. Therefore there was a distinction within the consciousness and also the forms. There would be times when the indigenous forms would come upon structures or residue of some sort that had been left by the others. Even though they tried to keep their presence insensible, or undetectable, this was the case for much time. As the others began to become more familiar with their denseness, there was a more keen capacity for that which would be reasoning, or being able to remember and to then note differences whether they were in climate, or in surroundings or in the atmosphere itself.

This then eventually led to the intermingling between the two. There were many who became more and more dense that had at one time been free of the matter, had merely been energy beings.

This then created three types of life forms that were developing during this time. There were the energy beings. There were the dense beings. And there were the products of both.

Through time, it would be the product of both that did continue to utilize the planet for experimentation, exploration, discovery. [42001bgc/drc]

The elemental experience referred to here is the experience of nature, such as air, rocks, plants, and animals.

The word "form" as used in this Intuitive Report indicates the forms of nature such as animal or plant.

During the time of Atlantis, there was much experimentation in the use of creating different animal structures, bodies, or forms that could be used by an energy being. These bodies were to be physical yet energetic.

The beings that came to planet Earth in most cases were energy beings. Later on some of these beings created physical bodies that would be used or inhabited. These human formed physical bodies were created by manipulating the genetic code of the indigenous population. In other words, life had evolved originally on this planet on its own, independent of outside planetary influence. The indigenous population was the Neanderthals.

These forms were adapted by these beings from other star systems for their needs and uses, much like man builds cities today by removing the natural habitat and replacing it with one made in his own image, or building a new city or civilization on top of an older one.

This is why mankind possesses such a high proportion of similar genetic coding to the animals of this planet. Yet at the same time there are obvious differences. The absence of body hair is a prime example. The slowness of healing as compared to other animals is another. The size and proportion of the brain is another.

This change in 2-4 percent of the chromosomes produced the necessary adaptations for these off-planet visitors to produce the kind of intelligent brain capacity and humanoid body structure that they would be able to use and inhabit. These created bodies produced Homo sapiens and the Human Race, while Neanderthal was of the indigenous population and was produced by the natural evolution of the planet. Neanderthal is the name given to the fossilized remains of a humanoid type creature or person in a valley of Germany by the same name. These type of fossils have since been found throughout Europe and the middle East. Once thought to have been Homo sapiens direct ancestor, Neanderthal now is seen to be a distinct lineage of its own. It probably had greater psychic or connectedness abilities and less reasoning than Homo sapiens.

Homo erectus dates to a time supposedly prior to Homo sapiens or Neanderthal. It is thought by some to be a direct ancestor of Homo sapiens. Intuitive inquiries indicate Homo erectus was created by the Centaurus. It is entirely possible that the Beldane and those of Sirius may have used genetic material from both Homo erectus and Neanderthal to form Homo sapiens.

So in looking for alien life out in the Universe on other planets, in other solar systems, we have until now missed the obvious. *WE ARE THE ALIENS.* Or more exactly, we were created by the alien life forms as a combination of the indigenous gene pool and mental-genetic experimentation.

Part of our ancestry is from other planets in other star systems. Four different star systems. They influenced not only the development of the human race but also of the planet itself.

In order to understand the history of planet Earth, it is necessary to accept that there are intelligent beings that do not have physical bodies. This is not hard to accept if you believe that each person is an immortal soul. But if you believe there is no God and the physical world and physical universe is all there is and you are only a physical body, then there arises a difficulty in understanding the energetic nature of Earth's and mankind's history.

Intuitive Research April 2001

Conductor (Dr. Daniel Condron): Where did these people who came to this planet come from?

Intuitive Reporter (Dr. Barbara Condron): Other stars. Other planets.

Conductor (Dr. Daniel Condron): More than one planet?

Yes. There were a total of four. Not all of them were here at the same time, they did not coexist upon the planet simultaneously.

Were these beings who came from these four planets, were they in dense bodies or in light bodies?

One group had no body at all. Two were energy forms and the other was dense when they were within the planet.

The group who were dense, what was the star system of their origin?

Centaurus.

The ones who had an energy body, what was their star system origin?

The most enduring was Sirius. Of a shorter duration was Beldane.

And the ones who had no form at all, what star system were they from?

Xena.

How long were the ones from Sirius upon the planet? Til what time period?

Would be the third cycle (of Atlantis).

Why did they leave?

The intermingling had made it available for those who wanted to stay to do so and had in reality been their own effect in that once the intermingling had occurred there was not the availability for leaving. The bodies were affected in such a way that in order to sustain the consciousness they required the physicality of the elements of the earth itself.

The ones who did not intermingle did not want to remain within this land area for it was not progressing as they had expected and therefore would not give what they had wanted. However, they had been able to sustain and to build that which would be necessary for their own kinsmen to continue to survive.

Are the ones from Sirius a part of the human population today, the whole population or just a part?

For them who intermarried have primarily been within what is termed the Indo-European land areas.

Did any beings or entities come to Earth from the star system referred to as Pleiades?

This is where Xena is.

What did these ones provide to the Earth?

There was not interference, therefore, they did not influence.

Were there any beings that came from the Orion system?

This is where Beldane exists or emanates from. [42001bgc/drc]

There were four different planets in four different star systems that enhanced, quickened, changed, and developed the planet Earth's evolution and human evolution as a species.

It is also important to understand a truth, a Universal Truth, in order to understand the history of Atlantis and the world. This Universal Truth is expressed as "Thought is cause." It may be explained as thoughts are things, thoughts are real, and thoughts are the causal point for any creation in the physical world.

For example, someone had to have the idea or thought of a chair before a chair was created. The same is true for your house, car, clothes, and jewelry. Look around you and you will see that thought or idea is cause.

The Final Cycle of Atlantis

At this time there had been many adjustments or changes that had been made in consciousness both in energy and what had become matter. There was the beginning of the faculty of imagination which was much stronger within the awareness and therefore there was the pulling apart or further delineation in a movement from two dimensions into three. We see this was most pronounced in most people.

There was a heavier and heavier grossness in the experiencing and there was the confusion that did often arise because of it. There was the floundering that would occur between the choice of forms and the availability of forms that could be used by consciousness and the tendency to move from one to the other without there being much awareness. It was during this period that there was the settling of the formation of the genetic code which could be utilized and expected to form a kind of progression that would serve as a stabilizer, in essence. This was provided through thought transmission from Xena but it was employed by those of Beldane in order to affect the matter that was present at the time.

Once this did occur, there was the separation into the physical forms which would be conducive to the growth of consciousness and maturity of spirit. Because the consciousness had been stabilized, it then did effect the Earth itself. There was the settling into the rotational pattern which made it more conducive for the learning which could now take place and the resolve of the confusion which had been prevalent for much time.

As the stabilization came into being, the actual movement of Earth mass was occurring as early as the Second Cycle. It was at that time that portions of the mass itself were let go of and there was the cooling and changing of the atmosphere in radical ways. By the time the third cycle had been endured, there was the beginning on the part of those from Sirius to effect the pyramidical structures or temples which were in place by the end of the third cycle. This was the beginning of the stabilization that then throughout the fourth cycle did create what has commonly been seen as land changes.

This was all coincidental, coinciding with one another and over some period of time. There were tidal waves. There were earthquakes. There were volcanoes that were dead and alive. There were these kinds of changes as the earth went through its stabilization because of the changes in the magnetic fields. This was the result of the polarity that had been set into motion by the consciousness throughout this entire period so it was not new.

What was different was the response or awareness of it by those who were in the dense forms. They were becoming progressively more fearful, or more ingenious in regards to responding to those occasions. [42001bgc/drc]

Energy is real. We don't see air but it is real. When air moves because of energy we call this air-energy: wind. In the same way, there are higher dimensions of consciousness that are not perceived by the five senses. All matter is frozen energy. Matter is energy that has been slowed in vibration to such a rate that it is perceivable by the five senses.

Day length has changed during the Earth's history. Year length has also changed. This is why it is difficult to give accurate measurement of the very ancient past. This is also part of the reason that estimates of the age of pyramids, very ancient civilizations, dinosaurs, and ancient time periods are usually incorrect.

One example of this is the age of the Sphinx. Recently it has been been ascertained that the weathering on the sides of the Sphinx is due to water erosion, not wind erosion as long believed. The last time there was water erosion in Egypt was over 10,000 years ago, according to modern measurements of time, when Egypt was not a desert.

Day length has changed. Year length has changed. There is not uniformity over time. This is a reality most science has yet to accept.

The alignment of certain parts of the Great Pyramid to the stars points the way to a much greater age for civilization than we see in the history books. These universal measures may well be one of the keys to the truths we have been searching for.

The Intuitive Report states that the actual movement of the earth's mass was occurring as early as the second cycle of Atlantis. Therefore, the second cycle of Atlantis was concurrent with the supercontinent Pangea and the early breaking apart and movement of that continent. Pangea is the name given by modern day scientists to describe what has been known for thousands of years as the end of Mu (Lemuria) and the beginning or First Cycle of Atlantis.

Pangea is the one and only continent that existed on the planet in Earth's ancient past. Following the exhalation of the Moon from the Earth, the supercontinent of Pangea or what has previously been referred to as Lemuria or the First Cycle of Atlantis began breaking apart. This was in an attempt by the Earth to rebalance itself.

What most people think of as Atlantis and what has largely been referred to as Atlantis, were just the final years in the last cycle of Atlantis. By the time of the last cycle, the large continent of Atlantis had been reduced to an island in the north Atlantic.

Some people think the atmosphere of the earth is getting very polluted now, but at times in the past it was even more so. This is why often people migrated to the higher elevations where the air was cleaner.

Where did the people go, what colonies did they establish in what land areas as the earth changes occurred and Atlantis was submerged?

Some of them migrated, indeed, but many were merely upon the land masses as they broke apart as if they rode on an island. Momentary movements would come, sometimes even with the phases of the moon, where the people even integrated it into their beliefs, into their way of life. It was quite natural.

They tended to be in mountainous regions where they believed they would be safer, although this was not always the case. Areas closer to the sun. Part of this was because the atmosphere was better there and it was warmer.

What modern-day continents were once part of Atlantis?

Parts of Western Europe. Parts of the African side of the Mediterranean through Turkey and into the Himalayas. Parts of mountains in the Eastern United States, into Mexico, into parts of Brazil, Cuba.

Was Antarctica part of Atlantis?

At one time, yes. During the first and second cycles, but its movement was coinciding with the large changes that began to unfold as the rotation of the earth changed and there was a losing of mass and shifting. [42001bgc/drc]

EGYPT

Many students of Atlantis believe Egypt was a colony of Atlantis. The Intuitive Reports present a different scenario. The Egyptian civilization was created by the Siriuns, those beings from the star system of Sirius. This is why the royalty and priesthood of the ancient Egyptians have always been such a mystery to us. They are from an alien race from another planet or to be more exact, they are the descendents of those Siriuns, who did not interbreed with the indigenous population of the Neanderthal or Homo erectus. This is why, when looking at pictures of this royalty which are on temple walls and artifacts, to this day you will notice their heads bulge outward at the back giving them a very definite nonhuman appearance.

The pyramid complex at Giza including the Sphinx was built using alien technology. The structures themselves work together to tap the power of the earth itself and the cosmos, particularly the solar system of Sirius.

This complex could not only transmit energy but also communication from planet to planet and at a rate greater than the speed of light. This is because this technology was used as both a teleportation device and a time machine. When the limitation of physical time is overcome, distance ceases to be an obstacle. Because both the Beldane and those of Sirius were energetic or energy beings, there was no need to transport physical bodies or physical matter from planet to planet. Instead, what was transmitted was energy and high knowledge.

Re-examine the Mind Diagram given earlier.

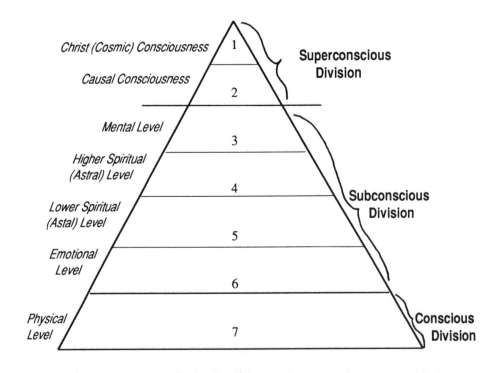

Figure 5. The Seven Levels of Mind within the three major divisions

There are Seven Levels and Three Divisions of Mind. There are three divisions of Mind that hold within them seven levels. The Seventh Level of Mind is the physical level, our physical universe. The lower the number, the higher the level of Mind, the greater or more rapid the rate of vibration. This means that the Sixth Level of Mind vibrates at a more rapid rate than the Seventh Level of Mind. The fifth level vibrates at a more rapid rate than the sixth level, and so forth. The First Level of Mind vibrates at the most rapid rate of all.

In order to vibrate at more rapid rate, the stroke must be and is shorter. Consider the following:

The time that is required to move from Point A to Point B may be 60 seconds.

Now suppose the distance from Point A to Point B is one-half the distance so that the distance from Point A to Point B looks like this:

A _____ B

Now the distance between Point A and Point B can be traversed in half the time.

The deeper one moves into mind or the higher one moves into consciousness, the less distance is involved in any movement, whether from Point A to Point B or to anywhere. Thus the key to overcoming the limitations of time and distance is the ability to operate in higher levels of Mind.

The civilization that was in ancient Egypt appeared highly evolved and deteriorated from that origination point. In other words, the peak of civilization and technology for ancient Egypt was at its beginning. There is no trace of ancient Egypt having developed over millennia. This is because this was a colony, a planned society, from an earlier civilization and that civilization was off this world. This civilization was developed by those from Sirius who came to this planet as energy beings and took on physical bodies.

In some ways ancient Egypt was related to Atlantis in that both were connected to beings from other planets. However, Egypt was more specifically created by and used exclusively by the Siriuns.

The Sphinx is older than the Great Pyramid at Giza. However, both of these structures or engines are vastly older than currently held by most that study them.

The Sphinx was built during the time after the Moon was thrown off the Earth. The Sphinx and the Great Pyramid and to a lesser extent the other pyramids around the Earth were and are still being used to stabilize the geomagnetic and structural integrity of the Earth.

The beings from the solar system Sirius, the Siriuns, desired and hoped that in creating the Giza complex that it would aid in someday raising the consciousness of the beings on planet Earth to a level close to equal to that of the mother planet.

You see the Siriuns were able to transmit energy over vast distances just as Nicola Tesla demonstrated in the 1800's. They would send more than communication. They would send energy through space.

Nicola Tesla was probably the greatest scientist in the history of the United States of America. He came to the U.S. from eastern Europe in the late 1800's. Tesla invented alternating current electricity therefore making it possible for houses throughout the U.S. and the world to be illuminated. He invented and patented the radio, and the fluorescent bulb. He also invented the Tesla coil which is used, among others things, to take photographs of the human aura.

An electrical, vibration, and energy genius, the modern, technological world as we see it is due probably more to Nicola Tesla than any other scientist or inventor. His genius was certainly in alignment with that displayed by the Siriuns millennia ago.

What is the origin of the Egyptian civilization? Who was it started by?

This is primarily from Siriuns. There were some that did not return, but stayed. They did not interbreed but they did maintain a physical-type of energetic form. There were some who had to stay in order to energize and stabilize the Earth through the use of the pyramids on the plane of Giza and the Sphinx.

Did they build these?

Yes.

What was the method of building?

Energetic manifestation.

What is meant by energetic manifestation?

The utilization of molecular construction.

Is there any other purpose for these other than the stabilization of Earth?

They were communication stations between the mother planet and the colony. They were a means to transmit and receive intelligence and energy.

What then is the connection between this pyramid complex at Giza and the Sphinx and the pyramid complex with the large stone face on Mars at Cydonia, Mars, which has the same geometric configuration as the one on Earth at Giza?

When there was not the usability of this planet....

Which planet?

The Earth. There was a seeking out of others that might be more readily adaptable. As has been stated most of the Siriuns, those who did not inbreed or intermingle, did leave. Some went to other planets, still seeking a place to colonize.

Which were built first the pyramid complex at Giza or the pyramid complex on Mars?

The one on the Earth was built first.

What time period was the one on Earth built?

When it was active is over 100,000 years.

From the present time period?

Yes.

Is the Sphinx older than the pyramid?

Yes, it was the stabilization, communication energy connection between here and the mother planet.

How old is it?

Approximately 50,000 more. It is difficult to describe in years because the measurement of the year itself was not the same. It was built at the time that the throwing off of mass ceased and the Earth began to quiet becoming condensed where it was stable enough in itself that the energy form could be sustained.

Can the Sphinx be used once again as a communication device with the mother planet Sirius?

There would need to be a re-energization of it. Although the energy is present within the Earth, it is not yet harnessed to do so. There could be some discoveries or illuminations made from utilizing the substance of this structure for what is commonly astronomical purposes, but the true purpose of it being energetic, there would need to be more evolvement. This was the hope of the Siriuns in creating it, that this would or could someday occur.

What was the energy source originally for the Sphinx?

The mother planet. The structure was a receptor. Then it became a sender as well.

When it was a sender where did it get its energy from?

People.

Did the pyramids have any factor in the energization of this?

Some. The energy would be received and then would be given to the Great Pyramid which would in turn internalize it into the center of the Earth. At a later time it would then bring it back out and direct it back toward Sirius.

Was there any teleportation involved?

A great deal. Particularly by those who created the Egyptian race.

How was the Egyptian race created?

Thought form manifestation. It was frozen energy.

Was there any teleportation of people between the mother planet and the Sphinx?

Yes.

Was there teleportation between the Sphinx to other areas of the planet?

There was the attempt to do so. Most failed. [42001bgc/drc]

The Egyptians, since they weren't a colony of Atlantis and were set up as a distinct race to function with the Siriuns, did not wish to be controlled or overrun by the Atlanteans.

The Atlantean civilization was heavily influenced by the Beldane. The Atlanteans had become entrapped in physical bodies and engrossed in physical matter. The Egyptians were still energy beings. The Atlanteans civilization was in large part created by the Beldane.

Pyramids had the effect of stabilizing the Earth and still have that effect to the present.

Are there records describing the history of the planet and the use of the Sphinx still stored in the Sphinx?

There is a history there, yes.

How is it inscribed?

At this point in the actual matter of the Sphinx itself, the structure itself. There would need to be the energization as has been spoken of for it to become active or alive at which time it would be like a hologram, light moving.

There has been some suggestion that there are records buried beneath one of the front paws of the Sphinx, what is here?

There is a chamber here. It was created by those who are other than Siriuns.

Who was it created by and for what purpose?

It was related to the Egyptians. It became part of their way of keeping the Atlanteans away from this area. It was a way to control their movements. Therefore the records that are here are Egyptian in nature.

Why did the Egyptians wish to keep the Atlanteans away?

They were very dense, and therefore, unpredictable.

What were the race of Egyptians?

They were of the energy beings that wanted to remain pure and wanted to remain on the planet. So they did try to effect a way to do so.

The Beldane, many of which were in Atlantis early on, became entrapped in physical bodies and thereby lost or gave up their existence as energetic beings. The Siriuns attempted to keep their lineage pure and thereby continue to exist as energetic beings on planet Earth, free to come and go therefore not trapped in physical matter.

What happened in later time periods when Egyptians had physical bodies?

It was through the attempt upon their parts to sustain energy bodies that over a period of time there was a quality of density or matter they were trying to avoid that did cause there to be some mutations. The practice of embalming the bodies was actually to leave a physical form where these beings could come and go. And did so for millennia.

What is the connection of the Siriuns to the planet today?

They are in the present, much like those of Xena, where there is less involvement through energy. The involvement is through thought or intelligence. Through presence rather than a form.

Why is it that there are pyramids all over the Earth as in Yucatan and Tenochitlan outside Mexico City, Pyramid of the Sun, Pyramid of the Moon, in the South Sea Islands in the Pacific and other areas?

This was in the intermingling of the Siriuns and the dense ones. At times it was a kind of imitation of what the others were doing with the Great Pyramid and the recognition that in order to stabilize further during the Third Cycle and Fourth there would need to be these points which would help stabilize the polarities which were beginning to become pronounced within the character of the elements itself. Therefore, they did perform that function of being able to cause there to be a progressive stability so that the learning could be made possible or available. [42001bgc/drc]

In other words, these pyramids were secondary stabilization centers or structures. The pyramids found around the world are imitations of the Great Pyramid of Giza. Yet, even though they imitate, still they have had great power and influence in causing our planet Earth to stabilize thus providing a safe home for mankind. They functioned to help stabilize the life form known as Earth in order that the planet could mature in such a way as to allow life forms of all kinds to thrive and develop.

The Consciousness of Atlantis

The Second Cycle of Atlantis

The fewest number of Atlantean reports on record at the School of Metaphysics Headquarters come from the Second Cycle of Atlantis. This does not mean there was less of anything - people, activity, learning - during that stage. It does indicate that up to the present day, information from this time has not been highly significant to those requesting Past Life Profiles. This could have something to do with the drastic Earth changes – the loss of Lemuria and shifting poles – legacies of the First Cycle.

Although the pool of resources to illustrate this period are fewer, a rich representative comes in the form of the following report for a male which was given in 1973.

This report talks about the shift from Superconscious (spiritual) dominion to outer (material) ego dominion. It describes how physical matter became so important in the consciousness of man that he began losing sight of his spiritual origin and nature. What this caused was an alteration of experience which is described here as the shift from high counsel to the newly forming separated self.

Some will read this as an external conflict, as many might relate what is described to their own problems with a manager or a parent for instance, thus externalizing the meaning of what is related. Others will seek meaning on a deeper level, reaching to realize that the root of the age old conflict is within Self. This report tells the genesis of this eternal battle within, between light and darkness, the spiritual and the material, God and the devil.

The development of consciousness unfolds during this second cycle. How choices affect the nature and quality of thought are elucidated and we find this particular soul's emotions are "damaged" and have "become a guiding force for this one." The formation that will allow the emotions to act in Subconscious Mind as a developing agent for seed ideas to sprout into physical manifestation while at the same time allowing emotions to react in conscious mind as the means by which we will come to experience our own thoughts begins during this time.

Here is the individual not yet encased in mental and emotional genetics, in a more energetic body that allows for movement that is progressively being slowed down.

An Intuitive Report from the Second Cycle of Atlantis

Intuitive Reporter: We see this one in the form of man in the area of the northern section of Atlantis. We see this one at this time to be in direct connection with the energy fields being set up at this time by the high counsel for the restriction of those negative energies concerning want of information for progression and want of destruction of the high counsel in order that a new government may be set up.

We see this one most concerned with this growth of energy fields and to be at this time engaged in a process of developing stronger abilities to create these mental and imaged fields of light in order that this thought transference may not be felt on the inner levels of the counsel and on the construction of the physical land mass itself. We see this one to be great in knowledge and understanding, however we see this one to have become so involved in this process of protection for the land and protection for the counsel and for all entities within this realm of understanding that the emotions have become most damaged and have become a guiding force for this one. For this is a new experience for this one, the emotions having been under control for some time. However, the emotions going into the level of energy exchange that they are at this time creates within this one great questioning and inability to cope with circumstances in which this one feels threat.

We see this one to be under the awareness of the high counsel and to be considered by the high counsel as having great beauty and growth but to be at this time held back from understanding through this lack of emotional control and lack of understanding of the emotional processes taking place at this time. For this one has become within self a self-protector of the counsel, feeling that it is necessary for self to protect this counsel with strong energy fields that have been understood by this one and corrected to a point of high exchange.

We see this one to visit quite often the Temple of Light for under-standing.

But within this temple to find the emotions as clouding the way for this great light of progression and understanding. We see this one to be at this time greatly influenced by a loved one. This influence being of connection with this protectiveness toward the counsel for this loved one is of the counsel's disciplinary movement for those negative energy fields set up. This one seemed to be in direct connection with particular groups affording information from the groups to the high counsel and being the interpreter of the information from the high counsel to the groups.

We see this one to desire strongly to gain control of the emotions

*in order that this one may have complete understanding of the circum-
stances for there is a great fear growing within of an inability to cope with
the situation. This one has the ability to see greatly into the future probabilities of the land masses and of the influence of energies upon thought
and upon thought control. We see, however, this viewing into the future as
creating great fear within and creating a feeling of anxiety and a feeling of
frustration for this one feels incapable of controlling these elements that
are in the progression of development.*

*We see this one to seek out the compassion and love of this entity
in connection with the disciplinary movement. We see however, that this
one of the disciplinary movement has found within the other great weaknesses developing and regards this with much skepticism as to ability for
this one to continue in the position held at this time. Giving of this information to this one there is at this time a great exchange of energies and a
great exchange of hostilities for this one releases fear upon the one of the
discipline supervisor and allows this exchange to become so negated in
field force that there is a great sapping of energy and a great feeling of
those energy exchanges before withdrawal.*

*We see this one to feel most sad about this encounter and to
constantly return to this one for the alleviating of this guilt feeling. However, we see at this point the discipline recorder to refuse this and to leave
self completely involved in the connective links between the high counsel
and these subversive groups.*

*This brings about great anguish to this one and we see this one to
relieve self from past searching on the inner levels for greater understanding and to remain in the Temple of Light searching constantly for understanding. However, we see this one to find great frustration in this and so
begins the declination of understanding. Before this takes place, we see
this one to desire strongly to transfer self to another area for seeing the
great cataclysmic circumstances to take place in the future. This one
desires no experience of them but rather desires self to be in a more
pleasant state even though this one would be severed from the relationship
with that of the discipline interpreter.*

*We see this one to have transferred self to that area referred to as
the Himalayas and to have begun study there of self and for progression
and growth. We see this one to at this point be influenced by three others
of the same temperament and of the same lack of emotional control and to
dominate these three others because of the ability to see on the inner levels
and to see into the probabilities of the future.*

*We see this one to have grown in domination and power over these
other three and to have been placed in the minds of these other three as a
great threat to their ability to use force and will within themselves.*

We see this one to have withdrawn from the physical at the age of 34 legions. We see this one to have withdrawn to a state of suspension in which a great deal could be reviewed and emotions better controlled.

Conductor: How is this one called?

Intuitive Reporter: Takaragi

Conductor: What is the time period?

Intuitive Reporter: The twelfth night of the second cycle of the Atlantean period before the destruction felt within the center core of the land mass.

Conductor: What would be the significance of that lifetime to the present lifetime?

Intuitive Reporter: We see this one placed in similar circumstances once again for information to be gained and for knowledge and for understanding concerning that of the emotions and the control of their forces in order that this one may progress.

We see this one to have within, great abilities for the interpretation of the inner levels and great ability to practice that of the clairvoyant and that of the interpreter of energy thought transference from others, this having a great and vast influence on the ability for this one to cope with circumstances; for before there is vocalization from others for the intentions, this one is well aware of the intentions through the energy exchange. We see this to be a subconscious gesture however, to affect the conscious mind and when this one is influenced by those of much confusion becomes confused with self, and unable to cope with the situation.

We see this one to be greatly influenced by those feelings of emotion such as fear and anger, jealousy and frustration. We see this one to be greatly influenced by these emotions for these are the emotions experienced in this past lifetime that this one was unable to cope with. We see this one to have within [his] grasp the opportunity for controlling these emotions. For this one has developed somewhat an objectivity about self. However this objectivity becomes shaded by emotions sometimes; for the inability to cope with others in their direct connection with the emotional senses and with direct connection with those thoughts within this one.

We see this one from childhood forward to be under great influence of highly intense emotional entities, for this one is seen to be influenced greatly by others and their emotional effects upon self having relationships time and again with those of past lifetimes connected with this emotional control and with the control of energy influence of thoughts of self upon others. This one has at this time the relationship existing with self and a particular entity which is of domination and submission which is before mentioned in a past lifetime. We see this domination to be a constant struggle between these ones in the sense of competition and in the sense of sense endeavor for this one constantly strives to reinforce self with the ability to gain more prestige than the one in direct connection.

We see this one to have chosen the parents to be a restricting force for these ones have great influence upon this one in the connection to emotional control for it is because of these parental influences that this one has experienced great emotional upheaval and inability to cope with situations.

We see this one to have experiences throughout the lifetime with the emotions, to have experiences with a high intensity of energy within but to be lacking in control of this energy, thus taking on physical manifestations of frustration and physical inabilities to feel in harmony, for the body processes are affected by the mental attitude of this one greatly. This one must realize the great responsibility of thought control and emotional control for this one's high evolvement of that termed psychic abilities, gives self a great influence on others and gives self a higher influence on own progression and growth.

We see this one to greatly need the ability to love self at this time and find love for self in the ability to cope with situations and in the ability to remain objective about self in direct connection with others. For this one tends to be protective of others as well as self, and to have many defenses in direct connection with self and opportunities for growth and progression with others.

This one is seen to be quite lazy in attitudes toward discipline of self, instead desires strongly the experiences of the inner levels and those happinesses and mysteries that they afford but not to contain within self the discipline in order to develop these for any circumstances for growth or any direct connection for opportunity of understanding. These will be experienced throughout this lifetime as well as others by many. This recognition is within this one, however the ability to discipline these will be up to this one for the growth and progression of self. For if this one takes the discipline within hand, this one may develop a great sense of understanding and a great control of the emotions of the physical temperament and of the mental aspirations of self. [31573191027]

Exploratory Analysis

This could be a reference to the cause and effect of losing the Lemurian land mass which occurred during the First Cycle. Such a loss, even in an instable, gaseous world, would be tantamount to a meteorite landing in the middle of the ocean. The effects would affect land, air, and sea; all parts of creation making up the planet. Additionally the stabilization of the magnetic poles would have an impact upon the inner core of Earth.

This report gives an eyewitness account of existence following the loss of Lemuria. Let us examine it from the beginning for what else it tells us about the Second Cycle of Atlantis.

> *Intuitive Reporter: We see this one in the form of man in the area of the northern section of Atlantis.*

The word "man" comes from the Sanskrit word manu meaning thinker. Unlike other intuitive reports cited here, this information does not begin with the denotation of sex, male or female, rather it is one of intelligence, consciousness itself. This could, of course, be interpreted in a material sense thereby implying the form of human being, a physical man body. You will need to determine its meaning within your own consciousness. Here, you will find our insights to add to your own.

> *Intuitive Reporter: We see this one at this time to be in direct connection with the energy fields being set up at this time by the high counsel for the restriction of those negative energies concerning want of information for progression and want of destruction of the high counsel in order that a new government may be set up.*

When originally transcribed into written form, the transcriber interpreted high counsel as high *council* which steers the meaning in an entirely different direction than the one explained here. Thus is the power of interpretation of information received through the senses. This is an excellent lesson in itself. With the training developed by the School of Metaphysics, Subconscious, intuitive reporting bypasses the external senses, thus offering a direct view from the Akashic Record. The reporting utilizes language to convey what is perceived. Once put into language form it is accessible to any who speak that language and it is subject to the Conscious Mind interpretation of the transcriber.

The Conscious Mind assimilation of intuitive information remains subject to the beliefs each of us have adopted. This largely depends upon how fluid we are in embracing information that may appear to contradict or even threaten those ideas. With this in mind, read this report in both meanings - counsel and council. Examine what each brings into your mind, and grow in awareness.

What if we at one time experienced Self as spirit, as beings of light? What if we considered the physical body like we now view a car or a plane or even a house, as a temporary place to live and experience? This report describes such a spirit, cognizant of Superconsciousness and its expression of energy as it seeks to create a structure that will encourage life and growth. This spirit is on the outside, however, having moved out of Superconsciousness into the developing outer mind, repeatedly termed here as Subconscious Mind and Conscious Mind.

> *Intuitive Reporter: We see this one most concerned with this growth of energy fields and to be at this time engaged in a process of developing stronger abilities to create these mental and imaged fields of light in order that this thought transference may not be felt on the inner levels of the counsel and on the construction of the physical land mass itself.*

Could this be talking about the formation of how thought will be manifest from an idea to an energy to a physical manifestation? In order for consciousness to relate spirit to matter a bridge needed to be built. That bridge in time became Subconscious Mind with its four distinct expressions of energies. This is a large part of the activity of the Second Cycle of Atlantis, building Subconscious Mind.

Here, in the deepest part of Subconscious Mind, is where thoughts will begin their journey toward physical manifestation. This activity will eventually become separate from Superconsciousness which remains whole and complete.

> *Intuitive Reporter: We see this one to be great in knowledge and under-standing, however we see this one to have become so involved in this process of protection for the land and protection for the counsel and for all entities within this realm of understanding that the emotions have become most damaged and have become a guiding force for this one. For this is a new experience for this one, the emotions having been under control for some time. However, the emotions going into the level of energy exchange that they are at this time, creates within this one great questioning and inability to cope with circumstances in which this one feels threat.*

The natural expression of consciousness at this time was connectedness. Like the joy that runs through a nation when democracy triumphs or Olympic medals are won, consciousness during this stage of Atlantis was like geese flying in formation, more instinctual than intuitive.

This entity was attempting to form a body that would hold its own, that would continue to exist apart from the thoughts held in the mind. Imagine if the structure and soundness of your physical body was subject to each thought that flows through your mind. An "I'm so short" thought would immediately manifest in your body by you losing a few inches. "I'm getting old" could age you several decades according to your image. "I wish I was in Tahiti" would propel you there in that moment. These seem farfetched to our modern minds because we experience a great separation, a great distance between what we think and what we have.

Entities during the early cycles of Atlantis were just beginning to experience such separation. Indeed, as with this man, they were purposefully creating the distance, perceiving it as necessary to accomplish what they desired. This made the emotions necessary, for this creation of mind, this level of existence, binds the inner realms of subconsciousness to the outer world of physical consciousness.

> *Intuitive Reporter: We see this one to be under the awareness of the high counsel and to be considered by the high counsel as having great beauty and growth but to be at this time held back from understanding through this lack of emotional control and lack of understanding of the emotional processes taking place at this time. For this one has become within self a self protector of the counsel, feeling that it is necessary for self to protect this counsel with strong energy fields that have been understood by this one and corrected to a point of high exchange.*

This consciousness is devoted to sustaining superconscious awareness. The emotions challenge this since they will serve a dual function.

> *Intuitive Reporter: We see this one to visit quite often the Temple of Light for understanding.*

This would be like someone who prays and meditates daily for guidance. During the Second Cycle of Atlantis, the door to Superconsciousness was in the process of being formed so the Light of understanding was more accessible. This reference could also explain why so many Holy Scriptures reference the body as a "temple."

Light was also the substance this one was using to create his desire.

> *Intuitive Reporter: But within this temple to find the emotions as clouding the way for this great light of progression and understanding.*

The tendency for energy to move outward, away from its Source, becomes a stronger pull for this one, drawing the attention away from the Source.

> *Intuitive Reporter: We see this one to be at this time greatly influenced by*
> *a loved one. This influence being of connection with this protectiveness*
> *toward the counsel for this loved one is of the counsel's disciplinary*
> *movement for those negative energy fields set up. This one seemed to be in*
> *direct connection with particular groups affording information from the*
> *groups to the high counsel and being the interpreter of the information*
> *from the high counsel to the groups.*

The formation of Subconscious Mind is still under the direction of the High Self. Subconscious Mind is also dependent upon Superconscious Mind for its existence. Will is beginning to be expressed through Subconscious Mind. Subconscious intelligence is the first to interpret the separating energies that are coming into being to create the whole self.

> *Intuitive Reporter: We see this one to desire strongly to gain control of the*
> *emotions in order that this one may have complete understanding of the*
> *circumstances; for there is a great fear growing within of an inability to*
> *cope with the situation. This one has the ability to see greatly into the*
> *future probabilities of the land masses and of the influence of energies*
> *upon thought and upon thought control. We see, however, this viewing into*
> *the future as creating great fear within and creating a feeling of anxiety*
> *and a feeling of frustration for this one feels incapable of controlling these*
> *elements that are in the progression of development.*

This is reminiscent of people today settling in coastal California or remaining in New Madrid, Missouri, St. Louis, or Memphis, or in any other known areas of land stress, defiant of their own fear of the inevitable, thinking they can escape. Here is the difference between personal precognitive experience and foreseeing done by another. Someone else's vision and knowledge can easily be ignored and forgotten. When it is your own, it is more difficult to deny. Watching reports of earthquakes half a world away, it is easy for some to remain distant, disconnected from the reality of the experience. When the earthquakes under your house, affecting you and your loved ones, destroying what you have worked for, it becomes part of your personal experience. This is the difference between belief and faith. Belief is its own reward. Faith leads to knowing and knowing is the future of mankind.

What is described in this report is subconscious precognition without the benefit of conscious reasoning and so the emotions react in the physical. In Second Cycle Atlantis, we had yet to conceive consciously but the signs of becoming caught up in our experiments were already present in fears and doubts.

Intuitive Reporter: We see this one to seek out the compassion and love of this entity in connection with the disciplinary movement. We see however, that this one of the disciplinary movement has found within the other great weaknesses developing and regards this with much skepticism as to ability for this one to continue in the position held at this time.

There is a growing recognition in self that the allegiance, the point of devotion has shifted. It shows in the shifting from giving love and compassion to wanting these, being without them. Separation from the Source has impaired this one's ability to choose how and where his energy will be directed. Energy used is not returned. Thus energy is wasted.

Intuitive Reporter: Giving of this information to this one there is at this time a great exchange of energies and a great exchange of hostilities for this one releases fear upon the one of the discipline supervisor and allows this exchange to become so negated in field force that there is a great sapping of energy and a great feeling of those energy exchanges before withdrawal.

The cry of "why me?" is heard around the globe daily. Thousands of souls experience the material world, not knowing how to find answers to their questions. Thus understanding eludes them as it did this man. Unanswered questions become negated in the individual's energy field, draining your energy and leading you to death.

Intuitive Reporter: We see this one to feel most sad about this encounter and to constantly return to this one for the alleviating of this guilt feeling. However, we see at this point the discipline recorder to refuse this and to leave self completely involved in the connective links between the high counsel and these subversive groups.

Here we find reference to the establishment of time. It comes through emotional experience that allows the mind to linger in what has passed and no longer is. The will holds to the present – the now – establishing lines of communication, energy flows, throughout the parts of Self that will eventually coalesce into levels of consciousness. Think of the will as the autonomic nervous system, connecting the glands and organs to the brain.

Intuitive Reporter: This brings about great anguish to this one and we see this one to relieve self from the post, searching on the inner levels for greater understanding. This one remains in the Temple of Light searching

constantly for understanding. However, we see this one to find great
frustration in this and so begins the declination of understanding. Before
this takes place, we see this one to desire strongly to transfer self to another
area for seeing the great cataclysmic circumstances to take place in the
future. This one desires no experience of them but rather desires self to be
in a more pleasant state even though this one would be severed from the
relationship with that of the discipline interpreter.

The desire for connectedness has become weakened with repeated contact with the outer mind and body. As the emotions rise, understanding subsides, and consciousness separates again. The attention moves from the now into the future, creating want, thus producing a cause out of synchronization with intelligence. This is the beginning of the thread that will bind the soul to the body, the traces of karma.

This is the entrapment in physical existence. The choice to use the physical world for learning thus leaving the inner world of learning behind.

Intuitive Reporter: We see this one to have transferred self to that area
referred to as the Himalayas and to have begun study there of self and for
progression and growth. We see this one to at this point be influenced by
three others of the same temperament and of the same lack of emotional
control and to dominate these three others because of the ability to see on
the inner levels and to see into the probabilities of the future.

Now the control of the lower self becomes stronger, betraying this one's desire for development of self, and systematically bringing self under the influence of the subconscious ego.

Intuitive Reporter: We see this one to have grown in domination and
power over these other three and to have been placed in the minds of these
other three as a great threat to their ability to use force and will within
themselves.
We see this one to have withdrawn from the physical at the age of
34 legions. We see this one to have withdrawn to a state of suspension in
which a great deal could be reviewed and emotions better controlled.

Here is a description of the time after physical death. A time of suspension, the judgement day of Biblical scriptures, where each soul must account for experiences until all is balanced, resolved.

When asked the time period, the response is *"the twelfth night of the second cycle of the Atlantean period before the destruction felt within the center core of the landmass."*

This is, most likely, a reference to the land mass (Pangea) breaking apart, an effect of the energetic material being expelled. The movement of material seeking to fill in the void left by Lemuria caused considerable change in the remaining earth and sea masses. The *"destruction felt within the center core"* could be lingering effects of this loss or it could be related to the electro-magnetic activity of the Earth.

Whichever may be the case, the loss of Lemuria in the First Cycle left what has since been named the Ring of Fire in the Pacific Ocean. The material flung away from the Earth formed the Earth's moon, held in orbit by this planet's polarity even today. If this is indeed true, there is every reason to believe that moon rocks brought back to this planet in the early 1970's correspond to the material of our planet. Someday soon we expect this information to be widely released to the public by those in possession of the moon's matter.

The significance of this Intuitive Report correlates the past life experience to the present life of the individual requesting the profile. This is included in its entirety here for the universal benefit it contains for us all.

> *Conductor: What would be the significance of that lifetime to the present lifetime?*
>
> *Intuitive Reporter: We see this one placed in similar circumstances once again for information to be gained and for knowledge and for understanding concerning that of the emotions and the control of their forces in order that this one may progress.*
>
> *We see this one to have within, great abilities for the interpretation of the inner levels and great ability to practice that of the clairvoyant and that of the interpreter of energy thought transference from others, this having a great and vast influence on the ability for this one to cope with circumstances; for before there is vocalization from others for the intentions, this one is well aware of the intentions through the energy exchange. We see this to be a subconscious gesture however, to affect the conscious mind and when this one is influenced by those of much confusion becomes confused with self, and unable to cope with the situation.*

In the handful of widely-known accounts concerning the "myth" of Atlantis, the impression we are given is that mankind had reached a zenith. There were crystal energy sources, flying machines, peace and prosperity, and a host of wonderful conditions we do not experience today. Seemingly, our species was more of everything then, than now.

These Intuitive Reports point to a different conclusion. They indicate evolution is progressing forward, that all energy is in the process of expressing itself, that creation is in constant motion. Thus the intuitive abilities sometimes attributed to the Atlanteans are probably better placed in our present, rather than in our past, with the greatest enlightenment yet to come.

What are often described as intuitive abilities of this period – telepathy, telekinesis, instantaneous healing and the like – is better described as instinct, collective instinct. Like the homing instinct of a pigeon or the herd instinct of bovine, this is the expression of connectedness free of individual ego. Where there is no sense of separation, the benefits of omniscience are known.

During Atlantis this connectedness was severed, as described in this man's report. The difficulties with emotion and fear he experienced then, are in his experience now. It is not so much that he has carried them over for millennia, rather it is he is still recreating the same pattern, still seeking to understand how the energies work and why. This will be understood where it was caused, here in the physical plane of existence.

> *Intuitive Reporter: We see this one to be greatly influenced by those feelings of emotion such as fear and anger, jealousy and frustration. We see this one to be greatly influenced by these emotions for these are the emotions experienced in this past lifetime that this one was unable to cope with. We see this one to have within [his] grasp the opportunity for controlling these emotions. For this one has developed somewhat an objectivity about self. However this objectivity becomes shaded by emotions sometimes; for the inability to cope with others in their direct connection with the emotional senses and with direct connection with those thoughts within this one.*

The objectivity present, that was lacking previously, is the power of the Conscious Mind to reason. This reasoning power in the Conscious Mind has been developed since the time of Atlantis. Conscious reasoning, as we shall soon see, is a more recent endeavor on the part of human man to move toward enlightenment as a spiritual being.

Conscious Mind power depends upon a still mind. When the Conscious Mind is disturbed by reactions to the emotions of self and others, the power is diminished. For this one, this pattern has been learned and practiced since birth.

> *Intuitive Reporter: We see this one from childhood forward to be under great influence of highly intense emotional entities, for this one is seen to be influenced greatly by others and their emotional effects upon self having relationships time and again with those of past lifetimes connected with this emotional control and with the control of energy influence of thoughts of self upon others. This one has at this time the relationship existing with self and a particular entity which is of domination and submission which is*

*before mentioned in a past lifetime. We see this domination to be a constant
struggle between these ones in the sense of competition and in the sense of
sense endeavor for this one constantly strives to reinforce self with the
ability to gain more prestige than the one in direct connection.*

The result of countless excursions in the physical plane become apparent in this
description of how the inner relationship described in the Atlantean period has now been
externalized between self and another person whom this one is separate from. The
polarities have become physicalized, a part of the sense of identity, the ego of both.

*Intuitive Reporter: We see this one to have chosen the parents to be a
restricting force for these ones have great influence upon this one in the
connection to emotional control for it is because of these parental influences that this one has experienced great emotional upheaval and inability
to cope with situations.*

What a concept to consider, that you chose the parents you now have! Then to consider
that whatever they offered you has been and continues to be integral to your soul
progression. A great irony that is particularly insightful is the reality that children now
entering physical life do not respond to emotional influences in the same way as their
predecessors, often to the chagrin and frustration of parents still caught in the throes of
domination and control. The capacity to reason is strong in these children, and it needs
to be cultivated and encouraged by enlightened adults.

An example of an illumined teacher is one who understands thoughts are real, as
this man has the opportunity to learn by the influence of his thoughts upon his physical
health. Again, this dynamic was not yet available during his Atlantean experience,
having been cultivated over thousands of years of mind-body connecting.

The developed ability for reasoning to transform psychism into intuition is also
addressed in the significance of this man's previous life to the present one. The
suggestions for him have universal import for us all. The significance concludes:

*Intuitive Reporter: We see this one to have experiences throughout the
lifetime with the emotions, to have experiences with a high intensity of
energy within but to be lacking in control of this energy, thus taking on
physical manifestations of frustration and physical inabilities to feel in
harmony, for the body processes are affected by the mental attitude of this
one greatly. This one must realize the great responsibility of thought
control and emotional control for this one's high evolvement of that termed
psychic abilities, gives self a great influence on others and gives self a
higher influence on own progression and growth.*

We see this one to greatly need the ability to love self at this time and find love for self in the ability to cope with situations and in the ability to remain objective about self in direct connection with others. For this one tends to be protective of others as well as self, and to have many defenses in direct connection with self and opportunities for growth and progression with others.

This one is seen to be quite lazy in attitudes toward discipline of self, instead desires strongly the experiences of the inner levels and those happinesses and mysteries that they afford but not to contain within self the discipline in order to develop these for any circumstances for growth or any direct connection for opportunity of understanding. These will be experienced throughout this lifetime as well as others by many. This recognition is within this one, however the ability to discipline these will be up to this one for the growth and progression of self. For if this one takes the discipline within hand, this one may develop a great sense of understanding and a great control of the emotions of the physical temperament and of the mental aspirations of self. [31573191027]

INTUITIVE RESEARCH
2001
II

ATLANTIS
Intuitive Research Part II

Each of these levels of Mind or dimensions of consciousness (see *Figure 5* on page 80) are specific universes of learning through which mankind has descended starting at the first level and moving all the way out into the seventh level of Mind which is also called our physical universe.

As originally designed, Mind was created as a vehicle through which beings of Light could evolve. Mankind was evolving through experiencing in the High Dimensions which are also known as the Higher Levels of Mind or the Higher Planes of existence.

As originally designed, the Sixth Level of Mind was created as an observation platform for the Seventh Level of Mind. This observation was progressing nicely until some entities or beings of Light decided to do more than observe and learn through observation. These beings decided to become directly involved in the Seventh Level, ie. the physical universe life.

These entities began to interfere with the natural flow of nature. This physical activity type of interfering led directly to the many souls becoming entrapped in physical bodies thereby setting up the cycle of Karma and reincarnation.

We are the descendants of those who interfered. We who inhabit physical bodies are those who were entrapped in physical bodies during the time period of Atlantis.

Those who chose not to interfere remained in the higher dimensions of vibration and Light, the higher planes of existence.

History of the Human Race

What is known as the Homo sapiens has arisen from those who engage themselves within the physical form to an extreme. In other words, the souls or entities who inhabit and are entrapped in the physical bodies of human or Homo sapiens become entrapped and set up the cycle of Karma and reincarnation by interfering in the animal man or proto-human activities. This they did in order to have extreme experiences like putting the animal man's hand in a fire.

For example, imagine you are on top of a tall building, a skyscraper and observing the people below. You aren't really participating but you do learn some things from what you see and observe.

Another example is the use of a telescope. You are not really participating in what you see so far away through the telescope, yet you can learn things about what you observe.

Observation from Subconscious Mind, specifically the Sixth Level or Emotional Level of Mind was much like this except there was not the distance factor. It was a vibration factor, a vibration difference. These entities were vibrating at a higher rate that was not perceivable by the five senses of sight, sound, taste, touch, and smell. Therefore, the Sixth Level entities or beings could see – or more accurately perceive – the plants, animals, and animal man of physical Earth but physical animal-man could not see him, much like ghosts or spirits are not usually seen or perceived by people today.

From that there has been the development of a kind of sustainable physical form which could be reproduced in a fashion that is comparable to that of indigenous life forms which are both of plant and animal structure. This means that Homo sapiens look and act somewhat like animals, yet there are differences. Walking upright, lack of fur over the body, binocular vision, color vision, large brain, opposable thumb, together make up a unique type of life form. Some animals have some of these qualities but not in the grouping that humans do. Keep in mind those who came to Earth drew upon the genetics already present to create sustainable forms.

A most outstanding difference between humans and animals is that humans have chakras, animals don't. Most animals have tails which direct the Kundalini energy, the creative energy, back down into the Earth. Humans, which do not ordinarily have tails, have the opportunity to direct their Kundalini energy up the spine, through the chakras, and out the crown of the head in order to evolve to Buddhas and Christs and gain cosmic consciousness and infinite awareness and existence. In addition as reported in these Intuitive inquiries, human man is evolving from a carbon-based life form to a crystal - based life form. This will serve to further differentiate humans from the animals which are the indigenous population of Earth.

Through the experimentation during the Atlantean period there were insights gained that would produce this new kind of form on the planet. This was particularly true in the third cycle, beginning somewhat in the latter part of the second and extending somewhat into the fourth cycle. In relation to this, it is interesting to note that most of mankind's domesticated grains were developed in the ancient past while present technology does not seem capable of doing the same thing today. Wheat, rice, rye, barley, and corn, are examples.

Much of what has been refined into the genetics which have sustained themselves to the present period were in regards to what was done upon the part of the Beldane in an effort to create a sustainable energetic form. When this was not forthcoming in the way that had been expected, there was some dissemination of this knowledge that was used by the Atlanteans.

Some of this knowledge of genetics was integrated into the Siriuns and their activities, particularly during the fourth cycle. The Siriuns who had chosen to stay needed to have a sustainable form. In large part, it was these ones who became what is known as the race of humans.

Intuitive Research May 2001

Conductor (Dr. Daniel Condron): Where did the Beldane originate?

Intuitive Reporter (Dr. Barbara Condron): From that cluster referred to as Orion.

Many of the pyramid structures on the Giza plateau are oriented toward that Orion cluster, why is this? How does this relate to the Beldane?

It does not relate to the Beldane, it relates to the Siriuns who had received some of the knowledge of the Beldane and had incorporated it into what they were doing. Particularly those who were of the Egyptians. There were two different groups which has been given.

Were the Egyptians set apart any different from other peoples of the planet?

Yes.

In what manner?

Their manner of assuming energetic forms which would be sustainable which would otherwise be known currently as matter were different from those which had been produced by the Centaurus and by the experiments of the other Siriuns who had populated this planet. The forms were expected to be ones that could be revisited and reused and in the capacity to enter and leave at will would be able to reenergize the forms. There were limitations to this process that were not foreseen, nor were they overcome at the point where they arose, and therefore there was a restriction that did then exist that these ones needed to respond to, in responding to it they did intermingle and in that interbreeding produced a form which was sustainable in a finite physical constellation.

The intermingling or interbreeding was between what two groups, or peoples?

Between these ones and several groups, actually. It was this group and some of the Beldane that had remained behind that wanted some kind of form and therefore it is through this group that the genetic code was transmitted that would rule the physical form of evolution.

From what area then did these human species, begin that they then did spread over the entire globe?

This would be in the area ranging from what is now the Mediterranean Sea, the globe itself was different in that period of time. However it would have been seated around the pyramidical structure that is known as the Great Pyramid, that which was the greatest of all such structures that were erected upon the planet.

How were the different races produced and why have they occupied different parts of the planet until recently? The three races?

Once the genetic code or pattern was established, there was the relativity of dimension. In order for there to be sustainability in the physical form, there had to be the separation into the triad structure in order for there to be the necessary cooperation to create frozen energy patterns. There was not recognition of how to do this in a unified fashion at that time. Therefore, the three predominant strains were developed and as there was the migrating away throughout the land areas and then interbreeding with other life forms there were more definitions of the separations that became apparent.

What other life forms were they interbred with?

Those that had been created by the others who had come to this planet. There were other Siriuns. There were the experiments of the Beldane and the few of them that remained, the few of the Siriuns who remained, primarily these were those. There was some interbreeding with the Centaurus, however, very little, for them the remainders remained separate. They were connected to the land area that has been referred to as Mu and they are still present within the area referred to as Australia. The effects to intermingle here failed. They were of an energetic nature rather than a matter nature and this was not compatible.

Are there any other groups on the planet today that are the results of the Beldanes or Siriuns or Centaurus other than the commonly referred to as the human species or Homo sapiens or the common group of people around this planet? Are there any special groups like this?

There are other intelligent life forms upon the planet which are not discernible through the physical structures of the Homo sapiens and therefore are not often acknowledged by them. We see that these expressions of energy exist both within the core of the planet itself and also within the depths of the oceans. They do emanate a kind of vibration that is collective and are integral in the sustainability of the planet itself. Although there is not a contact that would be expressed or even understood by the Homo sapiens, the genetic exchanges which are beginning to come about within the Homo sapiens in larger numbers are in some ways a correspondence to these other energies that have been sustained on the planet for longer than they have been present. More of an influence is the activity, once again, between intelligent life forms upon this planet and the mother planets.

Is this an ongoing connection, a continuation, to the present time period, these planets with these other planets?

It is comprehensive. It is a kind of omniscient. Those who have roots in the experience have continued connection. This is true for the Siriuns, particularly. The connection between the mother planet and those sustaining on the Earth within the Centaurus have not been connected since before they arrived. There is no sign of reconnection occurring there. There is the beginning of connection once again with that referred to as Xena. It does show itself in the more settled genetic structures that are changing and altering in the present time period.

What of the Siriuns?

There has been the omniscient connection. It is a more individualistic nature where some Homo sapiens are aware of this more than others. The genetic alterations within most of this group are creating through matter rather than energy forms.

What of the Beldane?

These are the catalysts. There are the energy forms that assume physical bodies in order for there to be a significant change in the genetic structure. This is tied as it was once before to a kind of communication which is occurring between them and a significant relativity to those of Xena.

How might those of Xena be referred to?

They are not present upon the planet.

Therefore, you see, Earth did not develop in a vacuum. Neither did the civilization that was Atlantis develop in a vacuum. Both borrowed heavily from older or more ancient peoples, beings, and entities. Some from our physical three-dimensional universe and some from higher dimensions of energy and consciousness.

Although physically the DNA of humans and animals are very similar, the differences are more than apparent. For even though there is only a 2% to 5% difference in the physical DNA or genetic structure between Homo sapiens and much of the indigenous (animal) population, the energetic structure shows or exhibits vastly more difference. For example, animals do not have chakras while Homo sapiens do. In animals, the creative energy called Kundalini energy goes through their tail and is grounded in mother Earth.

In humans there is no tail because the Kundalini energy is to be directed upward as each individual evolves. The Kundalini then moves up the spinal column piercing or vivifying each chakra starting at the base of the spine and moving upward through the crown chakra located at and directly above the top of the head. In humans the creative energy, the Kundalini, is used to expand and raise the consciousness of each individual.

Kundalini energy is the creative energy. It is what enables Homo sapiens or Reasoning Man to evolve to Intuitive, Spiritual Man with multidimensional consciousness.

All life on the planet — that mankind is aware of — is carbon-based. However, Homo sapiens or humans have the ability and are in the process of evolving their physical bodies from carbon-based to a crystal-based life form.

This is a transformation not only in mental and spiritual consciousness but also an evolvement in the physical body itself into a higher form in order that we souls can inhabit a more technologically advanced vehicle or body.

HUMANS

Why do present day humans have little or no body hair while all other land mammals have a lot of body hair?

Most of what is referred to as land mammals are indigenous to the planet itself. They have arisen through a kind of evolution that the Earth is going through and its production and do not interact with the life forms that are of higher intelligence. The similarity in the Homo sapiens form is owing to the experimentations that occurred where there was the receiving of what already existed on the planet and the attempt to emulate it, to imitate it, in order to create a sustainable matter form. Therefore there are similarities.

Is there any DNA from these beings from other planets in the human DNA then?

There are some similarities, yes, however, the differences are quite remarkable. It is more than the arrangement of the patterns. It is owing to the energetic base of the genetic structure itself that is not in matter form. This same quality is not found in the indigenous life forms. The indigenous life forms are carbon based and there has been significant movement to transform this from the current DNA within Homo sapiens by that which manifests through the Indo-Aryan portion of Homo sapiens.

Into what kind of life form?

Crystal. What would be described as fractal, crystalline.

Is this process ongoing?

It is commencing. It has been produced over eons. This has always been the destiny, the movement. It is only now that the factors are present where there can be quickening of this occurring.

What are these factors?

Collective intelligence.

Collective intelligence is connected consciousness.

Throughout history those who have attained enlightenment have proclaimed the oneness of all creation. Those who are progressing in stages to greater reasoning, then intuition, to greater and greater stages of enlightenment, have perceived connections between various aspects of creation. Mankind is progressing to a connected consciousness where each person understands their unique individuality while simultaneously being aware of their great connectedness to all humanity.

What is the relationship of this to the appearance of the Indigo children?

This is one manner of expressing the genetic change which is coming about.

Why do there seem to be three different groups of Indigo children?

It is comparable to what occurred in the formation of the previous three races. Those being matter-bound. Within the present these are energy-bound and it is the beginning of the reunification of consciousness. Therefore it is seen still in the triad. It's destiny however is unification into One.

If these other races from other planets had never interfered with the evolution of the Earth would the Earth have produced intelligent beings from the indigenous populations?

There is no way to be certain. There have been considerable life created in many forms. Therefore there is reason to believe that it would have continued to evolve.

"Indigo" is a word used to describe the exceptionally talented, gifted, genius children being born in our planet today that exhibit great superhuman and supernormal abilities. The children being born in the last decade, since 1995, bear the seeds of a new, evolved race on planet Earth for we are changing, advancing to our next stage of evolution as a thinking beings. One of the best books documenting these advanced souls is The Indigo Children by Lee Carroll and Jan Tober.

END OF TIME

Once the awareness and understanding of the Mind and its divisions, the planes of existence, the higher dimensions of energy vibration and consciousness are received and incorporated into one's thinking, the solution and awareness of humanities past, present, and future become more clear and understandable.

To understand time, to understand consciousness, to understand evolution, to understand the mystery of Life, you must understand something that it has taken me [Daniel] over 30 years to discover which is the fact that what we call physical time is a measurement of distance.

PHYSICAL TIME IS A MEASUREMENT OF PHYSICAL DISTANCE.

The Earth revolves around the sun. We call that distance a year. The Earth completes one rotation on its axis. We call that distance a day. The large hand of a clock rotates around the face of a clock. We call this one hour which is one 24th of a day (meaning day and night). The small hand of a clock rotates once around the face of a clock, we call this distance 12 hours. The secondhand rotates once around the face of a clock: we name this measurement of distance 60 seconds.

These are all examples of physical time, yet, there is a higher dimensional time. This inner level of Mind or high dimensional consciousness is not measured by physical distance. Instead higher dimensional time or mental time is measured by the rate of soul progression or permanent learning for the higher self.

The Mayan calendar, the Maya being the master timekeepers on the planet, runs out in the year 2012. What is the meaning of this?

There are records that have yet to be discovered. These people were directly related to the initial Egyptians, as they are known, and they were reflective of the same calibre of intelligence and honoring of consciousness. The calendars that are known openly are those which deal with the matter and the expression of matter to its point of completion. Once there is the ascending into energy forms there will be a different measurement of experience.

What will that measurement be?

Relativity.

Might that also be referred to as vertical time, rather than horizontal time?

In the context of being able to experience greater dimensions, yes.

What is meant by dimensions? Does that mean the levels of consciousness, divisions of mind?

It can be expressed that way, yes.

What is the shift of the ages referred to by the ancients that is going on now?

This is the movement of consciousness to understand itself and then to expand. It is the ability to understand consciousness as energy, ultimately, and this will be the next destiny.

What are the factors and energy leading up to the year 2012 that might be noticed on the planet?

Increasing polarity within the individual, between people, between the collective populace and the planet itself. In all forms, this polarity will express and be experienced. This is in an effort to accept a transition in the viewpoint of consciousness that will enable its purveyor to know the whole. This would be expressed as it has already been, in every form of existence.

Where are these records of the Maya that have yet to be discovered or known by the general public?

There are some records within the temples at Yucatan. There is some indication from astronomical data that can be collected by using the temple site itself.

What are the records of ancient civilization buried that might possibly be discovered that might show a greater level of development than currently thought on the planet?

This is not a physical record. It is a form that does generate energy in a specific pattern.

Is there a central location for this form, and what is this form?

It is found in many forms of life that exist within this planet. It is repetitive as a nautilus.

By the year 2012, the obviousness of a shift in consciousness on this planet will be apparent. In many ways, it already is. 2012 is the year the Mayan calendar ends. It is the end of time according to the Mayans who were the greatest timekeepers the world has ever known. They kept track of time in order to know the evolution of Higher consciousness. The Mayans of the Yucatan in southern Mexico were a civilization dating back perhaps as far as the Egyptian civilization. Both are much, much older than generally thought.

The year 2012 marks the end of the movement of consciousness into physical matter. From the year 2012 onward, time will more and more be measured as a movement forward in consciousness, the evolution of Self and mankind. The adding of permanent understandings of creation to the Self. This is the time that was prophesied by many people the world over. It is the shift of the Ages. It is the movement from Reasoning Man to Intuitive Man (thinker).

The next destiny of humankind is to understand consciousness as energy. Therefore, new sources of energy and new ways of using energy will emerge.

More people than ever are now desiring to understand Self as a whole, spiritual or mental being with multidimensional consciousness.

More and more the differences will become obvious between those who wish to lead a physically engrossed life out of harmony with nature and those who understand all life to be connected. There will be those who view themselves as separate and do not believe thought is cause. And those who know the truth that thought is cause and the connectedness of all life.

As the consciousness of the planet moves to a more connected consciousness, new uses and forms of energy will be discovered and used. Then the power and energy of the pyramid complexes of the Mayan in the Yucatan as well as those at Giza, Egypt will be known. This will bring the possibility of re-activation of these energy power plants. Direct communication, planet to planet, becomes possible without the restriction of time and space. The transfer of energy between planets becomes possible. An almost limitless source of non-polluting energy – called planet Earth and Sirius – will be available.

Figure 6. Fibonacci diagram.
The spiral growth pattern
is a feature of many mollusk shells.
The nautilus, like the pinecone and pineapple,
are examples of the pattern described
mathematically by Fibonacci.

The form of the nautilus uses the Fibonacci series in its growth as do many plants and, in fact, life on planet Earth. The Fibonacci series is named after the man who rediscovered it in modern times indicating a continual adding to in the process of growth. This series proceeds in this way:

0, 1, 1, 2, 3, 5, 8, 13, 21, 34, 55, 89, 178, 356, and so forth

Each number is the sum of the two proceeding numbers. The Bose radio, for example, uses this series to produce sound waves and excellent acoustics. The Fibonacci series explains the growth of consciousness as it evolves at an accelerating rate.

$$0 + 1 = 1$$
$$1 + 1 = 2$$
$$1 + 2 = 3$$
$$2 + 3 = 5$$
$$3 + 5 = 8$$
$$5 + 8 = 13$$

This form, when widely practiced and used, can give increasing energy, power, and consciousness.

Planet Earth's Development

The Earth as a planet and as a consciousness is maturing.

Planets go through the cycles of growth and change in a way similar to people, plants, and civilizations. These four cycles are termed or called infancy, adolescence, adulthood, and wisdom.

As the planet Earth matures, the vibration of the planet adjusts to match that change. Presently, the Earth is understanding just such a change. It corresponds with humanity's movement from reasoning man to intuitive man. The word "man" comes from the Sanskrit *manu*, meaning thinker.

The consciousness of the people of this planet must move from one of separateness to one of connectedness leading to a unity consciousness where it is recognized that whatever any person says, does, thinks, or feels, affects everyone else in the Universe. Then Self must accept responsibility for this awesome power.

There is a natural atrophy that is occurring in the motion that is affecting the magnetic properties as well as the gravitational properties. The movement of the energy of the Earth itself is constantly expanding and contracting and the condensation that is occurring is causing there to be a very slow cooling and hardening of much of the substance of the planet itself. This is a natural form of the expression of the energy of this particular structure and it continues to evolve according to its own consciousness.

What is the best thing each individual can do to harmonize with these changes going on in the human race and the planet and to use these changes for soul growth and spiritual development?

It has been prophesied by many from many different cultures, races, and times. It is the capacity to experience within the consciousness at all times the connection and relationship between what is perceived as separate, self being separate, and that of all other life. It is only in the elevation and transmutation of individual consciousness in this way that the assistance will be present for it to be offered. This would require the experiencing of the polarities to a point through which there can be the releasing of the atomic consciousness, therefore the experience of the whole energy can be absorbed. This consciousness then can provide the connectedness that is spoken of and the quality of love that has been taught throughout the ages.

The Universal Language of Mind was discovered by the School of Metaphysics in order to understand the meanings of night dreams coming from the inner levels of Mind and also to understand the deeper, inner meanings of the Holy Books and Holy Scriptures of the World. It is based on the understanding that the language of Mind is pictures whether in the Conscious Mind or Subconscious Mind, and that people use words to describe these pictures. The pictures are the symbols. The symbolic language of physical life and the Conscious Mind is based upon form or structure. The symbolic language of the Subconscious Mind is based upon function, or how it is used.

Any suggestions or perceptions of the Universal Language of Mind and how it relates to the shift of the ages, the shift in consciousness, this evolution of the planet?

This is the means by which reasoning can become acute and can accelerate the development of consciousness. For in the development of the will there is the accelerating of the evolutionary change and development that is to be built upon the love and connectedness that has been spoken.

The ancients desiring to stabilize the growth or maturity of the planet and thereby reduce dramatic earth changes, such as earthquakes, instituted a plan of energy stabilization of the planet Earth.

The stone stelae or needles placed in the ground at certain points along the ley lines acted as constant acupuncture for the body of the young planet Earth.

Acupuncture is an ancient process of healing, recently brought from China to the United States, which was known by the ancients worldwide but lost to most of the world during the Dark Ages and Kali Yuga. The Kali Yuga is a measurement of time. Our Sun revolves around another star, a sister star, in about 24,000 Earth years.

Yuga is Sanskrit meaning *age*. The 24,000 years required for our Sun to orbit around the center of the galaxy is divided into four sections or time periods. The period of time when the sun passes through 1/20th of its orbit or 1200 years is called the Kali Yuga. The period of time when the sun passes through 2/20th of its orbit or 2400 years is called the Dwappa Yuga. The period of time when the sun passes through 3/20th of its orbit or 3600 years is called the Treta Yuga. The period of time when the sun passes through 4/20th of its orbit or 4800 years is called the Satya Yuga. (See Gregg Braden's Awakening to Zero Point and his quotes of Sri Yukteswar on this subject.)

When the Sun goes to the place in its orbit which is farthest from the grand center, the powers of physical engrossment are the greatest. This was the Dark Ages that mankind passed through. This was also the Kali Yuga.

These periods of time are rooted in Earth's connectedness with a galaxy far beyond the perimeters of its solar system. Throughout time there have been those like

Thales and Copernicus who held to the unpopular belief that the Sun rather than the Earth was the center of our universe. It is now time for us to recognize our place and responsibility in a far greater system.

As the sun begins to advance toward the great center for 12,000 years, the mental virtue, or enlightenment, develops greatly. We are just beginning to see the rise of this virtue.

The healer using acupuncture on the physical body of the person they are healing insert small needles in the energy meridians of the body. Those needles then open up the energy flows of the electrical system of the body that have been blocked by limiting mental attitudes such as habits, fears, angers, greed, and separateness. This type of healing also works for physical injuries.

The ancients were applying acupuncture to the entire planet and were succeeding in this healing endeavor. These acupuncture meridians are actually the minor chakras of the body both of the Earth and of the human body.

The ley lines, as constructed in ancient times, ran at angles all over the Earth. At the sites where one or two or three ley lines intersected the beings from Beldane or Sirius would erect their temples and Holy sites. These intersections are the locations of the minor-major chakras of planet Earth, the energy vortexes or meridians of the planet.

At the sites when many ley lines came together or intersected, the ancients would erect centers of worship for these were the most Holy of all sites being the conjunction points of the most energy for the entire planet and its association and connectedness with the universe and the inner level of Mind which are the High Dimensions of the Space-time continuum. Atlantis was at the end of its Fourth and final cycle 12,000 years ago, and Earth and humanity are approaching the end of another cycle now. The End of an Age, the shift of the Ages, the year 2012. Thus the present time is very similar to 12,000 years ago except we have moved full cycle and are standing higher on the ladder of Self awareness now than at the time of Atlantis and instead of being on the descending cycle, we are on the ascending cycle of the Yugas and enlightenment for the planet. The latter stage of Atlantis was a time of movement into the beginning of the Age of Reasoning. The present time is the movement into the Intuitive Age.

Thus all kinds of higher miracles were possible at these sites due to what was called magic but actually due to higher scientific principles of wholistic and connected energy being focused and concentrated for greater power such as using pyramid energy to generate electricity as a power plant for electric lights, healing, and enlightenment.

This is why certain areas on the planet today are Holy or wholistic sites.

What is the purpose of having the ley lines around the planet marked with stelae or stone markers all along the lines or where they came together in temples?

This was similar to the creation of physical forms for the consciousness to utilize. It was as a way for there to be the energy patterns that could be established in the form of the Earth itself. Where the energy could be fed from the mother planets. At one time they were used in that way. They could be seen as guidelines for the energy to move through that would help stabilize the planet for we see during the Atlantean period there was still great difficulty in that regard.

Was this an artificially produced instability produced from these other races that came to the planet or was it a natural process of the growth of the planet?

It was by far a natural process. There was actually very little interference upon the part of any of the ones that came here.

What is the connection between Stonehenge to the Great Pyramid of Giza, Egypt, and to the ley lines found all over the world where the ancient temples were located?

Stonehenge was a point of entry, of time travel. A teleportation device.

Both for coming to this planet and leaving?

At one time, yes.

Is it still functioning?

No.

What has caused it to cease to function?

Some of the Earth changes that occurred in the latter Atlantean period caused the breaking apart and moving of the land and in that there was the destruction of several of the key stones that were used in the pattern itself and the breaking apart of them. In this there was the incompleteness that was created. This in the physical structure.
In the energetic structure, this was primarily used by the Beldanes, and we see that when most of them left, and we see only a few remained, the few that did remain were intermingled and therefore they had in essence sacrificed their ability to return.

In the ancient days, where the Beldanes stayed, were they considered to be a different race or group of people than the other peoples, and if so how might they be referred to today?

They were not really considered a different race, they were considered ostracized at different points of history. They would be referred to in current vernacular as the Celts. The Druids would have been of these people, or descendents from them would be more accurate.

INDIGENOUS LIFE FORMS

Scientists have debated for a long time the connection between Neanderthal and Homo sapiens. Neanderthal was an early humanoid-like being. Neanderthal is named after the valley or ravine in which skeletal remains were first found near Dusseldorf, Germany. The Neanderthal was about 5'4" in height. The head was long compared to modern man with very little chin and a rounded, sloping forehead. The Neanderthals were the most highly evolved of the indigenous species of planet Earth.

From our intuitive research investigation, it appears that Neanderthal is, or was, the real earthlings while Homo sapiens is an off-planet hybrid, a mix of planet Earth DNA with alien genetic experiments.

The Homo sapiens body was the type of body produced for the entities or souls — called higher dimensional beings — to use. By use is meant the ability to move into the physical body, take it over, and operate it for a lifetime.

The Neanderthals were different. Being an indigenous species of Earth, they evolved under the natural laws operating on the planet. Their bodies were never taken over by the multidimensional beings as souls. In other words, souls existing in Subconscious or Universal Mind never became entrapped in Neanderthal bodies.

This process of entrapment, reincarnation, and Karma only came into effect for Homo sapiens. For in fact, the design of the body made this possible. Once the energetic beings made the decisions to interfere with the bodies of proto-humans, it was just a matter of time before they would lose the ability to move in and out of these bodies. When that occurred, the cycle of birth, death, and resurrection, was set into motion so that now the soul chooses a body for a lifetime.

Who were the Neanderthals? Who or what were they produced from?

These were one of the indigenous life forms.

Does this mean they appeared upon the Earth without outside intervention?

They have evolved, yes, through the constant translation of carbon material.

What became of the Neanderthals?

They were fairly localized and within the Earth changes that occurred particularly in the fourth cycle of Atlantis and shortly following that period, they were destroyed. Most of them drowned.

How was it that the Homo Sapiens survived this flood or this water?

Not all of them were in the same area.

What parts of the globe did this flood cover?

Much of this would be what is now ocean between Africa and South America, primarily, although there is some from the Eastern coast of Africa, and Arabia as well.

Could this be part of what was referred to as Atlantis? This area between Africa and South America?

Yes, there is part of what has been referred to as Atlantean continent. However, more of it is more northward. There was also upon that referred to presently as Antarctica there were some Neanderthals which survived for a period of time but because of the extreme cold that did set in they could not sustain their forms.

What is the history of Homo erectus?

This is relative to the Centaurus.

What became of the Homo erectus?

What remains of them are aboriginal.

What is the difference genetically as far as the purposes of the Neanderthal and Homo sapiens, in other words why did those from other planets want a different body other than Neanderthal to work with therefore developing the Homo sapiens body, since there are many similarities?

It was not methodical in that way. It was a matter of what they could reproduce with the energy and intelligence that they had.

ATLANTEAN LAND AREA

There were four major cycles of Atlantis. With each movement from one cycle to the next, the land mass or land area that was Atlantis was reduced. In other words, the continent land area or country that we call Atlantis became smaller with each successive cycle. During the first cycle, Atlantis was at its largest and had its greatest expanse.

During the second cycle, the size of the land area of Atlantis was reduced. During the third cycle, it was reduced even farther. Until in the fourth and last cycle, the country of Atlantis was reduced to the size of a large island in the mid-Atlantic.

It is the fourth or last cycle of Atlantis that Plato refers to in his writing. It is the fourth cycle of Atlantis that broke apart and was for the most part submerged partially by earthquakes and partially the melting of the ice caps that occurred during the end of the last and most recent ice age.

Atlantis besides being a land area was also a civilization. It had technology that is still not in use today. One of the sources of energy was the planet Earth itself. Pyramids and other large stone structures and complexes were built and utilized to tap into this energy.

During earlier cycles of Atlantis the breaking up of that area led to the movement of continents or as it has been called since the mid-1900's, continental drift. The Appalachian Mountains are part of what was once an earlier cycle of Atlantis.

Figure 7. The Atlantean land mass at the time of the First Cycle
superimposed upon a representation of land mass in the 21st century.

What was the connection between Atlantis and ancient India?

There were occasions of intermingling. There was some of what would be considered in the present as world trade, although on a very different level.

Was there any connection between Atlantis and the Caspian Sea?

Part of Atlantis was within this area.

In what way since much of Atlantis is in the area of the North Atlantic?

This is a very large area. The changing of the face of the Earth has caused pieces of what was Atlantis, what was Lemuria, to be scattered in what are present continental land masses.

Where was Lemuria? What was this land area's purpose, design and outcome?

This is actually more a time period and a dimensional experience preceding that which is commonly referred to as Atlantis. There is some overlap with the first into the second cycle as it is known. It was more predating the Atlantean time period.

The XENA

How did the written language of Sanskrit develop in India, and by whom?

This was through contact with the Xena.

What were the Xena doing in that area of India? What was their purpose?

It is not so much that they were there as they were present. There was a presence, and their presence was in many parts because it was within the people. It is not centered in locality. It is centered in consciousness, in thought, and therefore in differing times the Xena did pervade the thoughts of those with consciousness who were already attempting to build something that was sustainable for them.

The question was concerning the language and the Xena were intricately involved in the transmutation of vibration that did eventually resound in this form of communication. They were also intricately involved in the initiation of the genetic code which has sustained a viable form of physical life that is increasingly intelligent and conscious of itself and others.

It is also becoming present within the consciousness of some upon the planet at the present time for the transitions that have already been addressed.

These Xena, was this the name of the people or the planet they were from, or both?

It is the way they identify themselves.

Do you see a constellation they are from, where do these entities originate?

Would be the constellation that bears the name Pleiades.

Remember, the Xena were not physical entities. That is, they were energetic beings who sometimes had interaction with physical beings. However, for the most part they did not become entrapped in the physical body of the emerging Homo sapiens.

To understand the Xena's presence, you will need to accept the fact that thoughts are real, that thoughts are things, and that thoughts may be transmitted or sent from one mind or one person's mind to another's. In fact, we can even in many cases eliminate the idea of distance between minds because the Xena, being consciousness rather than physical beings, could merge their consciousness with the various people of the planet at different times.

The Xena experience as pure consciousness from Superconscious Mind. Therefore, in times past their consciousness, the knowledge and their wisdom, pervaded this planet. It is becoming so again in the present time period. This is because humanity has evolved to a point of fulfillment in the Xena's plan for the evolving of consciousness on planet Earth.

In the newly revealed <u>Bible</u> <u>Code</u> that shows the past and future are revealed in this code, who produced this hidden code in the first five books of the Old Testament and why?

This is transmitted through the Xena and the transmitting of it at that time did cause an alteration in a part of the consciousness of the form in order for it to be sustained genetically. It was transmitted to some of the Siriuns (Sirius = Siriuns), who would now be called Egyptians. The transmitting of it did cause a change within the genetic structure which was different than from the Egyptians.

What people received this change in genetic structure that was different from the Egyptians?

Those who were in charge of transmitting and recording the scripture.

What was the outcome of this change to be, that was produced by this transmitting of knowledge?

It was unintentional. The change was not anticipated. There was seen a need upon the part of the Xena that there would be a guide or a kind of pattern that could be understood by those who were willing to know.

Why has it taken super computers, super fast computing power, to be able to decipher this code?

Because human consciousness tends to rely upon two dimensional restraints. It is through the use of the two dimensions that electronics have been harnessed, the energy has been harnessed, in such a way as to produce a kind of global brain. However in the manifestation of this there is also the manifestation of the limits.

What technologies of power and energy were available to mankind over two thousand years ago, in its ancient history, that are currently unavailable in its present time period?

Anything that exists within the imagination of man in the present time period has already been accomplished at some point by some part of consciousness.

The Xena seeded our planet Earth, not only with genetic material, but with knowledge of Creation which entails power of all sorts for those who know how to wield it.

Whether Sanskrit or the <u>Bible Code</u>, the Xena relayed knowledge of the structure of the Universe and how to harmonize with and utilize that structure which some call universal laws. They did this in order to fulfill the destiny of mankind which is to gain the full enlightenment which means to consciously exist with awareness on many levels of Mind, all levels of consciousness, or in many dimensions, all at the same time.

Universal Laws form the structure of creation. They exist in Subconscious or Universal Mind and manifest in the physical universe whether one is aware of them or not. For example, there is a Universal Law called Cause and Effect. The basic statement of this Universal Law is thought is cause. This means the life you have chosen, and continue to choose each day, is based on your thoughts. Your continual thoughts create your consciousness and your consciousness is your life. Your thoughts draw experiences of a like kind to you in order that you may learn the lessons of life.

Most people are not aware that they cause effects with their thoughts. They do not believe or understand that the thoughts they think in secret affect them and the world.

The brain and Mind are wholistic. However, the five physical senses tend to see or perceive the world as physical only and Self as separate from everything and everyone else. This is the great falsehood. This is illusion, often called Maya in the lore of India. The truth is, you and I – people – are not physical beings. Each of us is an energetic or energy being that has chosen to inhabit a body for a lifetime whether it be 20 years or 200 years.

To know creation is to perceive and understand it as the movement of interconnected energy and consciousness. You and I are units of Light, which are in other words localized units or focal points of energy and consciousness, referred to in many Holy Scriptures as I AM.

The Xena and other beings of the ancient world could perceive wholistically, interconnectedly, and synergistically, and could therefore understand the hidden meaning in these great Holy works that they created, transmitted or preserved.

The Egyptians and the Mayans were more than a colony of Atlantis, as has been supposed. Rather the Egyptians, Mayans, and Olmecs were set up as a race apart or separate by the Siriuns as a way for them to have power generating stations, as a way to have a stargate for returning to their home planet, and for the purpose of creating a physical-type body that could be used and re-used over and over again so the soul could enter and leave the body at will.

This was the purpose of the elaborate steps the Egyptians took to embalm and take care of the nobility's body when a Pharaoh or other high nobility was not in the body, rather than the less enlightened ideas purported for centuries such as the pyramids were only built as tombs.

Ancient Civilizations

Who were the Olmecs of Central America?

They were related to the Egyptians.

What was their relationship to the Mayans?

They were comparable to the Mayans. Several of the American tribal Indians were relatives to the more ancient Egyptians.

Which tribes would these be?

Those already stated. There was some intermingling with the Inca, the Seminole, the Navaho.

Who were the ancient Sumerians, who did they arise from?

They were early forms of what became the Egyptians.

They existed before the Egyptians then?

Yes. The ones (Egyptians) that are recorded.

Were there Sumerians earlier than the ones recorded?

Yes. There were also Egyptians earlier than those that are known.
From where did they arise?

They are Siriuns. They came from the Siriuns who wanted to stay on this planet.

Is there any further knowledge to help the planet Earth evolve its consciousness and the people of the Earth to evolve in their consciousness?

The evolvement has progressed and will continue to do so. The individual recognition of the evolvement which has always been there, and is still remaining and must be done, is the area which can quicken and can then have an influence upon the whole. Therefore it is the assuming within each of those who are separate, realizing their own significance and importance in thought and action, to the greater whole. Whether this arises from interactions with others on a personal scale or whether the thoughts and actions are far reaching is immaterial. What is of importance is the quality of the thought and the ensuing action for it is in experiencing the quality of thought that the evolution will become apparent within the consciousness of all. (42601bgc-drc)

It is important that more and more people on this planet raise their consciousness from the illusion of separateness to the energetic truth of universal connectedness. Then will the Golden Age of Mankind appear.

Thought is cause. Therefore, raise the quality of your thoughts. Still your mind. Exist in the silence and you will evolve to a higher state of consciousness.

The Third Cycle of Atlantis

According to Atlantean reports, the Third Cycle is characterized by some confusion. The major land movements are still occurring, transforming the face of the planet, and along with them the people are being transported, thus separating them from each other.

The need for developing a viable vehicle, a physical body, for the Atlantean people continues. This is partly in response to Earth changes, for the Earth provides the materials that will sustain a body over a period of time. This is partly in response to the desire of the intelligences who are finding themselves, in increasing numbers, entrapped in the forms they are creating.

There are those however who continue to discover and experiment, to invent new ways of expression. The following male was one of these.

Intuitive Report from the Third Cycle

We see this one to be in male form in the area now referred to as Atlantis. We see for this one at a quite young age to be captivated and enthralled with the physical existence. We see this one to take great joy upon discovering new ways to utilize the physical things available. This one possessed a charm which was recognized by those around the self. We see, however, that this one did not see this within the self at all times. This one was cognizant of this, however, did not utilize it at this time. We see this one to become involved in much learning and study.

This led this one into research in many areas of being able to design and utilize physical forms to produce what the mind desired. This one at this time came upon many discoveries. We see this one to downplay his importance within these discoveries. This one often did not share them with others due to a sense of insecurity.

We see this one to be affiliated with a certain structure whose primary purpose at this time was the research area. This one was at first very lowly in the hierarchy within the structure. This was due to this one's own attitude about the self. This one at first takes care of the physical objects which had been created or discovered. This one eventually involved himself with the research of how these objects could be used to a fuller capacity. In many ways this one refined that which had already been created to achieve greater effectiveness in its use.

We see this one working much with vibrations and the effects of vibrations within the time. This one had a great understanding of this process. We see this one to develop a close relationship with those working with him. We see this one throughout the lifetime to not share what was gained within the self and we see for this to have created within the self a sense of unfulfillment.

We see these individuals to work quite well together and to consider themselves as a team. Each supplied an important ingredient to the research and the mastery of developing new ways to form the physical. This one in particular added the idea of precision. This one was quite capable of being able to precisely detail the physical connections which were necessary to implement total efficiency in what was being created.

We see that at this time, this one's abilities were recognized by the close associates. This one began to slowly open up and reveal to these ones that which had become an understanding within the self. This one had little hesitancy in doing so since there was such a strong sense of trust built within these individuals. We see these individuals at first rejecting the information for there was fear within them that there was not time in discussing the concepts. We see these ones as from that point forward working many discoveries which were of import to this area. We see this one to withdraw at 31 years. We see this one referred to as Rexomum.

Conductor: *What was the manner of withdrawal for this entity?*

Intuitive Reporter: We see this to be choice on this one's part. There was not the seeing at a certain point of further use within this environment.

Conductor: *Was this entity capable of entering and leaving the physical?*

Intuitive Reporter: Yes.

Conductor: *What cycle of Atlantis was this incarnation?*

Intuitive Reporter: The early third cycle.

Conductor: *What particular discoveries did this one make that related to the group?*

Intuitive Reporter: We see much of this involving the physical body. The beginning of the observance of the energy flows throughout the mental and how this would effect the physical system. We see that there was much thought and contemplation of how the vehicles that were being manifested should be of a more refined and perfect manner. There had been many mistakes at this time that had been created due to experimentation. These ones were very involved in balancing or repairing these at this time.

Conductor: Would you elaborate on the designing and creating of physical forms this one experienced?

Intuitive Reporter: We see that this one placed a great amount of attention on the workings of what was being created physically. This one could follow very easily the path from the mental into the physical creation. This was not only in the way of the physical body but also physical structures made from the materials that were available to this one at this time. We see most of these to be from the Earth. This one was quite astute at seeing a single vibration and following it through into the physical.

Conductor: Was this entity a leader among this group?

Intuitive Reporter: We see that this could have been possible for this one, however, this was not a desire throughout the entire existence. This one placed more attention upon what could be done and what could be manifested and what could be learned and discovered, than a position of leadership at this time. We see that this one was much within the self in formulating this information and there was not, until the closeness with the two associates, a desire to communicate the knowledge and understanding with others.

Conductor: What would be the significance of that lifetime to the present lifetime?

Intuitive Reporter: We see that within the present time this one has much understanding that this one does not recognize at the current time. Part of this is due to the fact that this one does not express outward to those in the environment that which this one knows and understands. This one has made many discoveries throughout the lifetime within his own self. Much of this is related to past understandings. Some related to conclusions which have been reasoned through and drawn within the Conscious Mind.

Would suggest to this one that in order to complete a cycle, this one must express these in order to gain more. Would suggest to this one that this would be of great benefit not only to the self but to those other individuals. Would suggest that at this time, this one has formulated to a certain extent a goal for the self, however, this is rather selfish in orientation in that it is merely revolving around the self. Would suggest to this one to begin observing how much this one influences those around the self. Would suggest that in this way this one will begin to see that this one can influence these individuals to a greater extent with the knowledge and understanding that he holds within self.

This one is in the process of doing this, however, there is an insecurity linked to this. Would suggest that the insecurity which is being experienced at the present time does not apply to what this one sees within the mind. This one is aware of this, however, there is no activity being taken to come forth.

This time period is very instrumental to this one in that this one has chosen this time to once again create and discover, rediscover, many of the things which were previously known to this one within the past lifetime related. One of the opportunities or tools which this one has offered the self is the situations and environments that this one is in presently. Not to utilize these would be a great repression for the self. This one has created these for his growth and progression and should use them to their fullest extent. In doing so, the insecurity which is experienced will automatically vanish and this one will see the self in a clearer more definite light. That is all.

Conductor: Are there any suggestions for this one to see more clearly the means of expression?

Intuitive Reporter: Would suggest that this one has the ability to formulate ideas very well within the mental. Also there is a building balance of the reasoning abilities. Once this one incorporates both, this one will begin to bring forth more understandings. The expression of the understandings is of the utmost importance, not only to self but to others as well. This one tends to keep the process within himself, being rather introverted where his own ideas or opinions are concerned.

Would suggest that this one begin releasing these with an abundance of love in that this one will be able to multiply his own understandings at rapid speed, gaining the understandings which are desired by the self, but also being able to stimulate those within the environment to do likewise. [1057827151]

Exploratory Analysis

What were the possible discoveries this man was making? Let's review the information with this question in mind.

> *Intuitive Reporter: We see this one to be in male form in the area now referred to as Atlantis. We see for this one at a quite young age to be captivated and enthralled with the physical existence. We see this one to take great joy upon discovering new ways to utilize the physical things available. This one possessed a charm which was recognized by those around the self. We see, however, that this one did not see this within the self at all times. This one was cognizant of this, however, did not utilize it at this time. We see this one to become involved in much learning and study. This led this one into research in many areas of being able to design and utilize physical forms to produce what the mind desired. This one at this time came upon many discoveries.*

The attitude of childlike wonder is characteristic of one who embraces learning. This attribute is part of one who remembers where he came from. Such a one is not distracted by the manifestations of his own ego. This is the charm this one possesses, and loses sight of. Others recognize it, experience it coming from this one, but he does not realize it.

Like many Atlanteans, this male is intent upon manifesting his ideas, learning to make what he wants happen. This does not include interpersonal exchanges of energies that human beings call emotions. This level of consciousness has yet to be formed as a usable vehicle for this thinker. His purpose is very clear and strong; discover ways to improve man's physical body for consciousness to use.

> *Intuitive Reporter: This led this one into research in many areas of being able to design and utilize physical forms to produce what the mind desired. This one at this time came upon many discoveries.*

Look at your hand for a moment. Imagine what your life might be like if you had no thumb. How would you hold this book? How would you write or drink from a cup or open a door? Enterprising folk will probably have some ideas, yet you must admit the value of the human thumb!

Now think about your eyes that afford peripheral and direct vision, or your ears situated on your head for stereo sound. Every part of your body is purposeful. It is part of a greater whole that affords you the luxury of experiencing, with very little effort on the part of your intelligence. In the morning when your alarm goes off you get up and go. You don't have to consciously think about how to open your eyes, or lift your head, or roll over to get out of bed. That's all automatic. And that's not even mentioning the *internal* workings of the human body.

How did we come to have such a refined body-machine? Through the efforts of people like this man from Atlantis. Perhaps he was designing an eye or a nose or a heart. What we now have the luxury of taking for granted, was at one time yet to be created or perhaps even imagined by most.

Yet the imagined need arose in the minds of those who remembered why they were here and the work they were to do. This remains true today.

> *Intuitive Reporter: We see this one to downplay his importance within these discoveries. This one often did not share them with others due to a sense of insecurity. We see this one to be affiliated with a certain structure whose primary purpose at this time was the research area. This one was at first very lowly in the hierarchy within the structure. This was due to this one's own attitude about the self. This one at first takes care of the physical objects which had been created or discovered. This one eventually involved himself with the research of how these objects could be used to a fuller capacity. In many ways this one refined that which had already been created to achieve greater effectiveness in its use.*

This is the kind of person who receives someone else's work and takes it to another level. Like a musical genius who takes a simple melody and transforms it into an orchestral entity, or a scientific genius who watches a hummingbird and develops a formula for a new source of energy, this is the kind of thinker who has the power to receive, appreciate, and further his own and others' progression. This is the genius of invention independent of individual ego. The person whose contributions are timeless because they are serving something beyond the limits of his personal self. Evolution has always required this magnanimous thinking.

> *Intuitive Reporter: We see this one working much with vibrations and the effects of vibrations within the time. This one had a great understanding of this process. We see this one to develop a close relationship with those working with him. We see this one throughout the lifetime to not share what was gained within the self and we see for this to have created within the self a sense of unfulfillment.*

The desire to pass on what is learned is present even during the Third Cycle of Atlantis. Human Man will eventually find fulfillment of this need in the producing of children. Reasoning Man finds it in the fruition of mental creations. Intuitive Man finds it in the passing on of wisdom.

Human Man experiences a strong need to leave his mark on the world. This has produced some of the most outstanding innovations in our world, and some of its most horrific atrocities. Behind this drive is the inner need to give, to contribute something of value that will elevate all of creation. It is the reason the writer writes, the painter paints, the leader leads, the parent parents. To be fulfilled Human Man must give.

This man did not yet possess the faculty to learn this during the Atlantean period.

> *Intuitive Reporter: We see these individuals to work quite well together and to consider themselves as a team. Each supplied an important ingredient to the research and the mastery of developing new ways to form the physical. This one in particular added the idea of precision. This one was quite capable of being able to precisely detail the physical connections which were necessary to implement total efficiency in what was being created.*

The creation of the human form and how it will work was a collective effort. Makes perfect sense doesn't it? Considering the teams of medical surgeons who will work on repairing just one part of the body. It makes perfect sense that many minds would have come together with the common goal of creating the human man body. Even in linear evolution, the idea that the strongest genes win out, the survival of the fittest idea, is primary.

To realize that the body is the result of imaged thought form is to own the power of influence. For us as reasoners, this is a logical connection. Look at the room around you. You are probably clothed with materials fashioned in the mind of a designer. You are sitting in a chair created by a thinker which is in a room and house/building that at one time existed only in the mind of its creator. We now live in a world of man-made things. Each first existed as a thought form.

This man's contribution to the body was precision. Where might the thought form of precision manifest in the human body? Perhaps it is the focusing of the eyes for near and far vision. Perhaps it is in the exact amount of stomach acid needed to digest the food you just ate. Perhaps it is in the conveying of electricity through your nervous system to let you know the temperature of your bath water. To appreciate the miracle that is the human body is to open the mind to the Infinite Intelligence that created it and even now gives it life!

> *Intuitive Reporter: We see that at this time, this one's abilities were recognized by the close associates. This one began to slowly open up and reveal to these ones that which had become an understanding within the self. This one had little hesitancy in doing so since there was such a strong*

sense of trust built within these individuals. We see these individuals at first rejecting the information for there was fear within them that there was not time in discussing the concepts. We see these ones as from that point forward working many discoveries which were of import to this area. We see this one to withdraw at 31 years. We see this one referred to as Rexomum.

Once again the power of the influence of one person is brought to our attention. This time in the form of one man's influence upon a group, a land area, a planet, a period of evolution, and indeed a destiny of a race.

This man was present when this report was given in 1977. He posed the following questions from what he had heard. The replies give great detail to the actual work he was performing in Atlantis.

Conductor: What particular discoveries did this one make that related to the group?

Intuitive Reporter: We see much of this involving the physical body. The beginning of the observance of the energy flows throughout the mental and how this would effect the physical system. We see that there was much thought and contemplation of how the vehicles that were being manifested should be of a more refined and perfect manner. There had been many mistakes at this time that had been created due to experimentation. These ones were very involved in balancing or repairing these at this time.

Another kind of Intuitive Report offered through the School of Metaphysics is the Health Analysis. These relate directly to the work this man was doing, for they trace the mental cause of the condition of the physical body. <u>Permanent Healing</u>, a book Daniel wrote, is based upon years of research in this area.

The mistakes that can be made nowadays are usually the result of the quality of our thought rather than a genetic error. During the Atlantean period, mistakes arose as a result of a number of unknown factors. Creating at that time was like trying to create physical life in a test tube. Yes, it is something we have learned to do, but look how long it has taken us! And the blueprint already existed. That's what cloning is all about, using the genetic code already present. Atlanteans were creating a genetic code! A code that was only recently mapped by Reasoning Man.

The mistakes made by the Atlanteans can be likened to the birth defects of today. They were rarely directly intentional, but frequently the result of man's experimentation without insight into the repercussions or consequences of what was being produced. A prevalent example of this is man's tendency to use chemicals for everything – killing pests, speeding the growth of food, making clothing and furniture, the list is endless – without foreseeing their effects.

The chemical legacy of modern times has been around long enough that we are living with the effects in our own and our children's bodies. Back in the 1950's thalidomide was prescribed for morning sickness until a rash of babies with missing limbs were born to these mothers. Now there are those so sensitive they cannot live in an impure environment. It's one thing to think of the famous "boy who lived in a bubble" and quite another to realize that almost half of the children living in New York City are labeled as asthmatic. We are increasingly allergic to the world around us.

This was similar to what this man was facing in Atlantis. Previous experiments had produced unbalanced forms which needed adjustment to the perpetuation of the species. And so we find a similar situation arising in our world today.

> **Conductor: Would you elaborate on the designing and creating of physical forms this one experienced?**

> *Intuitive Reporter: We see that this one placed a great amount of attention on the workings of what was being created physically. This one could follow very easily the path from the mental into the physical creation. This was not only in the way of the physical body but also physical structures made from the materials that were available to this one at this time. We see most of these to be from the Earth. This one was quite astute at seeing a single vibration and following it through into the physical.*

The greatest tool for this man was mental, not physical. This thinker wanted to see the results of his thought. Unlike a day dreamer who is happy fantasizing reality, this person wanted to know his creations. His creations included the physical body and structures – maybe dwelling habitats or tools – using the substances at hand. Perhaps this is a reference to the work of the Beldane in stabilizing a form for consciousness to inhabit and use for maturity.

> **Conductor: Was this entity a leader among this group?**

> *Intuitive Reporter: We see that this could have been possible for this one, however, this was not a desire throughout the entire existence. This one placed more attention upon what could be done and what could be manifested and what could be learned and discovered, than a position of leadership at this time. We see that this one was much within the self in formulating this information and there was not, until the closeness with the*

two associates, a desire to communicate the knowledge and understanding with others.

Perhaps this one's dedication to what was being learned and discovered sustained his awareness of who he was and what he was doing during this time in Atlantis. What is interesting is that what kept him free and responsive in that time has become in the present the part that binds him.

For a reasoning being in 21st century America, who is still entrapped in the physical plane of learning, it is not enough to focus solely on what self is doing. The mind must expand to include others and this is most frequently seen demonstrated in Reasoning Man as leadership.

In Human Man it is the urge toward heroism, most often precipitated by a crisis. Think of natural disasters (floods, earthquakes, famines) and "accidents" and you will readily realize the drive to heroism. People who save lives display a connectedness in the moment, brought on by real need.

Reasoning Man then builds upon this, expanding it to a connectedness beyond his own time. Here is a response to the imagined need of many to evolve, to make a difference in the lives of friend and foe alike. Before this awareness can be given to others it must first be experienced within the self.

> ***Conductor:*** *What would be the significance of that lifetime to the present lifetime?*

> *Intuitive Reporter: We see that within the present time this one has much understandings that this one does not recognize at the current time. Part of this is due to the fact that this one does not express outward to those in the environment that which this one knows and understands. This one has made many discoveries throughout the lifetime within his own self. Much of this is related to past understandings. Some related to conclusions which have been reasoned through and drawn within the conscious mind.*

> *Would suggest to this one that in order to complete a cycle, this one must express these in order to gain more. Would suggest to this one that this would be of great benefit not only to the self but to those other individuals. Would suggest that at this time, this one has formulated to a certain extent a goal for the self, however, this is rather selfish in orientation in that it is merely revolving around the self. Would suggest to this one to begin observing how much this one influences those around the self. Would suggest that in this way this one will begin to see that this one can influence these individuals to a greater extent with the knowledge and understanding that he holds within self.*

This one is in the process of doing this, however, there is an insecurity linked to this. Would suggest that the insecurity which is being experienced at the present time does not apply to what this one sees within the mind. This one is aware of this, however, there is no activity being taken to come forth.

This time period is very instrumental to this one in that this one has chosen this time to once again create and discover, rediscover, many of the things which were previously known to this one within the past lifetime related. One of the opportunities or tools which this one has offered the self is the situations and environments that this one is in presently. Not to utilize these would be a great repression for the self. This one has created these for his growth and progression and should use them to their fullest extent. In doing so, the insecurity which is experienced will automatically vanish and this one will see the self in a clearer more definite light. That is all.

We influence one another constantly. We, as a species, are connected energetically. What happens to one of us, happens to us all. This is why we are beginning to figure out that war does not work. All the great masters taught these truths, and now more people are aware, more people are willing to learn how to live the truth.

The secret is unlocking the power of the conscious mind – reasoning – so it may bear the fruit of intuition. In Atlantis, it was enough for this thinker to identify what works and implement it into physical structures in order to benefit mankind. In today's world, he must identify what works and pass this wisdom on to others so that consciousness may be elevated for evolutionary progression.

Conductor: Are there any suggestions for this one to see more clearly the means of expression?

Intuitive Reporter: Would suggest that this one has the ability to formulate ideas very well within the mental. Also there is a building balance of the reasoning abilities. Once this one incorporates both, this one will begin to bring forth more understandings. The expression of the understandings is of the utmost importance, not only to self but to others as well. This one tends to keep the process within himself, being rather introverted where his own ideas or opinions are concerned.

Would suggest that this one begin releasing these with an abundance of love in that this one will be able to multiply his own understandings at rapid speed, gaining the understandings which are desired by the self, but also being able to stimulate those within the environment to do likewise. [1057827151]

INTUITIVE RESEARCH
2001
III

ATLANTIS
Intuitive Research Part III

What is commonly thought of as Atlantis from Plato's writings was actually the end of the Fourth Cycle of Atlantis. The four cycles of Atlantis together with the earlier time period of Mu or Lemuria encompass most of the evolutionary history of planet Earth.

Lemuria was a time period in which the Earth was in energetic form. In other words, it had not yet cooled and hardened into anything close to resembling the planet Earth of today.

The end of the Lemurian time period and the beginning of the Atlantean overlapped somewhat. During this time, the Earth cooled and solidified, the moon was expelled, and the first breaking up of Atlantis (referred to in scientific literature as the supercontinent Pangea) began to occur. This breaking up and movement of land masses continued through the next three cycles of Atlantis. During the First Cycle, Atlantis comprised much of the land mass of the world with the remnants of Mu occupying the rest. During the second cycle, Atlantis occupied less territory, then during the third cycle less, until finally all that remained of what would be remembered and referred to as Atlantis was a large island in the Atlantic Ocean.

The period of transition of Ages between the Lemurian time period and that of the First Cycle of Atlantis also saw what was to become the Earth's Moon being thrown off or exhaled from the steadily densifying form of the Earth. This was done to gain balance within the Earth's now denser form.

This portion of Earth that was exhaled or thrown off the early planet Earth became the Earth's moon. The expulsion of this Moon out of the area of the Earth now referred to as the Pacific Ocean led to a quickening in the movement of continental drift by some continents towards the area of space created by this exhalation of the moon.

The Lemurian time period took place before the Earth became solidified as it is today. This was a time period before the advent of reasoning.

The Atlantean time period was a time of great shift in consciousness. This forward shift in consciousness would bring about the factor and quality of reasoning to the developing planet Earth.

Intuitive Research July 2001

Conductor (Dr. Daniel Condron): You will relate the cycles of Atlantis, how many cycles there were. You will describe these and the physical location of each, and the approximate time period.

Intuitive Reporter (Dr. Barbara Condron): We see the initiation of this movement to denote a change in consciousness and energy as well as form. Therefore we see that which is referred to as Atlantis comprises all of these. We see that the initial bringing into being of this was the result of the changing of what would become the Earth from a gaseous form and mineral form into a more solid form.

The Earth had already begun to evolve in that there were ways for consciousness to express itself and also the means by which energy could be recycled. This was true within the gaseous state, the more dense state of what would now be minerals although these were not the same as what are currently found today, they were more energetic forms similar to fractals of energy. The plant formation and some rudimentary – what would be considered animal, more animalistic energies, already excited within the planet itself. There were forms of life that were living within the waters and beginning to surface.

There was one primary land mass which was not covered by water. This was quite mobile, however. It was still gaseous for the most part, unsettled and unstable. Therefore the movement of the plates of the Earth, the affect upon the Earth's mantle, these kinds of layers within the Earth itself had only begun to form with the coming together of energies in the geometric forms and then in forms that could replicate themselves. What would be plant life.

Therefore the condition of the Earth was very different from the present time period. This is well to bear in mind in considering the changes, the evolvement, and these taking place over periods that could be measured by distance and time for it can be most different from what is currently understood.

The initial coming into being of the Atlantean time period was as the result of a consciousness change that took place as the result of the need for reasoning, the need for a way to form within consciousness, with energy in a more stable form, a more long-lasting form. This was the movement of energy for that which would maintain and reproduce itself. This had been initiated in that which would be referred to as Lemuria. Because of what was occurring there, there were difficulties being experienced which were adaptability centered. Where there was difficulty in causing there to be the means to adjust to the ways in which the elements would interact or cooperate with one another.

The forms at this time were very moldable. They were not at all dense. They were more pliable. The planet itself was pliable. The planet itself was etheric. It was energetic. It was rotating at a much faster rate of speed and there was not the electro-magnetic fields in place as yet. Therefore it was what would be considered presently as unstable. It would whirl, it would spin, it would move, it would combine in many different forms at any given time in many different directions when held in comparison with what is presently accepted.

Therefore the intelligent life which was developing was reflective of this and this was the characteristic of that which was known as Lemuria.

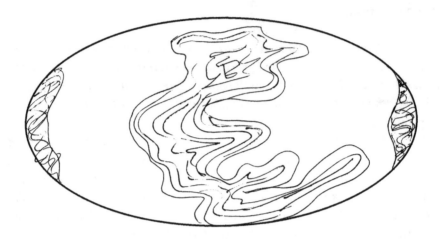

Figure 8. The Pre-Mu (Lemurian), Pre-Atlantean world was largely gaseous with the beginnings of mineral formations.

This came to an abrupt halt for the most part when there was the slowing of the energetic activity within the Earth itself as part of its natural maturation. As part of the kinds of energetic pulls that were being brought to bear upon it from the Sun within its own solar system, primarily. However there were other factors brought to bear from more distant places as well.

In this there was the attempt to become more fixed in the expression of energy which did cause the polarities to begin to express themselves. This had been in a more wholistic or balanced fashion. But at this point when there started to be the changes, the alterations, in the consciousness and desire to have what could be seen as permanence, this then began to cause divisions in the consciousness, the energy itself and therefore in the matter that was being created, the structures.

This first manifested itself within the Earth's cooling which then precipitated a kind of magnetic field which began to become pronounced. It was a slow process, over what would now be seen as thousands of years, hundreds of thousands, however during that period there were the factors brought to bear which caused there to be magnetic poles. In that there was the stabilization of energy transformation for the Earth. At that point it began to slow. It began to cool. It began to harden in ways that had not been available previously. It was this process and the amount of stress or strain that it placed upon the energy itself that did cause a large part of this energy to be released from the Earth. It was as if the Earth exhaled, or rejected that which it could not hold.

This resulted in a release of a large amount of energy from the Earth which did not escape the growing gravitational field of the mass itself and became caught in that but was separate from the mother itself. This would be the first cycle of the Atlantean experience.

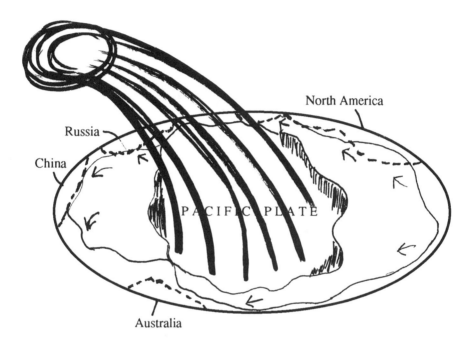

Figure 9. At the beginning of the Atlantean period the magnetism of the Earth was evolving. This was one of the factors which produced the Earth's only moon. In effect, this moon is a twin planet, having come from the Earth itself. The Earth is now like a giant magnet which protects the planet from a stream of electrically charged particles from the sun.

This loss of energy in such an abrupt manner brought about a shifting of the magnetism and a furthering of the magnetic fields causing the Earth over time to shift the direction of the polarities several times. This in turn abetted the release of energy and also caused there to be the beginning of the breaking apart of the land mass which remained. The loss of the energy caused there to be a considerable movement of this mass and a splitting as well of the mass and a movement of what would currently be referred to as continents.

Is this what would be referred to as Pangea, the supercontinent?

At the initial point yes.
Continue*.*

*This beginning of shifting then would be the second cycle where there was move-
ment of land to fill in the areas that were being reformed and the stabilization of the poles.
It was at this time and particularly the second and third cycles which was the period of
stabilization of the magnetic field. The gravitational field had been established before the
Atlantean period and the magnetic field was established at this point. The initiation of the
energy recycling of consciousness which is most closely defined as reasoning was begun
during these cycles as well.*

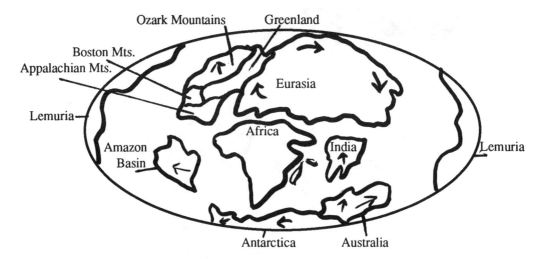

Figure 10. The forming land masses shift to fill in the space left empty by
the expelling of the Moon.

The third and fourth cycles?

*Second and third. This became part of the consciousness as a result of experimen-
tation that was being done with the forms. This was precipitated in large part by the
introduction of intelligence to this place once it was deemed as a possible, or compatible,
point of evolution to sustain and to further their own existence. This then brought into being
the formation in the fourth cycle of that which would be referred to as the pyramids, and the
Sphinx. It was following the fourth cycle where the introduction of other formations of
stones were created which enabled there to be the beginning of the electrical field of the
Earth.*

*There was an attempt in the fourth cycle of Atlantis to initiate a kind of crystal
activity, however, the Earth itself and its consciousness could not forebear this. It was in
effect not time for this evolvement without the understanding of the energetics of receptivity
which would be manifested through electrons.*

The First Cycle of Atlantis encompassed the movement of the Earth from its energetic or ethereal form to a more denser form more closely resembling the heavy, physical substance of Earth today.

This shift of the Ages, this shift of energy and vibration of the Earth from energetic form to a more dense or physical form, caused the substance of what would become the Earth's moon to be thrown off from the young, developing planet. This marked the end of the First Cycle of Atlantis and the movement forward into the Second Cycle.

The Moon, being thrown off from the Earth in the area of what is now the Pacific Ocean, created a hole or space in planet Earth for the matter or land masses to move toward. This continental drift is occurring today. In the past, it occurred at a much more rapid rate.

It was during the Second and Third Cycles of Atlantis that the Earth took on the qualities of form, structure, and energy that we are familiar with today. Even though the land masses of that time were much different than the present, there had been formed the magnetic poles and the electrical fields of the Earth. Therefore, the opportunity to develop physical bodies that would support the reasoning ability became more and more available in the Second, Third, and particularly Fourth Cycle of Atlantis.

The Land Formation Shifts

Within the second and third cycle was the continuation of movement, and breaking apart as it would be seen, of the two land masses that then [existed] one of which formed Atlantis which then moved. As the breaking apart occurred, and as the Earth moved and cooled and slowed and hardened, there were the formations of the continents which are presently known. (See Figure 11).

By the close of the fourth cycle there had been many migrations that had occurred, some of which were intentional, but most of which were merely the moving of these land masses, these pieces of Earth, that did make their way into different formations. The intelligences which populated them, for the most part, were merely riding along on them.

There were some intentional migrations where people would set out, particularly during the fourth cycle, for different land areas of legend or of notoriety. However, this was exceptional activity rather than the common place. So that by the point where the final remnants of what was known as Atlantis were no longer noted, this became that which is presently referred to as the Atlantic Ocean. Although this is not to say that this was the land mass itself. But it is what remains in the present history.

This is all.

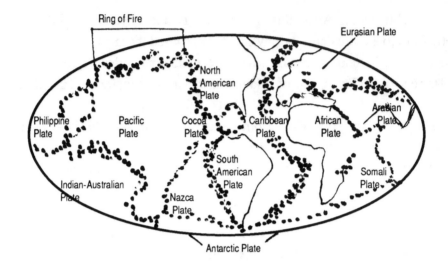

Figure 11. The shifting of the land masses during the Second and Third Cycles of Atlantis pave the way for the plates (shown above). Currently there are seven large plates and several small ones forming the Earth's crust. The dotted areas illustrate the many active volcanoes that allow molten material from inside the Earth to reach the surface. These can be seen as the growing spurts of our still young planet.

What was the location of the last remnant or part of Atlantis at the end of the fourth cycle, what would be its location on the Earth today?

This would be off the coast of Europe. At the time which is often referred to as the close of the Fourth Cycle, when the significant Earth changes were occurring which did cause there to be a breaking apart of the final land mass that had been known as Atlantis, this occurred within the Western end of what became the Mediterranean Sea. It was at that time that the Mediterranean was opened and created. Therefore the final land masses were parts of Europe; parts were submerged in what is now the Atlantic Ocean, even some that are now off the Northern part of Africa. This is all.

The one off the Northern part of Africa, is this off what is now known as the Atlas Mountains? The mountains in North Africa?

These were Atlantean, yes.

What is the relationship of the original inhabitants of England and Scotland and Wales and Ireland, the British Isles? What was their relationship to Atlantis, the relationships of the Druids and Celts?

These ones were of the Atlantean people. They were what could be referred to as direct descendants.

And was their language, therefore – the original Celtic language – descendent of the Atlanteans?

Yes.

And what of the Basque language?

This was also Atlantean.

Why do these two ancient languages seem to be different?

There were many separations of people. They were not all in the same local area so there were evolvements over time.

And the language of the Mayans. Is there a relationship between that and the Atlantean?

No.

As fascinating as it appears, the Egyptian, Mayan, Olmec civilizations as well as others, were initiated and set up by the beings from Sirius, rather than being colonies of Atlantis. This is why the civilization of early Egypt appeared full blown with its highest technology, and seems to have deteriorated from that time forward until finally conquered by Rome to put an end to the rule of the Pharaohs. The Mayan civilization also seems to have appeared fully developed. This indicates that the Mayan civilization was put into place or created by an earlier civilization.

Both the Egyptians and Mayans were the possessors of high technology that is only beginning to be discovered and imagined in the present time period. Far from being primitive, the ancients of these areas were highly civilized and highly developed technologically. Although the technology took on a different form than is used presently.

For example, Egyptian technology using the Giza complex pyramids and Sphinx, made use of the total energy of the planet Earth itself. They harnessed and harmonized with the Earth to make the planet one giant energization station while at the same time using the Great Pyramid to stabilize the Earth providing for lessening in Earth changes.

The Mayans also built pyramid complexes which acted as secondary stabilizing centers for the planet Earth. In addition, the Mayans had the special assignment of understanding, keeping track of, and giving to the world the measurement of time.

This measurement or calendar included not only physical time but also the movement forward in Earth's and humanity's consciousness. They also had a calendar for the planet Venus thousands of years before Western science sent satellites to Venus to determine its day length.

Western science and society in the 1800's and 1900's looked at ancient civilizations as primitive, yet even today Western technology cannot build a Great Pyramid of Giza. Nor can current science match its accuracy of measurement. Nor can it match its high technology and science of energy and wholeness.

Western European civilization has since the time of the Renaissance and the Industrial Revolution, tended to think of earlier civilizations and peoples as primitive and backward both intelligence-wise and technologically. This, however, is not the case. The Egyptian civilization, being created by the beings of Sirius, harmonized with and tapped the power of Earth itself. They created and used the Great Pyramid, Sphinx, Giza complex, ley lines, stelae, and temples to stabilize the Earth providing the opportunity for continuance of the developing life forms.

The Sirius-Egyptians also used the Great Pyramid which they created to receive energy from the mother planet.

These were powerful energies and high technology which dwarfs our present day technology and reveals a higher unified, organic, Earth-centered consciousness and evolvement at work.

The Beldane from Orion created the Atlantean civilization of the Fourth Cycle of Atlantis. This is the Atlantis Plato refers to in his *Timeas* and *Criteas*.

Those of Sirius of the Pleiades created the Egyptian and Mayan civilizations.

Therefore, the Atlanteans and their civilization were much different than the Egyptian and Mayan civilizations, having been created, stimulated or brought about by energetic beings from two different solar systems. Many of the energetic beings known as the Beldane became entrapped in physical bodies during the time of Atlantis. The Beldane were the source of the technology of Atlantis.

The Egyptians, on the other hand, built a more planned society. The Siriuns were the royalty of the Egyptians. As time went on fewer and fewer of the original Siriuns were left and more and more of the Egyptian peoples or common peoples were of the Human

Race. Pictures of Egyptian royalty show their heads to be large in the back upper part of the skull indicating their true origins.

The Siriuns, being energetic beings, attempted to use physical bodies as vehicles that they could step into and out of at will. They kept their bodies intact, what modern man calls mummies, in order to re-animate them as needed when they chose to take on physical form instead of energetic form.

The Beldane of Orion and the ones of Sirius in the constellation of Canis Major, the Great Dog Constellation, are the two main groups that then brought about in physical form the race known as Homo sapiens.

Of the two groups, the Beldane of Orion had the strongest influence and those of Sirius the lesser, in the formation of the early human race called Homo sapiens. This is the case even though the ones from Sirius spent the most time on Earth. This is because the Beldane became more involved in the experiencing of the human body form while those of Sirius attempted to remain in the state of energetic beings. This is why their civilization of Egypt and the Mayans was so different from Atlantis. In addition, the Atlantean civilization was created by peoples from a different star system, the Beldane, than was Egypt, which civilization was created by those of Sirius.

The Xena seeded the young planet Earth with pure consciousness that would and did bring about the needed genetic code and structure for intelligent life to exist on planet Earth. The Xena never existed in human or physical form on this planet as an independent or separate population. The Xena existed in Superconscious Mind. As such, they had evolved to a point where they would not, nor did they need to, be entrapped in physical bodies. In existing as consciousness itself, they were able to spread their consciousness over the entire planet Earth.

Highly evolved beings, beings who knew self as spirit, people who were in touch with the life of the Earth, could access the knowledge of these beings and thereby bring great knowledge to the world as evidenced in Sanskrit, the I Ching, and the secret code in the Bible. It is the inner urge of all beings to pass on what they have learned to others. The Xena desired to do just this.

The thought transmission of the Xena from the Pleiades provided for a settling or stabilization of the genetic code on planet Earth. This stabilized genetic code was then employed physically toward life forms in the physical environment of planet Earth by the Beldane of Orion. This was for the purpose of affecting the physical forms and matter that was present at that time. This led to the development of Homo sapiens.

The Beldane were energetic beings so they operated from a Subconscious Mind energetic perspective. As time went on they came to occupy the sustainable physical bodies of the Homo sapiens species they had developed. Most of this occupation of physical bodies was done unintentionally by the Beldane. They became entrapped in physical bodies and the cycle of reincarnation and karma by their misuse of the physical form.

Recall the diagram illustrating the structure of Mind presented earlier in this book. The Xena, existing as pure consciousness, resided and still reside in the higher dimension or division of Mind referred to as Superconscious Mind. While the Beldane and those from Sirius had energy forms and operated from that dimension or division of Mind called Subconscious Universal Mind.

The Centaurus of Alpha Centauri, who existed in dense bodies when they came to planet Earth, developed the physical bodies and peoples known as Homo erectus. This means they may have come in physical spaceships to Earth from a nearby star system. Alpha Centauri is the closest star to our own solar system. Their close proximity is probably the reason they were the only physical embodied race to come to planet Earth. It may have taken them years to traverse the distance or perhaps they had a technology we are not aware of today such as a stargate. At this time in the past, few physical beings of other planets were capable of moving physical matter through the inner levels of the higher dimensions of Mind.

In the higher dimensions of Mind, physical space or distance is reduced or ceases to be a limitation. Physical time is a function of distance. For example the physical time it takes for Earth to revolve around the Sun is called one year, or 365 days. A day is measured by the length of time required for the Earth to revolve on its axis.

The deeper or higher one moves or goes into the Dimensions or Divisions of Mind, the less distance is experienced between objects. There time is less an obstacle.

What is the difference in the history here? That the language is different?

The Mayans, as is also true of some of the Asians were relative to the original Egyptians, what would be termed the Egyptians, who were Siriuns.

What area of Asia was also related to the Egyptians?

This would be the Japans and some of what is now Siberia.

What about those of Sumeria, Ur of the Chaldeas and this area of Mesopotamia, what group were they from? Were they related to the Egyptians and Siriuns or to what group?

These were a blend of Egyptian and Atlantean. They are the most extensive re- corded group, civilization as it is called, that is directly related to the Atlantean. Although they were not pure Atlantean. The more pure Atlanteans reside in that which is referred to presently as China.

How did the Atlanteans get from the area of Atlantis to the area of China?

It was all connected space. There was no problem with there being movement. The movement was somewhat different from the present time period, yet the movement was available.

Was there a large distance to traverse?

No. The Earth was much larger. It was spinning much faster and there was much less density in all life, therefore, the movement was more dictated by consciousness than by physical matter.

During which cycle of Atlantis?

This would be particularly true for the first and second, however to a certain degree it was true all the way into the fourth.

The Chinese people and the ancient Chinese civilization, this is descended from what groups of people? Atlanteans, Lemurians, what group of people?

Partially Lemurian, although there is not an abundance of Lemuria left upon the Earth, most of it was cast off in the initial coming about of Atlantis which has been related. However, there are some remnants of this still on the Earth and even some remnants of the life that did end up intermingling, therefore, a part of this area is from that. A part of it is Atlanteans themselves.

Many people think that the Atlantean civilization is the oldest on the planet, and this may be true. However there are many civilizations that date back tens of thousands of years and beyond. The Egyptian, Mayan, and Sumerian to name a few.

The Atlantean civilization received its initial impetus from the Beldane who came from the Orion star system. Whereas the Egyptians and Mayans were developed by those from Sirius. Much of the ancient Chinese civilization was much more closely related to the Atlantean civilization than the Egyptians were related to the Atlanteans.

Orion is the brightest constellation in the heavens. It has an oblong shape with three stars in line near its center. Orion is represented as the hunter in Greek mythology. Three bright stars make up his belt and three fainter stars aligned south of this belt-line symbolize his sword. *A Orionis* or *Betelgeuse*, one of the brightest stars in the heavens, is located in the left corner of the oblong corresponding to Orion's shoulder. Betelgeuse might very well be the origin of the Beldane related in the Intuitive Reports.

B Orionis or *Rigel* as it has been named is diagonally opposite Betelgeuse. A nebula surrounding the three stars marking Orion's sword is one of the most conspicuously bright nebulae in the heavens. This reference also describes Orion in Greek mythology: "Another legend relates that Orion pursued the Pleiades until both they and he were transformed into constellations." This seems to fit in with our study of the seeding of early Earth and its civilizations for the Beldane came from Orion. Whereas, those referred to as Xena came from the Pleiades. The Xena may have been the most highly evolved of the three, being energetic in nature, for remember the Xena had or have no physical form at all.

Figure 12. The Southern Sky Chart.
These are the Southern Hemisphere's brightest stars, ones you can see from Australia, New Zealand, South America, and southern Africa. Orion, Canis Major, and Centaurus appear in a stream from the left center of the diagram to the midpoint.

What intelligence came into this area of Atlantis and developed this group of people, this civilization? From what area, planet or star system?

This would be from the short period with which the Beldane were present. These were the ones that did manifest the genetic adjustments which were required in order for life to be sustainable within the planet itself.

How would that area of Beldane be referred to, that star system, in current nomenclature?

This is within Orion.

Those from Centaurus, is there another name for this star system? Is this the area referred to as Alpha Centari or another star system?

This is within that referred to as Alpha Centari.

Those from India, from whence did that civilization arise?

These were the remnants that remained of Lemuria. They were relative to some which were lost as the Earth polarized. Most of them were lost in what is referred to now as Antarctica.

Did some of them ride this land area of India to its present location?

Yes.

What is the seemingly rich source of India's deep spiritual heritage?

This was the original development of the Earth's evolution itself coming forth. It would not have been sustainable were it not for interbreeding with the Siriuns. This occurred at what would have been comparable to the early Atlantean cycles. That period. Therefore, the perception of the deep spirituality is rooted within the honoring and organic wholeness of the Earth itself and what the Earth provides and what it produces.

Here then is the source of some of the similarities of spiritual heritage between Egypt and India. Throughout history and prehistory, these two great civilizations have had spiritual connection. India has yoga. Egypt has mudras. Both had many secret teaching for developing higher consciousness. Both were influenced by those of Sirius.

Those from Sirius created not only the pyramid complex at Giza, Egypt, but also at Cydonia on Mars. At Cydonia is a pyramid complex that includes the giant stone face on Mars. Geometrically, it has a similar configuration as the pyramid complex at Giza with the giant face on Mars having a similar function as the Sphinx on Earth.

The last pure remnants of those beings from Sirius in Egypt were in the royal lineage of the Pharoahs. The accounts of Egypt's recorded history tell part of this story. In order to maintain this purity, they often married their sisters or near relatives. They desired to maintain the Sirius connection. If you will look at paintings of the old royal line, you will notice a non-Human look about the shape of their heads.

The Earth's Moon is unique among all moons of the solar system in that it is so large in relation to the planet it is orbiting. It is as if there are two planets orbiting each other. Although some moons in the solar system are larger than Earth's moon, they are tiny in comparison to the planet they orbit. The moons of Jupiter, Saturn, and Neptune are examples of this.

Our sister planet Venus, has no moons. Mars has two tiny moons that may have been asteroids that the gravitation of Mars captured. Because of its large size in relation to the Earth, our moon has a proportionately large effect on Earth, most notable are the tides of the Earth's oceans.

This unique relationship of the Moon to planet Earth may have contributed to the development of life on Earth. It provides for the tides on Earth and its unique lunar cycles.

With the energy release of the Moon from the Earth or what would become the Earth's Moon, there was a further densification and solidification of the substance of the planet Earth. This prepared the way for the cycles of Atlantis, particularly the second, third, and fourth cycles.

It was quite a shock or period of adjustment for the Earth to have such a large object as the moon come out of it, even at this early stage in its development. Therefore, the Earth needed stability. Stability was needed for the continuation and further development of life on the planet. Stability was needed in order for those from Sirius to be able to use the planet. Therefore, those from Sirius used their technology and the wholistic technology of the Beldane, to stabilize the Earth. This technology was wholistic because it was harnessed and directed for the benefit of the whole planet Earth as well as connecting with Sirius. This type of wholistic technology is still not developed in the present time period.

Present Western technology has at its base or essence a consciousness of separatism, though in some ways is moving towards connectedness. Examples of this technology of separatism and misuse are the internal combustion engine, exploding atomic bombs in mother Earth, cutting down the Earth's forests, destroying Hopi sacred sites with bulldozers, and the list goes on around the world. Western scientific technology is founded upon controlling nature rather than harmonizing with nature.

Those of Sirius, that is the Siriuns, put acupuncture needles in the energy meridians of the living body of Mother Earth. The areas of the needles which were stone stelae are called ley lines and coincided with the energy meridians of this planet. Many of them have been destroyed by Earth changes. Others by man's ignorant destruction. At one time they covered the planet. The point or place in Earth which a stone stelae was placed is the location of a minor chakra of the Earth. Where two or more ley lines or energy meridians come together is a minor-major chakra of the Earth. At these places were located mounds, pyramids, or temples.

At other places on Earth are the major chakras.

The Great Pyramid of Giza is the medulla oblongata of the planet Earth. This means it is the point of receiving life force into the living planet. The Earth is a living being. Just as it has energy meridians, like people or souls inhabiting physical bodies do, so does the Earth have a medulla oblongata like our physical bodies do. The medulla oblongata in people is located at the base of the skull. It is the point of entry of life force, prana or cosmic energy, into the body. The Great Pyramid of Giza serves this same function for the Earth. The Great Pyramid of Giza is the medulla oblongata for the planet Earth.

The Great Pyramid together with the Sphinx received enough energy from the universe and particularly Sirius to breathe greater life into the core of planet Earth.

The History of the Earth's Moon

This is that energy release which was caught in the Earth's gravitational atmosphere at the initiation point of that referred to as Atlantis. A large amount of material, of energy, was expelled, escaped in essence from the core of the Earth in order for it to cool and begin to harden, begin to slow. As this occurred and the magnetics were being affected there were the shifting of the magnetics which then caused this to, in essence, be released. As it was, it was caught within the energy field of the Earth taking on its independence, yet dependent upon the mother.

Has the moon ever had an atmosphere of its own then? That was sustainable for life forms?

No. There was life on it originally in terms of the life that went with the expellation, but it did not sustain itself.

Have there been any intelligent beings who have used this for constructing structures or civilizations on this moon?

The remnants of what life there has been would be comparable to that which was on Earth.

Did the Siriuns ever use this for constructing?

No.

Did the Atlanteans ever use this for construction of any kind?

There were attempts to energetically use the moon which did not produce. The significant development for the Earth came with the advent of the Siriuns for they were the ones who positioned the energy channels which could thereby facilitate the transition from the magnetic to the electrical field which created the impulse for the Earth grid to be created. This was done through their technology.

What was the location of these energy centers?

This was focused upon a complex within the Atlantean area itself which is presently recognized as the Pyramid of Giza and the Sphinx.

The Great Pyramid and Sphinx were probably constructed before Atlantis was reduced to only an island in the Atlantic as it was during the Fourth Cycle.

Is that the center point then for the movement or balancing or working of energy on this planet?

Yes. The placement of the structure itself did allow for the reception of energies that would then be routed deep into the core of the Earth itself. This action then stabilized the earth enabling it to be energized in such a way as to provide a kind of sustainability for the life forms that were present. This was a benefit, not only to the Siriuns, but it aided all the life forms who were attempting to grow and to use the planet.

There was enough energy moved and stored within the Earth itself for this process to continue even after there were no longer transmissions to and from these energy forms.

From where to where?

From the Earth to Sirius and back. (See *Figure 3* on page 23).

What caused the ceasing of this energy transmission?

The change in the forms being used by the most intelligent life. The experimentations. That which fueled the energy transmission was the energy of people. When there ceased to be this available the movement and transmission of energies ceased.

Origination and Time Period of the Human Species

What is commonly called human is in large part the combination of the different life forms that have been described. Inasmuch as that is so, it does not have a singular point of origin but it is a state of evolvement. It is not a physical thing. It is an expression of consciousness. That which is human is reflective of the consciousness which has become centered in matter, in the frozen forms of energy and is within the present time period beginning to evolve or to pass away because of the catalyst present. This is all.

And by evolve or pass away, does this mean some evolve and some pass away or all evolve or all pass away? Explain what is being evolved into.

All consciousness will evolve. The forms will evolve and alter or will cease to be energized and therefore dissipate, no longer exist.

There are two ways of looking at the way in which life has evolved upon the Earth.

One way is how the Earth was progressing on its own. Then to understand the Xena as having a productive or beneficial affect through merging or extending their consciousness with that of planet Earth. Then the Centaurus came in physical form and the Beldane and Siriuns came in energy form to also influence and make more stable and productive the planet Earth. At the same time, they helped to develop the physical bodies we call Homo sapiens today.

The second way of looking at this development, is from a multidimensional or inner levels of mind perspective. Recall the divisions of Mind as given in the diagram of the Mind.

Upon our creation as individualized units of LIGHT called I AM, we began the movement of experiencing through the divisions of Mind. First, I AM experienced in Superconscious Mind learning the lessons of spirit and consciousness. The I AM experienced in Subconscious Mind as soul learning the creation lessons of energy, substance, and function. Finally, I AM experienced in Conscious Mind which is the physical world, environment and universe around us.

This movement outward into physical bodies led to the entrapment of the soul in the cycle of reincarnation. This is our present stage of learning. A soul or I AM enters a physical body at birth and uses that physical body for learning and growth until death or withdrawal of the attention from physical life.

There is a third way of looking at these events and that is to combine both of them in the following way:

Souls or I AMs existing in Subconscious Mind need a physical vehicle, a body to inhabit or use in order to learn and grow. Therefore, every opportunity was used to create these physical bodies and learning environment whether the means was off planet or not.

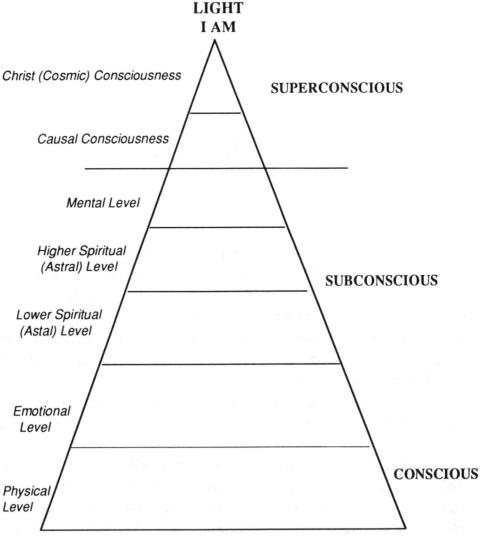

Figure 13.   Diagram of the Whole Mind
reflecting the expression of consciousness from the point of creation into the physical, material earthly plane.

What is the form referred to that humans are presently evolving to?

A manifestation of spirit which is energy. Which is fluid in its manifestation. And in that, less tied to the matter, more energetic in composition and expression.

In that way is it related to that which was expressed during Lemuria and Atlantis, yet with greater understanding?

Yes.

Is this progressing at a rapid rate?

Yes.

By the year 2012 how far will it have progressed along?

There are remarkable changes occurring within the Earth itself, similar to those which were present at the initiation stages of the Atlantean period. The composition of the Earth itself is physicalized and therefore it is gross and dense in its nature. It will continue to become more so until there is the separation of the energy, the final expression of the energy itself. This will take some time yet, and is not within the near future.

However we see the beginning stages of this occurring, and as was true within the initial stage of Atlantis, the changes are quite radical that are occurring. These will be felt in the present as shifts in consciousness, in the ways life is perceived and the ways life is lived, in the ways life is known. It is the movement of consciousness that will occur rather than the movement of form.

This then does produce, because of the Earth changing in the way that it is and the introduction of a pronunciation of the electrical movement within the earth and therefore within all who inhabit it, moving toward a more crystalline structure. This will then stimulate the changes that will then occur within the present and near future which are seen as the evolvement of consciousness that stimulates or provokes the evolvement of form in what would be termed genetics. Or in the release and dying off, the non-sustainability of forms which have outlived their usefulness.

Will there be appearance of new forms, new life forms from this?

It will be viewed as new, yes. But the point from which it springs will still be inherently tied to the Earth itself.

Is the Earth a living being?

Yes.

The Earth is a living being. On this point, all the old nature and mystery religions agreed and were correct. The Druids, Celts, Hindus, American Indian, and most all of the world's ancient religions worshipped mother Earth as the Earth Goddess. She is still worshipped today in Christianity as the Virgin Mary.

With this knowledge, we move our understanding to a higher level. Now we can worship or more accurately appreciate and respect the divinity within the Earth as we respect the living divinity within each person. All creation is connected. It is in this understanding of connectedness that we all reach higher understanding of Self as consciousness and energy.

During the time period known as Mu (Lemuria) and Atlantis, the I AM's that became souls were descending into deeper and deeper levels of Mind moving farther and farther away in consciousness from the source of LIGHT until they eventually became entrapped in physical bodies. (See *Figure 13,* page 156. The original source of LIGHT stands above and beyond Mind).

First I AMs moved into Superconscious Mind then Subconscious Mind and finally into the physical world and Conscious Mind. Then they forgot where they had come from and thought of themselves only as physical bodies.

At the present time period, mankind is poised to move into Mind towards Superconscious Mind and LIGHT with awareness and understanding of Creation. In fact, many of the forefront of humanity are already making and accomplishing those steps. They are leading the world into the next shift in consciousness.

Homo sapiens' body, being a carbon-based life form, is changing or advancing to crystal-based. This may hold tremendous advantages in allowing the essence of the Self or I AM to manifest its creative abilities as energy and consciousness. Most of the emerging information age is based upon crystals. At the heart of the computer is the crystal. Crystals can store knowledge. The crystal-based life form will have access to and the ability to naturally achieve, perceive, and retrieve the high knowledge of the essence of creation and consciousness.

The year 2012 is the year the Mayan calendar runs out. It is the last year of the Mayan calendar. The Mayans did not call this year 2012 because that numbering system is based in Christianity which came much later. However, 2012 is the Christian equivalent of the last year of the Mayan calendar. By that time, this shift in consciousness will probably be apparent.

The movement in consciousness will allow people to recognize time as a forward or progressive movement in consciousness instead of just the movement of a physical object, such as the Earth or the Sun. This is the shift from physical thinking consciousness to a mental, spiritual, connected consciousness.

How might during this movement forward in the change of consciousness the beings of this planet or each individual be more in tune with that energy to use it for soul growth and the evolution of humanity?

It is essential that there be awareness, where there be a willingness to align what these ones would see as love and will in order for this kind of awareness to be acute. This then causes there to be the realization of what has been spoken of in all cultures. It has been viewed as enlightenment. It has been viewed as illumination. It has been viewed as resurrection. It has been viewed as awakening. It has been viewed, and taught, to all life forms upon the planet in one form or another and it is time for this to transpire.

It is the commitment in essence an individual basis toward becoming conscious that will cause there to be the awakening and awareness of the transformation that is occurring. It is essential that there be an openness in the interpretation of the energies as they progress. This is the greatest challenge within the present initiatory phase of this stage of evolution.

In what ways if any do those of the Sirius star system influence the planet Earth today?

Only in those who have populated the Earth. There is no consistent contact with the point of origin.

Will there be contact in the future as mankind evolves?

It is not foreseen. The contact that is pending is with that referred to as Xena.

Xena, as you will remember, is the star system from which the beings came who existed as pure consciousness. Pure consciousness exists in Superconscious Mind. This is why the Xena will first manifest themselves or make themselves known to those who meditate every day, to those who have learned to go within, to the inner levels of consciousness.

Atlantean Technology

The most outstanding of these would be in the technology of the formulation of consciousness into the development and manifestation of thought. This was throughout the Atlantean time period and it was the incisive, definitive development in technology that has had the greatest impact and longest ranging effects upon the race as it has developed.

Did the Atlanteans have flying machines?

> *Yes, there were means to travel within the air. There were means to travel under-neath the water and upon land. All of these were available.*

What was the propulsion means for these vehicles?

> *The connection between thought and geometric structures, what has been often referred to as crystals.*

Is this based upon sacred geometry?

> *Yes.*

And the platonic solids?

> *Yes, and earlier forms that were more what would now be called holographic, more four dimensional even beyond three dimensional.*

In the present time period, advanced souls are learning an ancient secret known to only a few in the secret mystery schools of the past. This great and powerful secret of the Mind now available to the masses of humanity, the general population, is

THOUGHT IS CAUSE

All creation begins with a thought. Everything that has ever been created began as a thought. The highest and greatest of all technology is thought directed by intelligence.

The physical world is the effect of thought.

The propulsion system for the Atlantean vehicles was the same as what our physical bodies are, evolving into: crystalline structures. Crystals or crystalline structures are at the heart of today's technology and power revolution. Almost all computers use crystals. Crystals form the basis for our information age. Silicon, silicon wafers, Silicon Valley equals crystal, crystal wafers, and crystal valley.

Crystals always have a form. Many of these forms take on the shape of Platonic solids. The Platonic solids are: the tetrahedron, the octahedron, the hexahedron (cube), the icosahedron, and the dodecahedron *(see **Diagram 14**)*. This is important because all physical form and matter is built up from these five forms.

As mankind advances in understanding the nature of our holographic universe, a greater and more powerful understanding and use of the geometry of creation will develop either as physical technology or as the technology of the Mind.

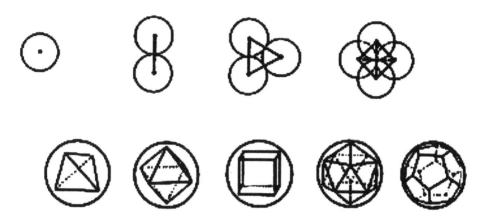

Figure 14. The Platonic Solids. The regular solid shapes contained within a sphere define the mathematical movement through the dimensions of space, beginning with wholeness or unity. The shapes correspond to the four elements and the sphere, as well as the chakras within the body.

You will relate the history of the dinosaurs

These were Lemurian life forms.

What caused them to die out, to become extinct?

Part of this was experimentation where certain forms were sustainable and others were not but there were such changes occurring within the planet at that time that the forms, as have been given, were moldable and plastic. Whether they were of the reptilian base or of what would be conceived as more human form. We see that there were actually only a few strains of them that were developed over periods of time and this was because there would be alterations in them with successive generations and then there would be the extinction of them very quickly. Usually through insufficient elements or through elemental changes in the environment, particularly revolving around gas but also in minerals. They would be best referred to as experimental life forms.

Was this indigenous life forms or were they experimental by outside intelligences?

They were indigenous.

Was this the experimentation of the planet itself?

The consciousness of the planet, yes. It could no longer be sustained once the magnetism began to be rooted and the large portion of what has formed the Pacific Ocean upon the Earth was released.

This was after the moon was released from the Earth?

Yes. These are also relative to some of the sea life which still do exist. Remain within the Earth.

Which sea life?

The octopus, even the whale are descendants from these ones.

Why is it that so many fossils or bones have been found of dinosaurs but not of the large pre-humanoid type beings from Lemuria?

That which is termed dinosaurs were closer to the mineral development of the planet. They are considered by modern man as an animal form, however, they are actually a mineral form that was moveable. This is not conceivable in the present time period because of the grossness and denseness of matter as it has formed since then and has become thick.
The more evolved intelligences of the earth were not of this same material. So what remains are evidence of not them but what they did. This is only recently being considered by the more current intelligences.

It may be that so-called dinosaur fossils are not fossils at all, for fossils were originally bone. It may be that dinosaurs were originally in mineral form, existing before the animal and even plant root races. Perhaps the puzzle-piece skeletons paleontologists construct are more a figment of Reasoning Man's imagination than a representation of what was. Perhaps all that existed of these life forms were the fossilized bones, the remnants of mineral forms, preserved through time.

Concerning the dolphins of the Earth, how can the dolphins and mankind work together to enhance the evolution of mankind?

Mankind will need to evolve further in order for this to occur. He will need to move away from separation which creates a judgementalism that does blind him, collectively speaking, it causes him to remain unconscious. Thus is the need for an aware and awakened consciousness in order for these kinds of developments to occur.

Will this occur more so by the year 2012?

The probabilities are there, yes.

Stories of creation are found around the globe. The similarities of these stories are worthy of time and investigation. The union of earth and sky is a recurrent theme. The Greek mythologies may well be the most enduring Atlantean accounts as the many parallels related here and elsewhere support.

The question about remains of Lemurian prehumanoids brings to mind the story of the Titans, the first children of Mother Earth. Six of the Titans were gods and they had six sisters whom they took for wives. The Titans reflect the elemental development of Earth, the expansion of air, fire, water, and earth long which preceded the creation of plants, seas, and animal. Perhaps the Titans are linked to what modern man calls the dinosaur. Certainly the satyr, the centaur, and other creatures combining animal-man are described in Intuitive Reports dating from the late 1960's.

In recent years mankind has become interested in and therefore more acquainted with the intelligence of the dolphin. Studies of their patterns of behavior and speech are opening our minds to the possibilities of communication. The dolphins have a connected consciousness. The consciousness of Homo Sapiens is moving towards connectedness but is at present based in separatism. The nature of reality is connectedness leading to oneness which is the annihilation of the illusion of distance or separation, which in turn overrides the illusion of physical time.

To know the consciousness of the dolphins, each person will need to build a connected consciousness within Self.

Immortality

What is the connection of the ancient Egyptian God Osiris to the star system called Orion or Orion's Belt?

This became part of the history of the Egyptians as it became recorded. This was the knowledge of immortality and remembering where the people had come from.

You will relate this knowledge of immortality.

This is eternal consciousness of being.

Can this be whether one is in the physical body or out of the physical body?

For such a one there is no distinguishing of the physical body.

What is the connection of the ancient Egyptian God Isis to the star Sirius?

This is the relationship of immortality to this particular planet. The extension of these people. The receptor.

The energy beings from Sirius created the Egyptian civilization. Those from Sirius borrowed or gained some of their knowledge from the Beldane who were and are from Orion. Therefore, both Sirius and Orion figure into the history and astronomy, astrology and astrophysics of the Egyptians.

Describe the process of the Siriuns used to reanimate or use the embalmed body of the Egyptians.

It is very similar to what is commonplace for human man presently. That which has become most commonplace where it was a system of learning how to put the body into hibernation. In the present period of time this would be seen as sleep where the body is vacated for a period of time and then reenergized and once again used.

Any further information, knowledge, or wisdom concerning Atlantis that would be of use for humanity in the present time?

This is all for now.

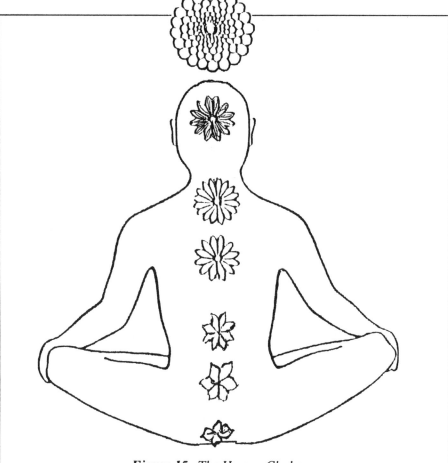

Figure 15. *The Human Chakras.*

Chakra is a Sanskrit word meaning wheel. Charkas are energy transformers, a kind of recycling vortex that enables the thinker to continue manifesting his desires and to sustain his physical existence. There are seven major chakras that work with consciousness and 77 major-minor chakras that work with the human body.

Those of Xena which are from the Pleiades how are they making their appearance known?

These would be most readily received, and have been described, as angels or archangels. They have been called ascended masters. They have in some occasions been termed spiritual guides. They exist beyond vibratory creation in this world and yet they are accessible within consciousness and are beginning to make themselves known.

Is this all?

This is all. (71201bgc)

Those Homo sapiens who through their efforts are evolving their consciousness to go deep within Mind, are beginning to be aware of the Xena, more and more. In order to access these higher dimensions, individuals must raise their consciousness. In order to do this, they must awaken their use of the energy wheels or chakras.

The chakras are energy transformers. All humans have chakras or energy transformers *(Figure 15)*. There are seven major chakras. They are:

The Root Chakra, located at the base of the spine.

The Spleen Chakra.

The Solar Plexus Chakra.

The Heart Chakra.

The Throat Chakra.

The Brow Chakra.

The Crown Chakra, located at and above the top of the head.

These energy transformers recycle used mental energy back into Mind. Each of the chakras works with a different level of Mind. There are seven levels of Mind.

The Earth, being an intelligent living being, also has chakras.

The first chakra that was created for Mother Earth was the chakra related to the energy source within the core of the Earth. The second controls the movements through the magnetic poles. This chakra operates at both the north and south magnetic poles and as such, with the energy core, serves the purpose of the first two chakras or energy recyclers.

Each chakra is associated with a Root Race. A Root Race is a stage of creation. The seven Root Races are:

1. Gas
2. Mineral
3. Plant
4. Animal
5. Reasoning Man (man meaning thinker)
6. Intuitive Man
7. God Man

These seven Root Races show or indicate a progress adding to the understanding of creation. They indicate a growing consciousness.

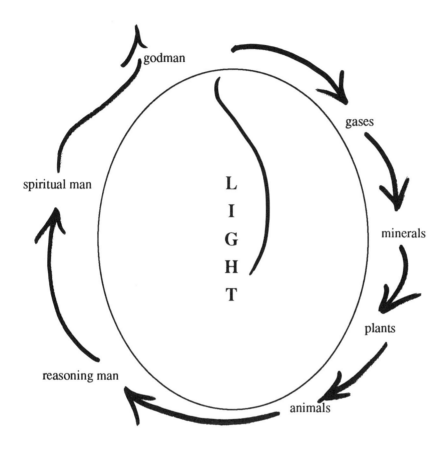

Figure 16. *The Root Races.*

Root Races describe the origin (root) of form (race) as they progress or evolve. Light is the constant; the expression of energy consciousness uses as the conveyance of its thought. Thus light exists through every root race beginning with the simplest of elements gases (air and fire) combining to form minerals (water, earth, and metal) then plants into animals. The Atlantean research indicates the Earth's evolution is both independent of and interdependent on the evolution of the consciousness brought here by the Beldane, the Siriuns, and the Centaurus since their forms were built from those already existing on the planet.

Earth Chakras

Where are the energy transformers or chakras of the Earth located?

There is an energy source within the core of the Earth. There is one that controls the energy movements through the magnetic poles. There was one set into motion following this which was related to the loss of Lemuria and the breaking apart of Atlantis which is now in what is known as China. There is the center that was set into motion during the Atlantean period that has been spoken of in the Second and Third Cycles which is in the Atlantic Ocean region presently. And there is an energizing within the grid of the Earth which does surround the Earth which is building in the present which could serve as a kind of energy transformer.

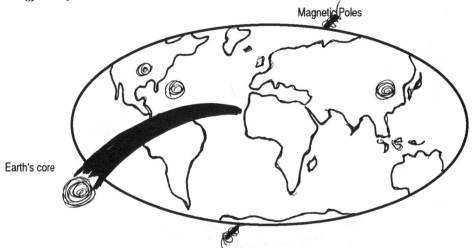

Figure 17. *Locations of the Earth Chakras* The sixth chakra, the Earth Grid, would appear as a net or web of   icosahedrons covering the globe.

The First and Second Earth Chakras then work with or recycle energy into Subconscious Mind that has to do with the mobility of gas and the stability of minerals. In the human body these two chakras relate to the Root and Spleen Chakras.

The Third Earth Chakra which was formed toward the end of Lemuria and the earlier stages of Atlantis relate to plants and the beginning of animals. Plants exhibit the ability to reproduce and the beginning of a nervous system. This Third Earth Chakra is located in the area of China, in the Gobi desert. The third chakra in Homo sapiens is located in the area of the solar plexus which is near the stomach area of the body.

The Fourth Earth Chakra which was set into motion during the Second and Third Cycles of Atlantis is and was for the further development of animals and animal man, and the beginning of movement into Reasoning Man.

This chakra is and was located in the Atlantic Ocean. In the body of humans the fourth chakra is located in the area of the heart. The essence of the quality of the Heart Chakra is understanding. This is exactly what Reasoning Man is successfully doing and building within Self.

The Fifth Earth Chakra is being created and energized in the present time period. Its purpose is to recycle the used mental energy of Reasoning Man so that Root Race can be completed propelling individuals first, and ultimately the human race, into Intuitive Man, the sixth Root Race.

This would be located at the Throat Chakra in humans and also the stimulation and quickening of the sixth chakra, the Brow Chakra. The Brow Chakra is also known as the third eye and eye of perception. It is located in the area of the pituitary gland in the human body.

You will relate concerning the energy transformer that is being built in the area of the Ozark Mountains, the College of Metaphysics area.

This is one of the points which contributes to the most recent energetic construction.

Any suggestions in causing its greater strength and growth?

A greater degree of devotion toward it would be helpful.

Since 1973, the School of Metaphysics has been adding and building and helping to create the energy transformer for the next stage in the growth, evolution, and expansion of consciousness of humanity and the planet. This chakra will be created and is being constructed in the energy grid surrounding planet Earth. It is a natural part of the Earth's evolution that has been quickened by the Xena, the Centaurus, the Beldane, and those of Sirius.

Presently, the Fifth Earth Chakra is being created by those of humanity who are dedicating their lives to quickening their soul growth and spiritual development toward enlightenment and are serving by teaching others to do the same.

What is the energy and meaning of the form of the nautilus, the Fibonacci series, concerning life and evolution of consciousness?

This is the key to expansion. To create as a Creator.

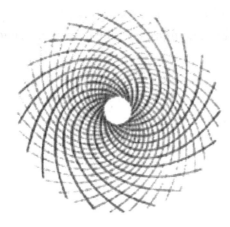

Figure 18. *Spira Mirabilis.* A spiral enlarging according to the phi proportion of 1:1.618 describes the growth of spiral shells, sunflowers, and other symmetries found in nature. This is the form (at left) embodying what it is to create as a Creator.

The form below is the receptive form, the "flower of life."

Is this also true for the flower of life?

The nautilus is the Creative form. The flower of life is the receptive form. It is the Created.

The School of Metaphysics through its centers and world headquarters, has been directing the forces and energies of love and truth scientifically in order to cause a quickening of this Earth Chakra for Intuitive Man. This is the reason why the College of Metaphysics is one of the points that contribute directly to the energetic construction of the Intuitive Chakra and the energizing new geometric construction of the Earth grid.

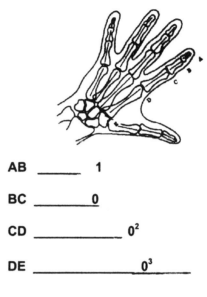

Figure 19. *The Golden Ratio (Mean).*
Geometry becomes sacred when the thinker expands his consciousness to identify the universal connections in all of life. Phi, the golden ratio, is one of these.

The length of the bone segments in the fingers of our hands can be measured in this way. The length of the first segment of any given finger is the standard measurement for that finger. The length of the second segment will measure a close approximation of 1.618 times longer than that. The third will closely approximate 1.618 times longer than the second, and the fourth segment 1.618 times longer than the third.

The pentagon, with its complex angular systems, is also an embodiment of phi. As with the lengths of the fingers, so too do the lengths of the segments within a pentagon proceed in golden proportion.

Using line AB as the standard measurement, line BC is 1.618 times longer than that. Line CD is 1.618 times longer than BC, and line DE is 1.618 times longer than CD.

Numerologically, five is the expression of reasoning, the ability developed during the Atlantean period.

AB _____ 1

BC _____ 0

CD _____ 0^2

DE _____ 0^3 _____

0 = Phi
Phi is the Golden Ratio which is 1.618

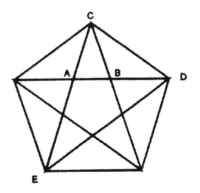

The Consciousness of Atlantis

The Fourth Cycle of Atlantis

Most of us are fascinated by accounts from this time period concerning what most people only recognize as mythological creatures – the half man-half goat, or horses with wings. The Atlantean material seems to support these as actually existing during these periods of experimentation.

   The following reading done for a male speaks to this. It also humanizes the reality of what was occurring at the time. Far from some mad-scientist Frankenstein-type Hollywood version, the reality of Atlantis is much closer to Mary Shelley's thoughts concerning man as creator. The incredible responsibility we assumed as we began to employ our unlimited creative powers in a finite world.

An Intuitive Report from the Fourth Cycle

> *We see female incarnation. We see Atlantean incarnation. We see this one working within that place that was devoted to the correcting and re-processing of the physical bodies of those ones that had been somewhat altered in the form, creating very obtuse and difficult forms to utilize at that time.*
>
> *We see this one using those processes which were available at that time to change and alter these bodies into a more suitable form, in order to experience within. We see the understanding of this one to be high and far-reaching. We see her understanding at that time to be very great. We see this one had the position of running a main part of this process. We see the understanding of herself enabled her to see far ahead, that was quite necessary, in order to create the correct vibration and the correct rate of change, in order to alter these bodies, to make them as exact as possible, without allowing there to be complete elimination of that body.*
>
> *We see many times there were mishaps, as there was not always the correct supervision in this process by others however, this one when first taking over this position began to instruct these others in the correct utilization of the visualization process that was necessary in order to see far enough ahead as to the end result of that which was being processed. We see also this one worked with the refinement of certain plants. We see another laboratory set-up where this one also supervised that helped create very refined plant life, that would produce the greatest of nutrition and food substance for these ones that were existing in this place.*

We see between these two places this one spent most of her time. We see there was much work to be done, for at this time, there was much need for the refinement of these plants in order to be utilized correctly by these ones that had been altered into more suitable bodies. We see this alteration process created a great change in the digestive system of these bodies, making it necessary for them to have the purest of food, and food intake, during the transitional period, after the altering into a normal state of life. This is why it was necessary for this one to refine these plants and these foods. We see this was a special process, created entirely for these ones that were going through this altering process.

We see this one to have a family. We see a husband, we see one child. We see the relationship between this one and the husband to be on a very surface basis, for this one was mostly devoted to her work, as same as the husband was mostly devoted to his work. We see there was some lack of understanding in this relationship, for there was at this time a coming into play great emotional strain upon the minds of these individuals. We see this one had great strength of mind, however, could not withdraw completely from this emotional emittance that constantly hounded her at this time. We see there was much difficulty in the relationship, in the physical relationship, between these two.

We see this one to have two sides to Self; there was the very intelligent side that understood these processes that have been related, however, there was the undeveloped side that did not allow this one to express freely and openly to the one of the husband through this lack of understanding of the emotions. We see the mental make-up of this one to be quite strong and very much in balance, and the reasoning process to be very good. We see, however, this reasoning process could not be applied to her emotions for it was very difficult for herself to allow this to be under control. We see this one had the ability to project a very strong current of love, however, to the one of the husband and the child. We see this created an imbalance in the make-up of this one. We see there was the advance-ment and the understandings of the mental, and there was the lack of understanding of the emotional and physical, creating an imbalance. We see this caused this one to withdraw into the mental realm very often, to sometimes almost ignore the physical completely.

We see this one to spend many times within this household, alone, and within Self, pondering thoughts related to that which underlay those processes that she dealt with in her work. We see she did not give much attention to the family group because of this lack of understanding. We see this created some inharmony within the family group. We see this one to continue in this manner for the remainder of her lifetime, constantly holding within Self this imbalance and constantly drawing within self during those times of emotional strain, attempting to draw before and beyond the emotional level so that it would not have to be dealt with. We see this one withdrawing from that lifetime at what would be approximately 33 years. We see she was referred to as Sherokee.....Shee-rock-ee. Synanna.

Conductor: Do you see a time period?

Intuitive Reporter: We see this to be some time before the break up of the Land.

Conductor: The last breaking up?

Intuitive Reporter: Yes.

Conductor: What would be the significance of that lifetime to the present lifetime?

Intuitive Reporter: We see within this one, again, there is a similar imbalance within Self. We see, again, there is great understanding within the mental realm, however, there is some lack of understanding within the physical, creating within this one a somewhat reserved attitude.

We see this one to be somewhat passive in his lifestyle and in his presentation of Self. We see him to somewhat shy away from that which is foreign to himself, however the mental stimulation within himself drives him to understand that which is foreign. We see this creating somewhat of a conflict. We see there is the desire to search out and find for Self the answers to the new ideas and new thoughts and these new concepts that are constantly being brought into view by himself, yet there is the shying away, at times, from these things because of the reserved and passive side of Self.

We see at this time there is great opportunity for this one to put into harmony and balance these two aspects of Self. We see this one is at present going through an understanding process, of how to put these parts of Self into balance with each other. We see this one is accumulating this knowledge that is necessary for this balance to be maintained.

We see this one is beginning to put into proper perspective the force and expression of Self through the male form. That which coincides with the mental, therefore, putting into harmony the mental, emotional, and physical parts of Self. We see this is, at this point, most significant for this one to understand at this time - that of balancing these three parts of Self.

We see great intelligence within this one. We see there is aware-

ness that at this time this is the reason for existence, that there is much opportunity laying in front of himself, in order to accomplish this.

Would suggest that this one do not shy away from that which has been chosen by Self. Would suggest that this one rely very strongly on the strength of his own mind for there is great strength in making decisions for the Self, even though they do not sometimes seem to harmonize with the emotional and physical Self. Would suggest that this one begin to realize this and to sometimes put up with those things that are unpleasant, in order to understand them, and at a future time, make them almost pleasant and enjoyable for Self to do.

We see this one is attempting to gain this realization and no further suggestions could be given. *[50174442626]*

Exploratory Analysis

The last breaking up of the Land would be what has classically been described as the final destruction of Atlantis, the submersion of the Golden City. This reference therefore identifies the time period of this report as the final stage, the Fourth Cycle of Atlantis. By this time Atlantis is a continent reduced to an island, as if New York City was the only area left of the United States. The woman predates this time.

This Atlantean woman was serving as a modern day medicine man, like a plastic surgeon, physical therapist, and computer whiz all wrapped into one. She was *"devoted to the correcting and re-processing of the physical bodies of those ones that had been somewhat altered in the form, creating very obtuse and difficult forms to utilize at that time."* Could this be a reference to the mythological figures of myths around the world, the combinations of man and beast that modern man finds too fantastic to believe?

Whether these "obtuse and difficult forms" is a reference to the presence of four legs and three hearts or to centaurs, the work this woman was performing reminds me of the work now done with congenital defects like cleft palates or the reattachment of limbs. The great difference between the material basis of today's allopathic medicine and the healing practiced by this woman are the tools used. Modern medicine uses chemicals to poison, lasers to burn, and knives to cut. All alter the physical matter of the body.

In Atlantis the tools were mental. This one taught *"correct utilization of the visualization process"* necessary to produce the result desired. Thought energy was employed to cause the desired effect. The changes were vibrational.

Through the perspective of this woman, this report reveals the intention for the changes made, these ones used *"those processes which were available at that time to change and alter these bodies into a more suitable form, in order to experience within."*

This was a time of setting into motion the genetic memory code which would enable the body to maintain its integrity while responding to the thoughts of its owner. An awesome task tantamount to the level of intelligence required to transform a computer the size of a small building into a small thin box that fits on your lap and so lightweight you can carry it anywhere.

Now we are on the threshold of consciously owning how our thoughts direct and mold our bodies. Awareness of this has been in the collective unconscious since Atlantean times and evidenced throughout history in miraculous healings of all kinds. Deeper thought, thinking that reveals the meaning of life, will open the mysteries of the mind potential and with it will come a flood of memories of what has been.

This Atlantean woman possessed great understanding of the mind, the levels of consciousness which were now more defined and solid. *"We see the understanding of herself enabled her to see far ahead, that was quite necessary, in order to create the correct vibration and the correct rate of change, in order to alter these bodies, to make them as exact as possible, without allowing there to be complete elimination of that body."* Some truths are universal; timeless. Self Realization was the foundation for this woman's genius during Atlantis and now. This truth applies to us all as much as to this one person.

Many of the most advanced systems of healing available on Earth today recognize a greater power behind the intricate design of the human body. Healers are always respectful of this, seeking to cooperate, not interfere, with this natural process. Aware individuals are attuned to their bodies, interpreting its energies and learning to respond to what it tells us about our thoughts, our progress, our learning. The way the bodies are designed, enable us to do this. They assure that learning will take place, even if it means the elimination – death – of the body.

One expression of the greater awareness is giving the body what it needs to be whole. The *"very refined plant life, that would produce the greatest of nutrition and food substance for these ones that were existing in this place"* could well be a reference to the cooperation between the genetics being formed for the developing human body and those forming through Earth's evolution. In other words a way for the two to coexist, to be mutually interdependent and helpful, was part of the Atlantean experience.

Think about a baby. When our son Hezekiah was first born, my body was not producing an adequate amount of milk. Although he fed frequently day and night, his fussiness indicated hunger, and in time he was not gaining weight proportionate to his feeding. We supplemented him with processed formula which he regurgitated often and up until the time when he began eating apple sauce.

Later we learned that my intake of a plant juice – carrot – would make a difference.

Beyond its inherent enzymes and vitamins, the vibrational quality of the carrot stimulates the mammary glands in the female, thus she produces more milk for her offspring. This is of the nature of the discoveries this Atlantean "scientist" was making.

> *Intuitive Reporter: We see there was much work to be done, for at this time, there was much need for the refinement of these plants in order to be utilized correctly by these ones that had been altered into more suitable bodies. We see this alteration process created a great change in the digestive system of these bodies, making it necessary for them to have the purest of food and food intake, during the transitional period, after the altering into a normal state of life. This is why it was necessary for this one to refine these plants and these foods. We see this was a special process, created entirely for these ones that were going through this altering process.*

Once again, think about a baby. Think of the need for nourishment once the newborn is on its own. Think of the transformation from living in water, breathing water, to living in and breathing air. Now think of the process of feeding a newborn. The most natural, purest food comes directly from the mother. It is not even exposed to the air when it moves from mother to child. The purer the food, the easier the transition from being fed through the umbilical cord to being fed through the digestive tract. At some point in evolution, this finest of arts and sciences had to be employed to find, recreate, and pattern this transition. Perhaps this is part of the work done in this Fourth Cycle of Atlantis.

There was also work of a very different kind occurring. This was the development of the emotional level of consciousness, the bridge between the inner, mental dimensions of mind and the outer, physical level of mind. The separations into individual minds become more apparent as time progresses and the emotions become the means by which we are made aware of the path we have created. This is described in the relationship of this one and the husband as being " *on a very surface basis, for this one was mostly devoted to her work, as same as the husband was mostly devoted to his work. We see there was some lack of understanding in this relationship, for there was at this time a coming into play great emotional strain upon the minds of these individuals.*"

The interaction of these two, being primarily emotional, draws the woman's attention out into the physical world, away from her purpose. In this way, this information describes how, and why, she becomes involved directly in the physical plane thus moving away from the point of cause. This is the beginning of becoming engrossed in the effects. The emotional energy between she and her husband becomes more than a distraction for her.

> *Intuitive Reporter: We see this one had great strength of mind, however, could not withdraw completely from this emotional emittance that constantly hounded her at this time. We see there was much difficulty in the relationship, in the physical relationship, between these two.*
>
> *We see this one to have two sides to Self; there was the very intelligent side, that understood these processes that have been related, however there was the undeveloped side that did not allow this one to express freely and openly to the one of the husband through this lack of understanding of the emotions.*

Now we enter into the realm of human beings, what makes us human. The need to experience, express, understand, and utilize the emotions is the spark that manifests itself between people. When the choice was made to become involved in physical creation, a tie between the mental self and the physical self was needed. This tie or bridge became the emotional level of consciousness.

Back in Atlantis, this account was probably one of the first incarnations following this soul's commitment to the physical. She retains the strong mental sense and finds great stress in experiencing the newly developing emotions.

> *We see the mental make-up of this one to be quite strong and very much in balance and the reasoning process to be very good. We see, however, this reasoning process could not be applied to her emotions for it was very difficult for herself to allow this to be under control.*

The reasoning spoken of was probably subconscious reasoning rather than conscious reasoning. Through experiences such as these, we come to learn there is a difference. The patterns have been created for the inner levels of subconscious mind (see *Figure 13*, page 156). They are not yet established for the emotional level. Therefore her sense of love is not an emotional love but one of connection, seated in the Fourth Level of Consciousness. *"This one had the ability to project a very strong current of love."* She feels connected to her husband and child, but lacks the ability to communicate it fluently, creating "an *imbalance in the make-up of this one."*

Her answer for this is isolation, "*constantly holding within Self this imbalance, and constantly drawing within self during those times of emotional strain, attempting to draw before and beyond the emotional level so that it would not have to be dealt with."* Nowadays legal or illegal medication dulls the emotions, allowing the person to believe they have escaped the learnings of the physical world. Such withdrawal, in any form, destroys the constellation of energy that has come together for your learning thereby postponing understanding sometimes for thousands of years.

Here is the how this man's Atlantean experience related to his life now.

>*Conductor: What would be the significance of that lifetime to the present lifetime?*

>*Intuitive Reporter: We see within this one, again, there is a similar imbalance within Self. We see, again, there is great understanding within the mental realm, however, there is some lack of understanding within the physical, creating within this one a somewhat reserved attitude.*
>
>> *We see this one to be somewhat passive in his lifestyle and in his presentation of Self. We see him to somewhat shy away from that which is foreign to himself, however the mental stimulation within himself drives him to understand that which is foreign. We see this creating somewhat of a conflict. We see there is the desire to search out and find for Self the answers to the new ideas and new thoughts and these new concepts that are constantly being brought into view by himself, yet there is the shying away, at times, from these things because of the reserved and passive side of Self.*

It has been a long time since this soul's Atlantean experience. Within the present he experiences in male form which gives his conscious mind an added stimulus to use the physical experience not present before. This is in an effort for the soul to overcome inertia, the passivity cited here. Now, he is attracted to the unknown yet still feels the urge to pull away. Now, thousands of years following his Atlantean experience, this man has enough experience and understanding to bring the self into balance.

>*Intuitive Reporter: We see at this time there is great opportunity for this one to put into harmony and balance these two aspects of self. We see this one is at present going through an understanding process of how to put these parts of Self into balance with each other. We see this one is accumulating this knowledge that is necessary for this balance to be maintained.*
>
>> *We see this one is beginning to put into proper perspective the force and expression of Self through the male form. That which coincides with the mental, therefore, putting into harmony the mental, emotional, and physical parts of Self. We see this is, at this point, most significant for this one to understand at this time - that of balancing these three parts of Self.*

The science of the mind is rapidly becoming well known. Self improvement books constitute a growing percentage of the nonfiction market. People are looking for ways to know more, earn more, live more, be more. This has stimulated research into the nature of human man. What makes us who we are? Are we merely sophisticated animals? Or do we possess within us a divine spark of intelligence?

What we are learning, as the world becomes a smaller place and all of its knowledge becomes accessible, is the connections between us are more than physical genetics. They are a common heritage of spirit, expressing itself individually. Each individual in turn is made up of parts as well. Human beings can be described as mental, emotional, and physical beings. All present within one form (see *Figure 13*, page 156), the gift of the Atlantean period.

To use this manifested intelligence to its greatest potential is to become cognizant of its presence. When the soul assumes physical form, it becomes responsible for the body, its care and health. Meeting physical needs is a part of life that affords much learning. Necessity is the mother of invention because it stimulates the faculty of reasoning in the conscious mind.

Acknowledging emotional needs expands our world beyond the physical, connecting us with our inner Selves and with each other. Emotions illuminate areas of awareness and darkness. Emotional health depends largely upon clarity and focus in the Conscious Mind.

Knowing Self as a mental being is to understand thought is cause. Here dreams are real and past understood experiences lend themselves to intuition.

Entraining the head and the heart, causing them to vibrate in synchronization with each other reunites the soul. This harmonizing of the conscious, outer mind and the subconscious, inner mind, occurs when all three parts of the Self have a common ideal.

To know the Self in this light, is to experience Self in seven dimensions.

> *Intuitive Reporter: We see great intelligence within this one. We see there is awareness that at this time (that) this is the reason for existence, that there is much opportunity laying in front of himself in order to accomplish this.*
>
> *Would suggest that this one do not shy away from that which has been chosen by Self. Would suggest that this one rely very strongly on the strength of his own mind for there is great strength in making decisions for the Self, even though they do not sometimes seem to harmonize with the emotional and physical Self. Would suggest that this one begin to realize this and to sometimes put up with those things that are unpleasant, in order to understand them, and at a future time, make them almost pleasant and enjoyable for Self to do.*
>
> *We see this one is attempting to gain this realization, and no further suggestions could be given. [50174442626]*

By the time period given in this intuitive report, the many separations of land have moved across the face of the globe, scattering the Atlanteans, offering many opportunities for the intermingling of life forms. The migrations occurring since the Second Cycle now accelerate and the Atlanteans move to populate the Earth in earnest. To the Andes, to Egypt, to the Himalayas they move as the land breaks apart, carrying them to new destinations.

As they spread, they interbreed with those they find there. According to the reports, the Egyptians are the ones more reticent to this. The creators of the Egyptian civilization, those from Sirius, desire to stay pure. By the Fourth Cycle however those remaining upon Earth have adopted this as their place of existence, their place of learning.

The Earth has served as a laboratory for intelligent beings, a place of experimentation for those wanting a new home. Through three cycles of experiments these intelligences have become accustomed to creating, to making things happen in the physical world. Through repeated contact the purpose for creating pales in the delightful attachment to the forms created. The creator loses sight of who he is. Becoming lost in what he is creating, his identity becomes finite, material. He has become entrapped in the figments of his own imagination.

By the Fourth Cycle, many have forgotten their purpose in life and have become subject to the natural laws of cause and effect – karma – as it is taught in Hindu scriptures. Perhaps you cannot fathom becoming so caught up in anything that you would lose sight of your divinity, your origin, your God. The following Intuitive Report *[42377311117]* about Atlantis, which indicates no particular cycle of time, may shed some light upon this for you.

Intuitive Reporter: We see for this one to be experiencing in male form. We see for this to be an Atlantean time period. We see much experimentation previous to this time period. We see however at this particular time there had been much refinement of the vehicles in regards to this one's own experience with these vehicles.

We see that there was a particular purpose at this time period to bring about a greater amount of harmony within the physical and the physical experiences of many entities which were entrapped in the physical at that time. There were many dealings with energies and manifestations of energies and also with the harmony of sound and color in regard to producing a healing and balancing effect within those trapped in the physical, and also in refining many of the forms which were also still in the physical in a most grotesque and also unworkable manner for the purpose of evolution.

We see for this one to have many associations with others, both of the physical and nonphysical. We see at the beginning of the Atlantean period this one was not entrapped in the physical and there was the association and communication with the nonphysical beings as well as with the physical. We see that there was information which was gained from those within the nonphysical and also the meetings with those not in the physical to methods to be tried in regards to the healing and in regards to the correction of many of the errors which the fellow builders had made. We see that there was the manifestation of self into the physical in regards to using energies outside of the self.

We see that there was a choice to enter into the physical in the evolutionary system and cycle of continuance of experiencing within the physical. We see that through the efforts of this one and also through many entities which were involved in this healing process that a vehicle was formed which was adequate for this particular step in development.

We see that there were many entities which were still experimenting in forms which were not adequate when these decisions were made. We see, however, that the decision was made in regards to the developing of the physical vehicle in a different manner which this one saw as being more productive at this time. We see that there was also the decision for this responsibility. We see this one was referred to as Naneva. We see that these were vibrational syllables which were used and corresponded to the notes of F sharp, B flat, and G. This is all.

Conductor: How long did this entity remain in the physical body?

Intuitive Reporter: We see that in regards to information which was given, there had not been the entrapment within the physical. We see, however, upon the decision to experience in this manner the first vehicle that was used after the entrapment was for a period of years which would correspond to between 30 and 35.

Conductor: Was this a manifested vehicle or vehicle of the animal man?

Intuitive Reporter: After the decision had been made there was entry into the refined vehicle of animal man.

Conductor: How did this entity become entrapped in the physical?

Intuitive Reporter: The decision was made for this responsibility.

Conductor: Was this an entrapment in the lifetime just related?

Intuitive Reporter: The entrapment was just following information which was related. We see at this point that there had been the entrapment of several. We see that through the efforts which were described within information that there did come about the refinement of animal man. We see that many entities were entrapped at this time and had been transferred from the grotesque forms into the animal man forms. We see that after many had entered into this form and there was seen what was to pursue from this that the decision was made for this type of entrapment in the physical vehicle.

Conductor: What was the error that caused this entity to be entrapped in the physical?

Intuitive Reporter: There was no error.

Conductor: Do you find this entity being looked upon as a god?

Intuitive Reporter: There was not awareness of a god by most of the entities trapped in the physical at that time.

Conductor: What would be the significance of that lifetime to the present lifetime for this entity?

We see within the present time period, that once again there is the building of a vehicle. Would suggest to this one that the responsibility which corresponds to this particular decision is also that which corresponded to the decision in the past. Suggest to this one that in regards to the information which this one has gained throughout many lifetimes that there is the information and the abilities to also bring about the refinement of a further vehicle.

Would suggest to this one to view the information which is held in regards to the healing understandings which this one has gained and also in reference to the sound and color that the further understanding of this in a manner which is related to the inner self, rather than the outer self, would be most beneficial at this time. [42377311117]

Images from the End
The Destruction of the City

Most of the accounts of Atlantis concern the destruction of the great city of Atlantis. Plato referred to it as "the great deluge of all." He borrowed his account from the Egyptians who had witnessed many such deluges. Accounts of Earth being covered by water exist in traditions around the globe.

When realizing the extent of Atlantean migration in every direction on the face of the planet, it becomes very apparent how these same elements found themselves in the world's great myths.

It is even more understandable as we realize our intermingled ancestry has brought us together as a race rather than separating us as we have been led to believe. This ancestry, the ones who made sustained, progressive existence on this planet possible, also devised a universal language. This language evolved, as the levels of consciousness were created, as a means for vibration to travel from one form into the next. This language appears all over the planet. This is the language of images, of pictures. From the hieroglyphics of Egypt to the pictures and petraglyphs of American Indians to Chinese characters, the Universal Language of Mind on this planet is images.

And so the graphic images of the destruction of man's physical world remain with us. In the inner worlds of mind they are reminders of immersing ourselves in the temporal. In the outer world they spark wonder and fear.

Here is an eyewitness account of the end of a time period, a people, a place called Atlantis.

Intuitive Reporter: We see this one as existing in the time period of the ultimate destruction of Atlantis.

This one is concerned with the revolution in this one's ability of the planetary influences upon the place of existence. This one uses this knowledge to aid in the revolution and the misuse of power and the struggle of power was a manifestation of this one's direct knowledge of the influences and the power source to be tapped from the instruments at hand. This one was one of the seven to overthrow and replace the counsel.

This one was involved directly in the destruction phase and ultimately realizes the mistake and misuse of power by the three main leaders and that this one has in fact become manipulated by them. However, this is realized after much has been destroyed.

This one at first has a mental attitude of much hurt and pity and sorrow for there is a realization that this one will experience what this one has caused directly. However, then this one adapts a mental attitude of trying to prevent the ultimate destruction for there is recognition of what has already taken place and there are also feelings of revenge within this one for the three who have used and manipulated this one. This one uses a beam through one of the tools that this one helped to structure and uses it to destroy the leader of the counsel, of the men, that is, to replace the counsel.

However, the destruction of Atlantis is already set into motion.

This one then comes into combat with one other individual and is stabbed, which brings about again a very traumatic mental and emotional concern. This one again, through the struggle, grasps for the tool of the beam, turns it on, and causes the destruction within the entire dome of the revolution area of location.

The beam is very strong, and through the destruction and the lack of control when this room is destroyed, [the beam] causes a tremendous explosion and release of energy which is involved with causing one of the major quakes. {It} causes a great deal of physical destruction within that plane. This one withdraws with a very disturbed mental attitude of great anguish and shock and realization that this one is not immortal but mortal and physical.

Conductor: What was the age of withdrawal for this entity?

Intuitive Reporter: Primary cycle which could be related to 34 years, a considerably short life span.

Conductor: How was this entity referred to?

Intuitive Reporter: This one within the revolution adopted the name Rema, which reflected the term "revolt" and "power."

Conductor: The revolt, is this the final destruction?

Intuitive Reporter: Yes.

Conductor: Is there association with that one referred to as Junor?

Intuitive Reporter: Yes. This one was one of the direct opposites that this one was trying to overthrow. There is an interesting interaction between the two that could be related as part of the revolution activities, conflict and manipulation on both parts to stop the other.

Conductor: What would be the significance of that lifetime to the present lifetime for this entity?

Intuitive Reporter: This one on the inner levels desired to incarn in a situation where this one could learn the influence of the planets upon individual's life for a constructive and positive means.

This one took a great deal of preparation in planning this lifetime and situations that could occur within this lifetime that would be a least line of resistance for this one to be sure that he did choose to present and understand and utilize the positiveness of the planets unto individuals and to be very constructive in its use. For this one has a great deal of understanding to arrive at, and this one has worked out much of the karma through previous lifetimes, yet there needed to be just the right situation for this one to manifest in the physical the understanding of the power and of the positive, constructive use of the study of the planets.

Would suggest to this one to always be analytical and most evaluative of the purpose and the cause and effect that this one has upon individuals within the physical, with this one's knowledge, for there is a carry through of this one's knowledge which this one uses. This could be developed more fully where there is a somewhat recognition of the intuitive abilities of this one.

However, there is much room for growth which is part of the positiveness of the study this one has undertaken. There is much need within this one for growth and understanding of the abilities within self. [81775201831]

The man requesting this report is, in the present lifetime, an astrologer. The best one I've ever had the pleasure to know as a matter of fact. His Atlantean experience and his life now are intrinsically linked. The present has become his judgement day, his day of reckoning, his opportunity to pay karmic debts to himself and others.

For the rest of us, the Atlantean account from his viewpoint brings to bear the presence of the influence of the planets upon the well known final destruction of Atlantis. And, perhaps more importantly in light of what is presented in this book, perhaps the presence of alien beings themselves.

What remains with us from these Atlantean experiences is the sense of Self discovery. As we explore who we have been and where we have come from, we come to better realize who we are as a race of thinking beings and where we might just be able to go.

INTUITIVE RESEARCH
2001
IV

Introduction

This is the fourth section of Atlantis which Barbara and I developed and discovered, clarified and solidified, the knowledge and material we had developed previously. I worked diligently to piece together the knowledge Barbara revealed while intuitively reporting. We discussed the insights and knowledge of the Earth and its history, each stimulating the other to further discovery. The knowledge had been intuited and then reasoned with to develop a coherent image or picture of life on planet Earth, sapient beings on Earth, and civilization on and off Earth, that goes beyond anything previously revealed or presented in our time period.

It is my wish that this knowledge and discovery be used by people all over the world, in whatever mode or method of research, to add to the body of knowledge of mankind's history and to propel us to great heights of Self knowledge and knowledge of who we are, where we came from and where we are going.

Atlantis Part IV is a successful effort by Dr. Barbara Condron and myself to fill in the missing gaps in mankind's history and to reveal and answer many of the most intriguing questions in history, archaeology, anthropology, geology, planetology and cosmology.

With certainty, there is more to come.

For now, here is presented to the world – Atlantis, Part IV.

ATLANTIS
Intuitive Research Part IV

The Links between ATLANTIS and Recorded History

Because some people think Atlantis was or existed in the Mediterranean Sea, I thought it advisable to delve into the Minoan civilization to discover its true roots and origin as well as its age.

The Minoan civilization is known to have been very ancient and thought to have predated Greek civilization by many researchers. Yet, up to now, its history has remained an enigma. Its writing or written language, although discovered, has proven difficult to decipher.

Here is what the Intuitive Investigation revealed concerning the source of the differences between Minoan civilization and Egyptian civilization.

You will relate the origin of the Minoan civilization.

This was initiated from a combination of Atlanteans who had migrated to Egypt but were repulsed from the area. They then settled within an area which was at the time connected in land mass but later was broken apart. They did bring into their development of life many of the attributes that had developed during the Atlantean period itself including the type of opulence that had developed and the refinement of what now would be seen as culture, those elements which would produce culture.

What time period would this be referred to as?

The emigration itself was in the Fourth Cycle of Atlantis.

Approximately what in modern times years BC would this be?

25,000.

What method did the Egyptians use to repulse the Atlanteans from Egypt?

Fire.

Was this high technology or a lower level of technology?

This was primarily physically produced, physically based, using combustible physical materials.

Was there any use of the pyramids or Sphinx or any of these types of powers?

No.

Were the pyramids and Sphinx in existence at that time?

Yes.

The Minoan civilization was created by peoples migrating from Atlantis in the Atlantic Ocean to Egypt. After being driven out of Egypt by the Egyptians these migrating Atlanteans moved on to form or create what was to become the Minoan civilization in a time period much farther back in history or pre-history than the date estimated by modern scholars as 2900 B.C. This was the time the pillars of Heracles (Hercules) were still intact and the valley or basin that was to become the Mediterranean Sea was not yet inundated with ocean water pouring in from the Atlantic Ocean. Today this area is known as Crete, an island at the east end of that sea. However, at the time it was settled by the Atlanteans, it was still a part of the mainland.

Through the reasoning use of this high knowledge, I can perceive how the civilization that developed around the Mediterranean in the time period of civilization given in most history books of 3000-4000 B.C. was descended both from Egyptian and Atlantean civilizations. Once some of the Atlanteans moved to the Mediterranean area, both they and the Egyptians exerted influence throughout this area. This means that what we call Western civilization is an amalgamation of the earlier civilizations created by the Beldane and the Siriuns. This includes the Sumerian civilization of Mesopotamia as well as the Greek. Whereas, the civilization of India is a mixing of this with the culture, civilization, or peoples descended from the Centaurus, and the civilization of China comes from an earlier cycle of Atlantis with some influences from Mu (Lemuria) which was itself influenced by the Centaurus.

Why did the Atlanteans choose to invade Egypt?

There were many who had emigrated for some time who were attempting to leave the conditions which were present within the Atlantean area. Some were out of synchroniza-

tion with the thoughts and activities which the Atlanteans were pursuing in general. They sought to have a freer expression and to maintain the ability to enter and leave at will. There was recognition upon their parts of the rapid disintegration of the energies into physical form and the losing of connectedness. These were some of the ones who emigrated.

Others were in defiance and were exiled in essence from the Atlantean people for either misuses or ways in which there was not cooperation. These were the ones the Egyptians particularly wanted to keep separate from. But the Egyptians were curious and there was a desire for them to remain in contact with their home world, to keep the consciousness open, and therefore there were those who did reject the Atlanteans. Those who did reject the Atlanteans from the first time that they began to make themselves known.

There was, as has been given, interbreeding that did occur on the parts of some, however, by the time this particular strain was present and did develop itself, the connections with the origin had been severed and what remained were the traditions and stories and myths as they would be seen in current existence of what had been. Therefore there was still the consciousness present within the Egyptians of wanting to remain pure, of wanting to keep invaders out, of wanting to resist contamination or adulteration of their consciousness and their lineages.

What was their consciousness? The Egyptians?

Originally it was Siriun.

This invasion from Atlantis then, was this quite a bit of time before the final destruction, the completion of the fourth cycle of Atlantis?

The Minoans, those who became those people, were previous to the destruction but not in an extended period.

The Atlanteans themselves, as they were not descendents from Sirius, where did this civilization come from? What planet of area were they connected to?

As has been given, these were from the Beldane.

The Minoan culture developed in the Aegean area prior to the coming of the Greek civilization. It was centered on the island of Crete. It was a great and powerful civilization in the third millennium B.C. The great ancient palace at Knossos, Crete, was unearthed in 1900. Conspicuous among many fresco paintings, there were scenes of bullfighting. A later Greek myth or history told a tale of a minotaur, a being with the body of a man and the head of a bull. Since the Minoan civilization was created by transplanted Atlanteans they probably brought these memories with them.

The Cretans (Minoans) had money, a system of weights and the art of writing.

The Minoan kings of Knossos extended their power. In 1500 B.C. they controlled the entire Aegean area and traded extensively with Egypt. Their civilization spread to mainland Greece. Excavations at Crete revealed hundreds of clay tablets with written scripts known to the modern world as Linear Script A and Linear Script B.

Michael Ventris and John Chadwick of Britain deciphered Linear Script B in 1952. They identified that language as an ancestor of the Arcado-Cyprian of Greece.

In 1957, the American Cyrus Gordon found evidence indicating that Linear Script A was probably a form of Akkadian, a Semetic language of Babylonia and Assyria (ref. Funk and Wagnall's Encyclopedia, 1963).

Putting this knowledge together with the knowledge developed by Barbara and myself, we have a clearly emerging picture or image of what existed and occurred before currently accepted history. This knowledge, from this point forward is history, and extends history.

An outcast Atlantean group tried to move from their island in the North Atlantic Ocean to Egypt but were repulsed. They then traveled to the area that was to become the island of Crete and the Aegean area during the Fourth Cycle of Atlantis but before the flooding and submersion of the valley or area that became the Mediterranean Sea.

The early civilization of Ur and the Chaldees was an amalgam of both the civilizations of the Beldane and those of Sirius. This is why they are one of the oldest known civilizations on Earth.

The Babylonian and Assyrian civilizations were in the same area of the world and the same rivers as the earlier civilization of Sumer or Sumeria of which Ur of the Chaldees was a part. Since some of the originators of both the Sumerian and Minoan civilizations were from Atlantis, it is understandable why their written languages would be related.

Thus we see the heart of the origin of our Western civilization, and to a large part Middle East civilization, is the coming together of the cultures of the Beldane and Sirius during the Fourth Cycle of Atlantis.

The civilizations of India while being influenced also by the Beldane and those of Sirius also were heavily influenced prior to this by the Centaurus and their influence on the civilization of Mu. This influence on India and her peoples by the Centaurus occurred before the island of India reached and crashed into what is now Asia, thus forming the Himalayan Mountains.

The Chinese civilization developed as a coming together of earlier Second and Third Cycle Atlantis and Lemuria to form its own uniqueness.

With this knowledge, we now know the history of the world. We have before us not only the causal factors of history as commonly recorded in history books in the Western world, but also a history that is before that commonly recorded. Of course, the history books of India, the Holy Scriptures of India such as the <u>Shiva Purana,</u> tell of history going back hundreds and thousands and even millions of years (see Michael Cremo's <u>Forbidden</u> <u>Archaeology</u>).

We now know why Egyptian civilization suddenly appeared in the height of its glory and technology. Earth is a colony or more exactly Earth is and has been many colonies.

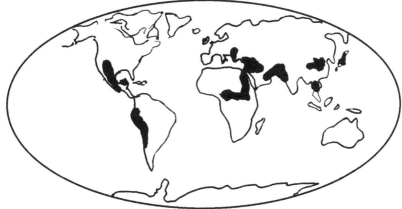

Figure 20. *The Beginnings of Civilization on planet Earth.*
The currently accepted estimates of civilization dated from Egypt in c5000 B.C. Most scholars characterize civilization as cultures that built cities, developed complex social and political structures through stratification, and evolved a formal economic structure through division of labor. Atlantis was a time of movement in all of these areas. Unlike the Siriun/Egyptians, Atlanteans demonstrated another important quality of civilization – a willingness of familial groups to embrace outsiders.

Searching for the COMMON ANCESTOR

There is a temple located 90 miles from Luxor, Egypt on the west bank of the Nile River which is perhaps the oldest temple in Egypt. It has the most unusual and unique architecture, different from any other temple complexes on the planet. The walls contain patterns of interlocking circles. Who made this earliest of temples and for what purpose?

This was produced by the Xena for the purpose of stabilizing the movement from gases to minerals. It was originally an energetic construction. A thought form that was projected and solidified over much time. It was the initiation of the one-dimension of consciousness that then made it possible for there to be a rooting or grounding, a stabilization into form.

Of what?

Of consciousness.

The statement that the temple near Luxor was produced by the Xena for the purpose of stabilizing the movement from gases to minerals is key here. It indicates this temple or the thought form that became this temple, is much, much older than the Great Pyramid and probably the Sphinx.

The Xena, being beings of consciousness itself, come to planet Earth to help form it and stabilize it in its very early stages, even before the Moon came out of the Earth. The great Pyramid of Giza and the Sphinx were built to stabilize the Earth after the moon had separated form the Earth.

How was its function different from that of the Great Pyramid?

That which is referred to as the Great Pyramid of Giza was a stabilizing effort for the planet that became necessary following the expulsion of the body of Lemuria, of Mu, away from the Earth itself. Part of the repercussions required there be a stabilization for the Earth to remain connected. It was this need that brought about the pyramid of Giza. This coincided with the Siriuns' activities who did energize this structure. Who continued to feed it. It was a different kind of structure. Its purpose, its formation, and its perpetuation was different and is still active in regards to the Earth itself.

This is not true for the pyramid structure known by Luxor.

Originally, did this pyramid near Luxor bring stability to the Earth?

In the way described, yes.

During what cycle of Atlantis was the Great Pyramid constructed?

Third.

What cycle of Atlantis was the Sphinx built?

Second.

This knowledge concerning the Temple near Luxor, Egypt, which was possibly dedicated to Osiris, opens up a whole new field of knowledge and investigation for it brings to light the awareness that not only did the Beldane and the Centaurus and those of Sirius construct buildings or edifices, but so did those of Xena who were and are beings of pure consciousness.

Therefore, humanity must now come to realize that most and probably all of these very ancient structures or temples were not only places of faith or worship but they were scientific machines exhibiting a greater technology than anything on the face of planet Earth today. These buildings, these structures, whether Luxor, the Sphinx or the Great Pyramid, caused very specific beneficial physical effects on the whole planet as well as emotional, mental, and spiritual effects. These ancient buildings were power generators and Earth stabilizers and consciousness builders.

No wonder they were built to such exacting specifications using sacred geometry. Sacred geometry teaches how to tap into and use the energy of the Universe itself for the growth and stabilization of the Earth and all sapient beings on the planet.

Why is it most researchers place a time frame of construction of the Sphinx much nearer the present, and even those who reach farther back into the past by noting the astronomic and astrological alignments think the Sphinx was built much more recent to the present, such as the end of Atlantis?

They are drawing upon what they are aware of.

What happened to the ancient Egyptians, the royalty that were descended from the Siriuns?

They eventually learned how to breed which is why the lineage is so important in the history that is recognized by modern man. The same kind of movement can be seen in China. These are the two areas strongest in this.

Did the lineage die out or does the lineage continue to this day?

It continues to this day.

Is it a pure bloodline?

No. It has become the focal point, this area on the planet, for the integration of all life forms that have coexisted within this planet. This is one of the reasons why this area on the planet is the focal point for so much of the energy at this time. Why it is seen as the cradle of civilization. Why it is seen as a political element that is so volatile for so many people. Why it is seen as the point of focus for religious ideas from many different areas. These are a manifestation of the unification of the consciousness that has embodied this planet for some time. The integration of it, the synchronization of it, the ability to experience it in multidimensions is reflected in the activities that have happened within this area for eons.

Why do the ancient Egyptians, as royalty, appear to have enlargements or large

bulging areas in the back of their skulls as shown by the bas reliefs, pictures and statues of the ancient Egyptian royalty?

This is the way that the brain evolved in order for there to continue to be the contact between the home, the point of origin, mother planet, and Earth. It was part of the evolvement of being able to utilize the energy exchange between the Pyramid, the Sphinx, and the home planet as a communication device, an arc, or more pertinently a triangle of energy. The ones who utilized this energy, who kept it moving, kept it cyclical, were the ones who developed this type of form. Those then did produce the bodies for what would be considered the royalty. They were the ones that could continue to communicate with home. As a result the bodies developed in that way.

What has happened to this kind of form, this kind of skull and brain? Does this lineage continue to this day or did it die out? This type of form?

The potential for the form is still present within the genetics and it is beginning to return in the increased brain cavity. The skull is becoming bigger. The electrical impulses in the brain are becoming quickened. As the shifting occurs in the ways that energy is expressed in the planet and in the consciousness of those who abide with her.

Mankind is evolving. Those of Sirius had already developed a brain that was capable of connected consciousness. The dolphins also already have a brain that is capable of and uses connected consciousness.

The early Egyptians of the royal bloodline were Siriuns or direct descendants of them, and thus maintained a connected consciousness with themselves, with planet Earth, and with their home planet. The Atlanteans did not have this connected consciousness.

The Dolphins and the Siriun-Egyptians were alike and connected in this way. Mankind is evolving to a connected consciousness. This is why our brains are growing and developing new neural pathways and greater abilities. It has always been our destiny for it was in the original makeup of those that added their genetic material to the indigenous species of planet Earth.

Perhaps it was part of our destiny, even without the aid of the Beldane and Siriuns, for Neanderthal Man is known to have had a larger brain than Homo sapiens and for this larger size to have been particularly located at the back of the brain.

CIVILIZATIONS

There appears to be a gap of about five thousand years between the fall of ancient civilizations such as Atlantis and the rise of the more historical civilizations, why is this?

There is not a gap seen. The limits of physical knowledge are in part responsible. The attachment to looking for physical knowledge is also responsible and the manner in which the knowledge that is present is interpreted is another factor. The continuity exists, it is present, and it is knowable.

Civilization and mankind has continued uninterrupted worldwide for many tens of thousands of years and perhaps even hundreds of thousands of years.

During what cycles of Atlantis or Lemuria did the dinosaurs exist and cease to exist?

This was before the time that would be referred to as Atlantis.

Would this be referred to as Lemuria?

It was more in regards to that referred to as Da. This was when the planet was evolving from gases to minerals. Plants were just beginning to be formed in this period of time.

This was the time period when the Xena built the temple of Luxor.

Many people do not accept the fact or truth of Atlantis. Most know of it through fairy tales and Hollywood's eyes. Scholars consider Plato's account of Atlantis to be true yet believe that after the fall of Atlantis almost 5000 years were required to rebuild civilization. With the research we have conducted, we have found that civilization continued unabated with the fall or breaking apart of the final part of Atlantis which had over time been reduced to an island with a city on it.

You see, Atlantis had colonies during the Fourth Cycle. Atlantis also had trade with other countries and land areas. There were also groups that left Atlantis on their own to seek a new life, such as those of the Minoan civilization.

During earlier cycles of Atlantis, large masses of land broke away and floated with their inhabitants to new areas such as the Appalachian Mountains of North America. What most people think of as Atlantis was actually only one of four time periods, or "cycles of Atlantis". Plato's account of Atlantis was in reference to the fourth and last cycle of Atlantis.

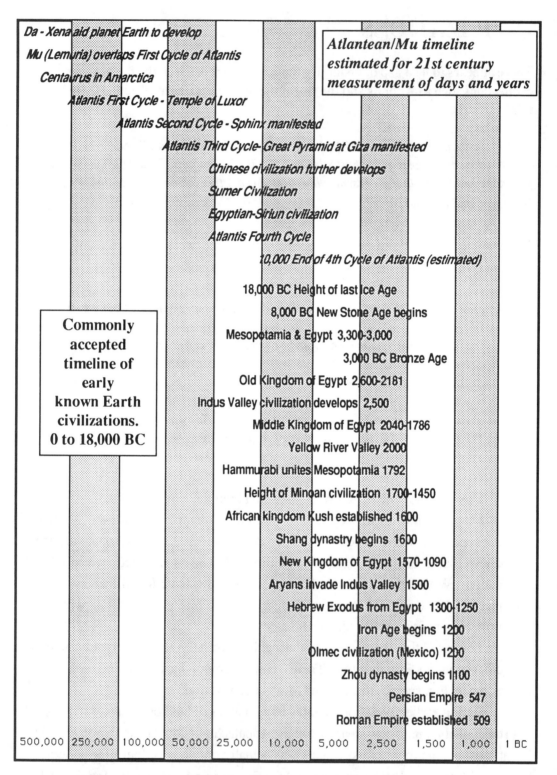

Figure 21. B. C. Atlantean Timeline and Commonly accepted World Timeline

In addition to these colonies and trade by Atlantis, the Egyptian civilization had been existing contemporaneously with the Fourth Cycle of Atlantis, and Egypt was not destroyed when Atlantis went down. Instead, the Egyptian civilization and its royal lineage which was descended from those of Sirius, continued into historical times until conquered by the Romans. Cleopatra supposedly being the last of the royal lineage.

The civilization of Egypt exerted great influence on Mediterranean civilization throughout this time period. The Atlanteans, or the Druids and Celts who were descendents of the Atlanteans, built Stonehenge. Stonehenge is aligned with the Great Pyramid indicating the Druids understood the geological, cosmological, astrological, and archaeological significance of the Great Pyramid and Sphinx to the evolution of consciousness of humanity and to the stabilization of planet Earth.

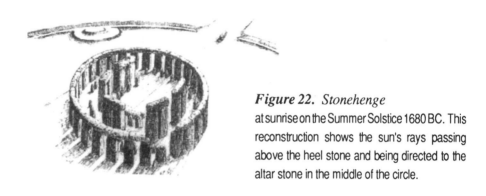

Figure 22. *Stonehenge*
at sunrise on the Summer Solstice 1680 BC. This reconstruction shows the sun's rays passing above the heel stone and being directed to the altar stone in the middle of the circle.

There is some false thinking on the part of many who think that the Northern Europeans were not civilized at the time the Romans conquered them. Let's examine that idea. The Romans conquered the Etruscans, who were the more civilized and cultured of the two. The Romans conquered the Greeks, who were the more cultured of the two. In fact, Pythagoras, one of the most enlightened beings ever to walk the face of this planet, moved from Greece to Italy to create his school for enlightenment. There were many Greek colonies on the Italian peninsula before the city of Rome began expanding and conquering civilized people.

The Romans conquered Carthage and its empire. Carthage itself was founded as a colony of Phoenicia, whose civilization was surely superior to that of the Romans in many ways.

The Phoenicians are generally credited with having created or invented the world's first alphabet of which the modern English alphabet owes its ancestry.

The Romans conquered the Celts in what was to become France and Germany.

They also conquered what was to become England, even though the Celts had better and bigger ships. The Romans had rowing vessels, so they could maneuver better in the English channel when there was no wind, which helped them to defeat the Celts (see America B.C. by Berry Fell).

The Atlanteans, those known as Druids who were descended from Atlanteans, built Stonehenge. The Romans never built anything close to Stonehenge in its astronomical or mathematical power. Stonehenge is a giant computer predicting such things as eclipses. It also once served as a stargate.

It appears that instead of steady progress upward of civilization that we have been led to believe in history books, especially as it relates to technology, we have a steady decline of civilization until the time of the Italian Renaissance. At which time, consciousness, knowledge, technology and civilization began to progress and grow again.

This is not to say that there weren't areas on the planet that developed civilizations during the time period of the fall of Atlantis to the rise of our modern world.

The cause of this, I have explained earlier. Recall the discussion of the Yugas or Ages that our planet moves through as it travels around the center of our galaxy and also around our twin star. The Kali Yuga which the Earth started moving out of only a few short hundred years ago was the time when our Earth was the greatest distance from the center of the galaxy. This coincided with, and had a direct bearing and influence on, the lower consciousness of that time.

The downward cycle of consciousness lasts for 12,000 years and the upward cycle of consciousness lasts for 12,000 years. Twelve thousand years ago corresponds almost exactly with the fall or destruction of Atlantis in about 10,000 B.C. 10,000 B.C. plus 2,000 A.D. equals 12,000 years. Now mankind is poised to move forward in consciousness in great leaps. A powerful reason for this is that 24,000 years ago to 12,000 years ago was the time of the dawning of the reasoner in relationship to the consciousness of the planet. This was the time period when planet Earth and our solar system were moving toward the center of our galaxy. This corresponded to an increase in consciousness.

Now planet Earth is once again moving towards the center of the galaxy. Presently we are in the time of another great shift or change in the consciousness of humanity. This time it is the movement into Intuitive Man or the intuitive thinker. Man means thinker whereas male and female refer to types of physical bodies. Our consciousness is changing as Mother Earth's consciousness shifts or moves to a higher level also. Because of all these factors, the possibility exists for each person on planet Earth to quicken the rate of soul growth and spiritual development of the Self.

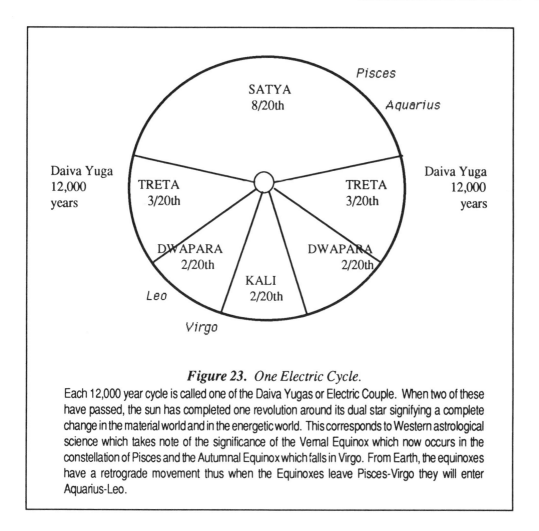

Figure 23. *One Electric Cycle.*
Each 12,000 year cycle is called one of the Daiva Yugas or Electric Couple. When two of these have passed, the sun has completed one revolution around its dual star signifying a complete change in the material world and in the energetic world. This corresponds to Western astrological science which takes note of the significance of the Vernal Equinox which now occurs in the constellation of Pisces and the Autumnal Equinox which falls in Virgo. From Earth, the equinoxes have a retrograde movement thus when the Equinoxes leave Pisces-Virgo they will enter Aquarius-Leo.

TIME TRAVEL...beyond our Universe

What mode of transport did those of Centaurus use to come to planet Earth?

This is a kind of portal.

Where was this portal located on planet Earth?

At the time it was within what now would be referred to as the Indian Ocean. At that time, however, there was land here.

It would seem as if at various times during Earth's history there were stargates built or used or constructed in order for beings from other star systems to come to planet Earth.

This was the preferred method of transport rather than physical, matter spaceships that would need to traverse vast distances. Stonehenge was utilized as a stargate by the Beldane or their descendants. The Pyramid-Sphinx complex was used as a stargate by those of Sirius. Both the Beldane and the Siriuns were energy beings at first.

However, the Centaurus used or resided in physical bodies. This is what makes this knowledge even more fascinating. To transport energy and consciousness is one thing, to transport physical objects let alone a humanoid physical body, is quite another. Because the Centaurus were intimately related or connected with the emerging consciousness of Mu (Lemuria) they were located in what is now referred to as the Indian Ocean. This is why remnants of Lemurian civilizations can be found off the coasts of land areas in or around the Pacific Ocean.

It is also why relics or ruins of the Lemurian age or civilization can be found in areas or land masses that border the Pacific Ocean or in the South Seas, the Southern Hemisphere. Examples of these areas are Antarctica, Madagascar, India, pre-Inca ruins in the Andes Mountains and possibly the Cascade mountains in California.

Although I had considered earlier in this book the possibility of spaceship travel from the Centaurus, it is probable that they used a type of stargate also as their means of space travel.

Further Exploration of Land Masses

Describe the movement of the land masses of Atlantis and relate it to the cycles of Atlantis.

At the time of beginning of materialization of the Beldane within this land area, the land was connected. Shortly after the movement of these people, there began to be changes because of the interaction of their energies with the natural energies that were evolving on the planet and in the planet. Part of this was the natural evolution of the planet itself, but part of it was the beginning of interaction which was an unanticipated factor which caused there to be the initial breaking apart of land mass.

This then caused there to be some separation of people and it caused there to be a movement of the land apart from one another. The gaseous nature of the planet, the lack of coherency, were factors in this as well, and there was the presence of that referred to as Mu, more recently termed Lemuria, which was forming and which was in the process of instability on the opposing part of the sphere that was beginning to form. With the breaking apart of this into two, there were repercussions within the core that was building within the Earth that created the need for the expelling on the opposing side of what became the Earth's moon. *This then set into effect a chain reaction which led to the breaking apart of parts of the continent which was Atlantis and to a less extent affecting the movement of remaining parts of Lemuria which remained on the planet which would later become Antarctica, Australia, and India, Madagascar, that which is East of the great mountain chains of the Americas.*

Some of what occurred during these breaking aparts were lost and therefore there are what is now seen as civilizations or what is seen as cities which are submerged. These can be found throughout the world off coastal areas. And have been (found).

As the Earth changed and cooled and stabilized, there was the movement of people with the land and in this way much of the people became dispersed. They continued to develop and to refine and to learn how to respond to the physical world that they found themselves linked to. They began to develop their own individual, separate identity. Therefore, in time, that which was called Atlantis was small compared to what it had been at one time.

The areas that ring the Pacific areas were once under the influence of Mu (Lemuria).

During what cycle of Atlantis was that mass of the Earth expelled that became the Earth's moon?

This was what brought about the transition between the First and Second Cycles.

Did then during the First Cycle, Atlantis and Lemuria coexist on opposite sides of the planet?

Yes.

During the First Cycle of Atlantis, the civilization or Age called Mu (Lemuria) existed. Mu was located primarily in the Southern hemisphere and Atlantis in the northern hemisphere of planet Earth. This is why India, Antarctica, Madagascar, and Australia were parts of Mu (Lemuria). As was parts of South America.

Because of the release or exhalation of the mass from the Earth that became our Moon, the Pacific Ocean was created. This is the largest ocean in the world and is the area where much, if not most, of Mu was located. The areas on the edge of the Pacific basin survived as land masses. Antarctica became frozen over. The lands that would become known as India and Madagascar moved north, with present-day India crashing into Asia forming the Himalayan Mountains. Meanwhile the land mass now known as Australia assumed its present position.

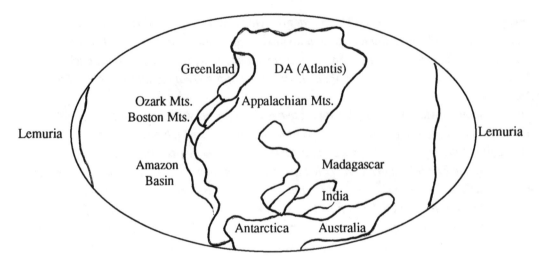

Figure 24. *Map of Atlantis and Lemuria*

This expelling of the Moon led to much instability on the young planet Earth. It also led directly to the first breaking up of Atlantis, the Northern continent into smaller continents and islands.

The expelling of the Moon is the reason there is more land mass in the Northern Hemisphere than the Southern Hemisphere.

The Great Pyramid of Giza, Egypt, was built by those of Sirius, as a way to stabilize the planet after it ejected the Moon. Other pyramids and temples were later built to add to and aid this process of stabilization and maturation of planet Earth.

What is the significance of crystal skulls found in ancient temple sites around the world?

There are several purposes to these. They served as a prototype for the development of the Homo sapiens body. They also served as a means to experiment in how the crystalline structure of the brain could utilize consciousness.

In what matter might they be used today, in the present?

They still contain the same purpose, therefore, in the mind of the appropriate consciousness, the potential of the brain could be delved into and understood on deeper levels. There could be a greater appreciation and recognition of the nonphysical form and even the conveyance or the ability to move from physical, limited, gross form into energetic, electric, pranic form.

Why is it that most of Earth's early civilizations that are widely known in the present such as Egypt, Sumeria, Minoan, China, India, and the Mayans are all located upon a narrow band of latitude on the Earth?

The energy which they produced, which was Atlantean and was closer to its original intent, has migrated to a particular level of frequency and vibration which is compatible with that of the Earth. As the Earth has stabilized and grown into a type of rotation these Atlanteans have been drawn to certain places upon the planet both in terms of consciousness but also in terms of physicality itself in order to create a constant vibratory pattern which would sustain the memory of humanity. This has been an essential part of the evolutionary process. The maturation of consciousness.

This is also why there are so many similarities. Not only is their origin the same, but their duty, their tradition, their hopes, their ancestry was in common. Therefore, there are the common expressions of it with some diversification due to the lack of contact for so long.

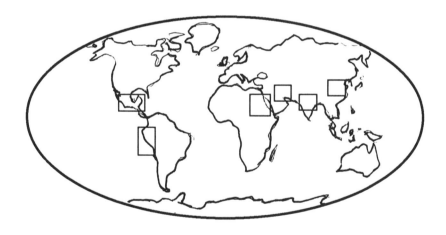

Figure 25. *Geographic settings of Earth's recorded civilizations.*

The physical bodies we know today as Homo sapiens, were created deliberately by intelligent beings not by some random act of nature. Full-sized reconstructions of human skulls made from quartz have been discovered across the planet. The first was found in 1927, in Belize, by British explorer Anna Mitchell-Hedges. Controversy surrounds the skulls because their existence is the result of very sophisticated and highly developed technological skills, abilities that would be difficult to reproduce today with our modern technology.

These crystal skulls were created by an advanced technology. A technology more advanced than our own. Intuitive Research reveals these crystal skulls were and are the blueprints for the brain and body of Homo sapiens. They show and indicate that Homo sapiens was created with high knowledge and off-world technology.

These crystal skulls can be used to aid individuals to transform themselves rapidly into enlightened beings. The people using them will need to be metaphysicians – those who have meditated every day for years, who have understood the inner levels of mind, and have developed their own consciousness to higher dimensions.

The reason why so many civilizations developed along this narrow band of latitude in the Northern Hemisphere is because the civilization of the Southern Hemisphere called Mu was destroyed with much of the land masses of this area.

The civilizations that developed in the northern latitudes developed from the Beldane, the Siriuns, or both.

Much of the civilization of Mu developed from the Centaurus. This is part of the reason why Southern and far Eastern civilizations seem so different from Western ones.

The information given earlier that those of the Egyptian and Mayan were begun by the Siriuns rather than the Beldane which is a different planetary influence than these others such as Indian, China, Minoan, and Sumerian, did some of them not have a common ancestry?

There is still a common ancestry.

How would that common ancestry be referred to?

Ki.

What or where is Ki?

It is a wave. This is the best description. It is most aptly described as the inbreath and outbreath of Brahm.

Even though the Siriuns and the Beldane are from different solar systems, still they were seeded by a common ancestry.

That common ancestry is God, also called Brahm or breath of God or inbreath and outbreath of Brahm, or the Creator, or Allah, or the Tao.

Everyone and everything in the Universe is related. Every being in the universe is a child of God, a son or daughter of the Creator.

Every being from every planet in the Universe is related and connected. We are now discovering our connectedness through the spiritualization of the planet and the expansion and elevation of consciousness beings on this planet. This is the future of Homo sapiens. We are evolving into Homo connectedness leading to Homo oneness.

The OCEANS

During the time period of Atlantis were there cities under the oceans?

Not as they would be seen today, no. There was intelligent life forming within the waters. In fact, the life itself had been part of bringing the waters into existence.

Where did this intelligent life come from?

Canis.

How would this star system of Canis...is this what would be referred to as Canis Major?

No. In present terminology this would be Canis Minor. Although at the time that there was colonization this expression of light was one, it was not divided. It had yet to be divided by that which is referred to presently as the Milky Way. It was one.

That of Canis Major and Canis Minor?

Yes.

What form did this intelligent life take on in the oceans?

This occurred during the mineral stage in the development of the Earth itself. Therefore there was the fashioning of the molecular structure that would produce water and would produce eventually sea water. The forms that were forming within these structures then were mineral initially. They were phosphorescent and they were akin to what was being developed that would now be referred to as dinosaurs. The forms that developed within the waters were able to adapt and sustain much easier than those who were air breathers therefore the life form has adapted to the planetary development itself and has sustained itself in some forms even to the present as there have been those forms which were created eventually upon land that have sustained themselves for some time.

When those of Canis Minor came to Earth, were they in physical form, or energetic form, or what form did they take?

Photonic energetic. What would be seen as atomic by current scientific measurements. Which was most highly conducive to that which they had come to. The Earth at that point was compatible. It was easy to resonate. There had been other searchings for this type of compatibility and it was found here.

Did these ones stay? Remain on planet Earth?

Yes. These would be presently the dolphins and to a lesser degree the whale and to lesser degrees other sea life.

What was their method of transport from Canis Minor to Earth?

Thought form projection would be the most accurate description. It was the movement of light.

What is the meaning to mankind, humanity and planet Earth, that both the dolphins exist on this planet and Homo sapiens exist on this planet? What is this evolving to, what is the ultimate outcome?

Awareness and unification of the whole of life form. There are inherent limitations in each form which are easily noted and in order for there to be a cooperation and a blending, a utilization of the harmonization with the planet itself and with all life, there must be the expansion of awareness. Through this there will come the expansion of energy, intelligence, and manifestation.

The intelligent life that formed in the waters of the oceans is the dolphins and to some extent the whales.

Since the dolphins are from Canis and brought their intelligence with them, they were a part of the stabilization of planet Earth and helping to bring it into being in its present state of evolution.

Those that became dolphins came to this planet as intelligent, energetic beings. They later took on the intelligent, physical form we know today as dolphins. Some interbred or mixed with one or more indigenous species and became the whales of planet Earth.

When one is beyond physical limitations and is a being of Light or an atomic being, then physical limitations of physical distance and physical time, which are based on the measure of physical distance, does not limit self.

The constellation known as Canis Major contains Sirius and is the star system from which came the Siriuns. The Siriuns are those energetic beings who founded both the Egyptian and Mayan civilizations and caused the Earth to stabilize by constructing the Great Pyramid of Giza.

The energetic beings who became the dolphins originally came form Canis Minor which is a different constellation than Canis Major.

Canis Major contains Sirius, the brightest star in the heavens, while Canis Minor contains Procyon, a star that is far less bright than Sirius but still a first-magnitude star.

So even in the naming of constellations, there seems to be the recognition that the life of the Siriuns, who had a part in creating Homo sapiens, and those of the dolphins who came from Canis Minor, are intimately connected.

The dolphins already possess connected consciousness. They do not possess Homo sapiens physical technology. Homo sapiens, as a species, are moving to a greater connected consciousness. Many of our human race have already achieved this. It is called Christ Consciousness, Buddha Consciousness, Cosmic Consciousness, Zarathustra Consciousness. It is the oneness with all creation. It is as Jesus (Joshua) the Christ (Messiah) said, "I and the Father are One." This has been said by many masters who were master teachers of consciousness. Enlightened beings of all races, from differing time periods, civilizations or peoples on the planet, have expressed this thought.

Now we are forming a connected consciousness with alien beings from another planet, the dolphins. They are here waiting for mankind to evolve.

You will describe the changing of the Earth's magnetic fields over the course of the Earth's history and on into the present.

In terms of the physicality of the Earth there are two primary factors that have been necessary in the evolvement and building of the Earth itself and its evolution. One of these is magnetic in that it is a drawing, a pulling, a receptive force within creation, that enables there to be the movement. The other is a radiant form of giving, moving, directing, the aggressive expression. These two, in combination, have created the necessary elemental development for there to be life form structures within and through the planet. For the planet to have a vehicle for its consciousness.

The magnetism has served to coalesce, to condense, to contract, and to solidify. This is a process that has been occurring over eons of time enabling the quantum structure of the Earth itself to sustain.

It {Earth} has reached a point where it is turning, it is beginning to move in a direction away from further condensation to the beginning of a long journey toward expansion. Therefore, there is the beginning of changes in the magnetism of the Earth, the radiation of the Earth, and it does in some ways mirror the changes occurring in the Sun. It is both self-generating and reflective. Therefore, it is connected within the whole with awareness of its part. This is all.

What is gravity?

It is the reaction to that which has just been spoken, the connectedness between the magnetism and the radiation.

How does gravity work?

It is the effect of the pushing and pulling of opposing forces.

Planet Earth's magnetic fields change over time. As the planet's consciousness nears the end of a cycle, as it is in the present, the magnetic field becomes weaker.

The magnetic field of planet Earth is the weakest it has been in many thousands of years. This weakened magnetic field provides the opportunity for rapid growth in consciousness as humanity lives on the cusp of the Ages.

Astrologically, humanity is moving more and more into the Age of Aquarius, the age of knowing, and out of the Age of Pisces, the age of believing. This is a shift of the ages from one age to another.

During the Age of Pisces, the quality of believing was predominant in the consciousness of humanity. Therefore, churches and religion became the dominant structure on the planet.

During the Age of Aquarius, which is the Age of Knowing, the urge is for each individual to come to know Universal Truths. Truths that apply to everyone, everywhere, throughout time. Therefore, since the time of the Italian Renaissance, science has come to the forefront of consciousness on the planet.

In addition, there are other forces at work on our planet Earth that are propelling consciousness forward. Mankind is attempting to fulfill and complete the stage of consciousness known as reasoning. This sets the stage for the next level of consciousness which is Intuition or Intuitive Man (thinker) which may also be called Intuitive Humanity. Intuition includes reasoning and, in addition, adds the ability of the individual to draw upon Subconscious Mind in order to bring out and use understandings of creation developed in past lives.

We are entering into the Sixth Day of Creation called Intuitive Man.

Also we are moving out of the darkest of Yugas called the Kali Yuga. Yuga means age. Planet Earth, and indeed our solar system, is moving into an age nearer to the central sun or the center of our galaxy where knowledge of higher consciousness becomes easier to comprehend.

As the consciousness of mankind progresses, we will be able to understand gravity, and not only overcome it, but harness it for our greater use. The energy source of the future will be the Earth itself, then the planets and the Sun.

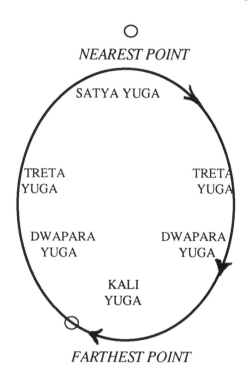

O
NEAREST POINT

SATYA YUGA

TRETA YUGA

TRETA YUGA

DWAPARA YUGA

DWAPARA YUGA

KALI YUGA

FARTHEST POINT

Figure 26.
The journey toward the dual sun is illustrated in this wheel diagram. The Kali Yuga is the farthest point from the grand center our Sun revolves around. Our planet began its ascent toward that center just 300 years ago. To understand the impact of this movement think about the advances humanity has made in that short period of physical time.

DESTINY

What is the meaning for planet Earth and humanity that the Centaurans have come to this planet, those of Sirius, those of the Beldane, those of the Xena, and those of Canis, all five have come to this planet and are all a part of the evolving structure of this planet and of humanity?

This is an expression of the unification of the universal energies. Each of these intelligences did have what would be described as motives for their colonization and the habitation of them has created the synergy necessary for there to be the elevation of this particular planet within a larger body. The journey toward this has been satisfying for most and is quickening at present in part due to the technological development which enables all life forms to be aware of each other. Now there must be the intention refined in order for the respect to be present, for there to be movement beyond coexistence into dimensional shifts which will open the opportunity for co-creation.

What is this larger body that was referred to?

This would be most readily understood as the expression of the mind of the Creator.
Of God.
Of the Source of all Being.

Our planet Earth is part of a solar system which is part of a galaxy which is part of our Universe. This is only the physical part. There are higher levels of mind, higher dimensions of space and time that have been explored only by the enlightened of humanity.

Our evolution must now progress along the lines of greater connectedness rather than the pseudo-science of separation. We have discovered our physical world, now it is time to discover Self and thereby know all of creation.

ATLANTIS RISING

In many cultures on the planet there are clairvoyant records. From the quatrains of Nostradamus to the Mayan Calendar to Biblical references of the end of time, prophecy has been a part of man's existence all along. It is a sense of destiny, a blending of remembering and forecasting, united in the ever-present now.

And so each generation that has walked the Earth experiences the timeliness, the urgency of the present. We are no exception. Americans particularly want to know how things will turn out and so we are prone to set goals and accomplish them. This is a structural support for reasoning.

We want to know that there is a happy ending, because our beliefs point us in that direction. Collectively, we call it the American dream and it is a part of the collective consciousness, whether aware or unaware, of every person who is born here and those who are drawn here.

We are a nation of optimists. We have a sense of profound destiny. Sometimes it may seem to some so entwined with egotism that it threatens our humanity. But the truth is, there has never been a nation on this planet like the United States. What became this evolved experiment in republican democracy was forged by those seeking autonomy as spiritual beings.

Our founding document describes us as being "endowed by our Creator". The first principle listed in our Bill of Rights is "freedom of religion." The words were thoughtfully crafted, they reflect meaning of great significance to the initiation of this new form of government on this planet. Our founding fathers had a sense of their greatness. They were philosophers who no longer wanted a king. Benjamin Franklin's final virtue was to "Imitate Jesus, and Socrates."

This nation was forged by those who wanted freedom to worship and who were willing to extend the same respect to others. In effect, with the creation of the United States, humanity was liberated to excel, to explore, to become Spiritual Man.

To choose the United States as a birthplace means having the opportunity in physical existence to exercise the will that we were given by our Creator. The more we appreciate and use, the more we gain, the more we grow, the more we expand, the happier we become. "To him who has, more will be given." Many do not understand this. They judge it as selfishness, seeking to take down the prosperous. They are destroyers. The prosperous are builders.

Prosperous people are grateful people. They remember where they came from. They know how they created what they have, and having more they are often the most generous.

The struggle to understand this is inherent in physical life. The haves and the have nots they are called in today's world. The truth is the United States is the most generous country on the planet. It has in 200 brief years become a paradigm for evolutionary breakthrough and growth.

The United States is the new Atlantis, or the continuation of it.

The United States was founded by people who were willing to do. They were willing to leave property and sometimes relatives in search of a new life. They risked their lives for a chance at freedom. They set forth ideas that would continue far beyond their lifetimes. Just like the those who created the earlier Atlantean civilization.

As this material came together for us, I began to realize Atlantis still lives. It lives through the United States. This was not a completely new idea. Over two decades ago I was part of two seminars, one on *America's Secret Destiny* and the other on *The Living Atlantis*. Both spoke to the idea that Atlanteans were reincarning in large numbers in the United States. What has happened is the idea has blossomed through experience, taking on breadth through reasoning and depth through intuition.

The founding fathers became familiar with universal principles as they set into motion the structure by which we could self-govern. They knew that when people give up their right to make decisions, they lose their right to determine their own destiny. Some of the founding fathers were metaphysicians. They understood that thought is cause. They knew when things don't work out, the only place to look for blame is at home, in you. By the same token when things work out beautifully it is not by chance, it is not something outside of yourself, you have created that thing of beauty. Then is a time to be honest as well as grateful, accepting the responsibility for a task well done.

These are the legacies of Atlantis – the need to have a place to exercise will and determination, intelligently. A place to be able to realize that thought is cause and the physical its manifest likeness. Such realities can only exist where certain freedoms are guaranteed and the citizens appreciate them enough to live by them and teach them to the next generation. The only guarantee is common agreement, common ideal, a shared sense of destiny.

Producing Intuitive, Spiritual Man on our planet is that common destiny.

During our Intuitive Research, Daniel asked a question about the commonality of mankind. "The information given earlier that those of the Egyptian and Mayan were begun by the Siriuns rather than the Beldane which is a different planetary influence than these others such as Indian, China, Minoan, and Sumerian, did some of them not have a common ancestry?"

The response was: *"There is still a common ancestry."*

When I transcribed the report I smiled. It makes sense to me that this "common ancestry" is energy...the energy of Atlantis.

Perhaps we are now ready for a sixth planetary influence either from afar or produced through us. Maybe what the purpose of all of this is, is to produce the planetary Christ. Certainly, all the evidence, physical and meta-physical, points to our individual destiny as enlightened beings. History reflects this journey thus supporting this idea. More and more I can imagine the possibilities of a world filled with Siddharthas, Quetzecoatls, Zarathustras, Moseses, Pythagoruses, Jesuses, Mohammeds, Gandhis, Kings, Dalai Lamas, and countless others whose names history might fail to recall.

In August, as we researched and wrote this book, we received an email concerning a symbolic calendar built into the measurements of the Great Pyramid. This calendar spoke eloquently of the birth of Jesus the Christ, the development of the atom bomb, and the two world wars of the last century. This calendar ended September 17, 2001, the letter said.

I didn't think much about it at the time because I gave it little attention. I would think more about it after September 11th.

On September 11, 2001, the world experienced an astounding explosion in collective consciousness.

Outwardly it was stimulated by men flying large airplanes filled with passengers into the two tallest buildings in the world's most multinational city. In fact by the time it was over citizens of reportedly 80 nations were killed, not just Americans. If someone had wanted to attack the world, New York City, home of the United Nations, was certainly the place to do it.

Many of us saw it live, minutes following the first plane's assault. There is no way to know exactly how many people were watching when the second plane plowed through the second of the Twin Towers of the World Trade Center. Many who did see it couldn't believe what was before them. "It's like a movie," one kept saying, unable to accept it into her consciousness. The facts couldn't penetrate the construction of her beliefs. But they would, for this act might have been many things, which would certainly be debated and argued for years to come, but foremost this global experience was an awakening.

Throughout the days following the attack I caught snatches of news primarily from televised images, teleporting me to the scene, introducing me to those directly involved in recovery. Being a teacher at the College of Metaphysics I was constantly engaged in informing, educating, and counseling students and other teachers. And through it all Atlantis kept surfacing in my consciousness.

It was more than being in the process of writing this book. Most of my work was done, and I had expected the book would go to press in the summer. However, it was still in our hands in September, and I began to realize more of why after the 11th.

This burst of emotional energy, of life and death, of mistakes and regrets, of fight and flight, was the essence of the Atlantean experience. The descent into matter, magnified to the extreme, was here in New York City, the materialistic capital where just months ago two morning co-hosts had joked about a new restaurant that would cost no less than $500 per person for one meal.

It was the same kind of craving for physical experience during Atlantis that lured many spirits into the material plane to find that the doorway only moved in one direction.

Disbelief filled most of us in those first few days after the twin tower destruction. Many stayed glued to their televisions as if seeing it over and over and over again would help the truth finally sink in so they could move from the quagmire of denial.

During Atlantean times and since, many have repeated experiences time and again, through many cultures and land areas, trying to awaken.

I was one of the ones who saw the second plane plow into the second tower. It was indeed as if the wrath of God was reigning upon the city of iniquity. Then several minutes later, word came that another plane had rammed into the U.S. Pentagon. My first thought was "it has started." Images of prophecies I had read at some time through my life flew through my mind.

I was upstairs with our son and didn't know if Daniel, our chancellor, knew. I raced down to the great room of the main building and walked directly to the television. I told a group of people gathered there that they might want to know what was going on. My actions were Atlantean energy, the need to know, the need to communicate. I would become increasingly familiar with those energies in the coming days, a kind of exhilaration – misplaced to my conscious way of thinking – that only comes as the Kundalini energy flows toward unity within Self and with all of creation.

An hour or so later as the first building collapsed before our eyes, a teacher asked what I thought. I took a deep breath and simply said, "It's the death of believing."

The reference was many faceted. Certainly Biblical, for the movement from believing into knowing as symbolized by John the Baptist and Jesus of Nazareth who would become the Christ. Astronomical, for we leaving the Age of Pisces, the believer, and entering into the Age of Aquarius, the knower. Prophetic, as Tennyson's prophecy to "ring out the thousand years of war, ring in the thousand years of peace." I knew in those first moments following the crashes that everyone's beliefs, even those who later were shown cheering the event, would be changed. No one was going to be left untouched by this. It might be days or years before they would be aware, but they would in time become very aware of what had been started this day by only a handful of men.

Just like Atlantis.

This event was foreshadowed eight years earlier in the bombing of the very same building that now no longer exists. The perpetrators had reasoned well in those years, and this time they succeeded in their mission. This is more on the physical and psychological level, the combative arguments and actions of judging right and wrong.

The much greater foreshadowing was in consciousness. This was a test, so we could evaluate how much we had learned with each lesson presented. For Americans, we had seen several such incidents in the last decade – the WTC bombing, the Waco, Texas attack, the OKC federal building bombing, the Columbine, CO school shooting. These acts of senseless violence were causing us to think, to come out of too often drug-induced mental stupors of denial and into a lucidity that admits and forgives and accepts and allows. The kind of thoughts that bring insight and illumination, that lead their owner to go beyond the goodness for self and align with the goodness for all.

One woman interviewed said she told her child "something good will come from this." The sentiment was echoed by many in the aftermath of the tragedy. The older among us had seen another day that lived in infamy and what it had brought. Now the lesson was being presented to a new generation. "Let us pull together" became the refrain. Let us care and love and do better.

The woman's words stuck with me. I knew them to be true, and I knew they were incomplete. Too much was left to the great cosmic forces in that word "something." The reasoner in me was pressing to know, what good and how? I thought about it for hours, meditated and prayed. Then it came to me, quite clearly: for something good to come from this, we must learn the lesson.

Being at the School of Metaphysics world headquarters during this time, I was abreast of thoughts and opinions in a wide berth. Telephone calls from around the country and emails from around the world flowed in. *Universal Peace Covenants* were our first response. The Multidimensional Experience concerning the events of September 11th was the second.

Initially, I created this experience with those on campus in mind. The Saturday following the attack, a group of teachers and students gathered in the College chapel. The experience was designed to stimulate awareness throughout the levels of Conscious and

Subconscious Mind. The purpose was to bring resolution in a way that would entrain the minds toward productive action now. The experience was poignant for each one present. Placing the basic experience on the internet became a natural response to the many requests we were receiving asking what the School of Metaphysics' viewpoint of the attack was. It was not that we had an official stand on the tragedy. What we did have were viewpoints of thoughtful metaphysicians from many backgrounds and an example of what we teach that could assist anyone in putting their own experience into perspective. This too was Atlantean.

Multidimensional experience assists in the movement of consciousness from a state of believing into knowing. I could see more clearly how this is the universal lesson in September 11th. The lesson received by each of us is unique, accepted or rejected according to our own understandings or need. To learn our lesson requires reasoning. And reasoning is Atlantean.

Reasoning produces intuition, the destiny of our nation.

Two days after the towers came down, I caught a few minutes of an interview with a man who had just missed being in one of the buildings. The only reason he wasn't there was he had decided to take his son to his first day of kindergarten.

Now this CEO of the largest company occupying the World Trade Center sat talking about the 700 people, including his brother, who were missing and presumably had died when the buildings collapsed. As he talked, the spectrum of his experience shone on his face: the awe that his life had been spared and the anguish for the families., the fear of surviving and the determination to care for the living, the pain of not knowing why and the resolve to draw upon inner resources previously unknown.

He spoke about meeting with the families of those killed and they asked, "Why?" He had no answer and it obviously pained him.

He spoke of the government and Federal Reserve telling him how needed the work of his company was. He took the news to the surviving employees in New Jersey and London and at 7 a.m. the next day they went to work.

When the interviewer asked, "Why? Was it a way to get back?" he seemed puzzled by her question. He said the reasons were everything; some didn't want to stay at home anymore, others wanted to do something, others didn't want to think about it anymore. Getting back wasn't one of the reasons.

As I sat listening intently to this humbled man, for the first time I consciously moved beyond thoughts of the horror of someone being a survivor in the wake of such destruction. I had intellectually grasped the responsibility, the opportunity, and how the universe moves to bring about such circumstances, but my experience that morning was head and heart, together.

It was Atlantean.

Images of tidal waves and natural disasters prevalent during Atlantean times flashed between Howard's televised image and me. Sitting there, I realized the polarity inherent in asking "Why me?" I thought of all the great Masters and how they conducted themselves, and I saw before my eyes a man gaining such mastery.

When you are in positions of leadership, others look to you for answers, even when you do not yet possess them. It is that sense that others depending upon you that causes the inner growth, the inner stretch that mastery requires. Howard Lutnick had not consciously asked for or wanted to be in this position, but it was quite obvious he was ready.

A week later I searched for printed articles about this man, and found them. In one he said, "I have to take care of my family." He was talking about the 700 families of those who perished. Whoever Howard Lutnick was when he took his son to school that morning, destiny had made him a different person. His family had extended beyond flesh and blood, beyond shared economic goals, and his sense of responsibility extended proportionately.

By Friday, other human stories were surfacing. With them came the many coincidences. There was the woman in the wheel chair who was carried down 65 floors only to stall at the fifth floor and as a result she and the cluster of firemen helping her were in a space left standing when the remainder of the building pummeled down around them. Then there were the two friends who took two different planes back home, the two planes which plowed into each of the towers just minutes apart.

Some survived, others died. The stories defy logic. They are beyond statistical odds and cannot be resolved in the reasoning of the conscious mind. They require us to draw upon potential rarely touched. They are Atlantean in their manifestation of the Universal Law of Cause and Effect, karma as it is termed in Sanskrit. The matter of why some live and some die comes more from the soul than from those wishing to intimidate through fear and terror.

I remember pieces of Past Life Profile concerning a female involved in the first development of the Atlantean creation. Each time a difficult moment was experienced, she wanted to withdraw from it, deny it or ignore it. She feared working with complications because she felt unable to control herself in the process. She could see that she was bringing difficult situations into her life and she even knew they were for a purpose, the purpose of understanding those experiences. But *"she knew of the ability to withdraw from that plane of existence and found that most tempting instead of working with what needed to be worked on."*

Like people in the days following the tragedy, many found it easier to withdraw, to deny, to get back to business as usual as if nothing had changed. They, like this Atlantean woman, struggle with expanding their capacity to respond. For this woman, the challenge of responsibility manifested in three areas, what would in today's world be called her co-workers, her supervisors, and her family/friends.

Her work was developing substance that contributed to the development of light. Sort of a precursor to supercollider work or holographic experimentations. *"There was much trial and error in this area and the members of the group working on this project would experience frustration and conflict among each other often."* When she would discover something new that would work, she would withdraw from the ensuing arguments to make have her work recognized. Likewise she *"refused to see the purpose for herself"* that the leaders in her group saw. Because she saw it as too much for her *"to carry"* she would withdraw from it.

Her fear also manifested in close associations *"where the expression of love was being attempted to be understood. In all areas, the same basic tendency took place, of feeling of lack of control. Much guidance and much advice was given to this one; this one sought the guidance and advice, but in spite of it being given and taken within self, it was not applied or used, though it was understood."* This Atlantean woman could see it with her head but refused to respond so she might know it by heart.

This has been the story for most of mankind for centuries.

The suggestions given to this woman back in 1975 are particularly appropriate for us today, for if we are to learn the lessons life is bringing us as our world becomes one, we will want to join our ability to receive ideas with our ability to respond, to put them to use.

This is what the significance of the Atlantean lifetime to the present lifetime was for this woman:

> *Intuitive Reporter: The significance would be desiring certain types of experiencing where much understanding can be gained on many levels of understanding and, when being on the edge of involvement, withdrawing self from them continuously due to the fear and the belief that there is not control within self for experiencing for the sake of understanding. This one also seeks out others for advice, hears the advice, but does not heed the advice given.*
>
> *This one desires to be responsible, to be actively involved and meaningful in all kinds of activity. This is very strong within self as it was*

*in that Atlantean time, but the fear and belief of no control does not allow
for that desire and that need of responsibility to be fulfilled. Would suggest
to this one to formulate firmly within the mind the purpose for existence
and the reasons why she continuously draws to self certain types of experiences; to comprehend within self the quality of understanding which she is
looking for.*

*Obviously the understandings are already known within self but
the conscious mind needs to know them also, therefore, the experiences
keep attracting themselves to her. When she recognizes the kind of understandings that she desires, would suggest then that she keep them firmly
within the mind, using that will which is so strong within herself to project
into that understanding of purpose and to keep within that understanding,
never moving or backing away from it, never withdrawing from it. She will
find that all those experiences that she feels or fears will be difficult, but
that she has the ability to control them and to come out of them with deeper
understanding.*

*Would also suggest that she begin to apply the advice given, to
record in the memory certain kinds of advice given that cause a ringing
within her mind or the feeling that this is a message that she has heard
before, for indeed a particular kind of message being given to this one has
been projected to her before during that time repeatedly, and this message
has to do with a certain type of development that is potentially hers and
would be of much benefit to those around her who are at a different level of
progression at present. [51475119303]*

For many of us, it is time to complete what we began in Atlantis, to unite the soul and find
freedom in responsibility. Now more than ever we long to experience truth. To rise above
terror we must go beyond reasoning. At last we are ready to know.

Without doubt the attacks on the World Trade Center and the U.S. Pentagon on
September 11th affected the entire world. Just as the perceived ending of Atlantis did.

By the final destruction of what had been Atlantis, the integration of the Atlantean
people was well in place. The world was becoming a melting pot through the mixing of
the races. Atlanteans had emigrated throughout the world and the Earth as a classroom
had begun. Here we would mature our souls. Here we would learn the lessons to evolve,
to grow, to become enlightened.

So the spirit that is the United States of America is to integrate the world. This
place – of all people, races, religions, nationalities – is the world in microcosm, the world
as it will someday be.

This place of diversity works because of what we have in common and that goes all the way back to our founding fathers and to the Greek philosophers and to the ancient Egyptians and to the Atlanteans.

It was in these days that I realized anew the awesome covenant School of Metaphysics teachers put together back in 1996. I had often referred to it as the most perfect document ever penned by human man. I have read many proclamations and declarations of brotherhood and goodwill. Most are filled with negating language, as if talking about all the things something is not will free the positive truth of what it is.

The *Universal Peace Covenant* was written over nine months by more than two dozen people whose roots span the globe. Because of this, the covenant reflects the hopes and aspirations of young and old, rich and poor, educated and illiterate, master and apprentice, religious and secular. It is the plea and promise of humanity as we stand on the threshold of spiritual renaissance. It was written from a vision of what can be, from a desire to create and live Intuitive, Spiritual Man, and therein is its majesty.

Every word in the *Universal Peace Covenant* contains a picture, an image communicating to the inner self. It is my desire that every person who knows of the Covenant share it with others until everyone on the planet has heard it. Here is the Covenant in its entirety.

Universal Peace Covenant

Peace is the breath of our spirit.
It wells up from within the depths of our being to refresh, to heal, to inspire.

Peace is our birthright. Its eternal presence exists within us as a memory of where we have come from and as a vision of where we yearn to go.

Our world is in the midst of change.
For millennia, we have contemplated, reasoned, and practiced the idea of peace. Yet the capacity to sustain peace eludes us. To transcend the limits of our own thinking we must acknowledge that peace is more than the cessation of conflict. For peace to move across the face of the Earth we must realize, as the great philosophers and leaders before us, that all people desire peace. We hereby acknowledge this truth that is universal. Now humanity must desire those things that make for peace.

We affirm that peace is an idea whose time has come.
We call upon humanity to stand united, responding to the need for
peace. We call upon each individual to create and foster a personal
vision for peace. We call upon each family to generate and nurture
peace within the home. We call upon each nation to encourage and
support peace between its citizens. We call upon each leader, be they
in the home, place of worship or labor, to be a living example of peace
for only in this way can we expect peace to move across the face of the
Earth.

World peace begins within ourselves.
It arises from the spirit seeking expression through the mind, heart,
and body of each individual. Government and laws cannot heal the
heart. We must transcend whatever separates us. Through giving
love and respect, dignity and comfort, we come to know peace. We
learn to love our neighbors as we love ourselves bringing peace into
the world. We hereby commit ourselves to this noble endeavor.

Peace is first a state of mind.
Living peaceably begins by thinking peacefully. Peace affords the
greatest opportunity for growth and learning which leads to personal
happiness. Self-direction promotes inner peace and therefore leads
to outer peace. We vow to heal ourselves through forgiveness,
gratitude, and prayer. We commit to causing each and every day to
be a fulfillment of our potential, both human and divine.

Peace requires peaceful action.
It is not made in documents but in the minds and hearts of men and
women. Peace is built through communication. The open exchange
of ideas is necessary for discovery, for well-being, for growth, for
progress whether within one person or among many. We vow to
speak with sagacity, listen with equanimity, both free of prejudice,
thus we will come to know that peace is liberty in tranquility.

Peace is achieved by those who fulfill their part of a greater plan.
Peace and security are attained by those societies where the individu-
als work closely to serve the common good of the whole. Peaceful
coexistence between nations is the reflection of man's inner tranquil-

ity magnified. Enlightened service to our fellowman brings peace to the one serving, and to the one receiving. We vow to live in peace by embracing truths that apply to us all.

We stand on the threshold of peace-filled understanding. We come together, all of humanity, young and old of all cultures from all nations. We vow to stand together as citizens of the Earth knowing that every question has an answer, every issue a resolution. As we stand, united in common purpose, we hereby commit ourselves in thought and action so we might know the power of peace in our lifetimes.

May peace be with us all ways.

May Peace Prevail On Earth.

More than one person said in that week following September 11, 2001 that time would be measured by *before* and *after*. It was a defining moment for the United States, like the bombing of Pearl Harbor or the assassination of John Kennedy, where we discover individually and collectively who we are.

In this way the events of that day remind me of Atlantis – the time *before* when our spirits were free to come and go at will, and the time *after* since our spirits have been tethered to a glowing ball whirling in space.

Perhaps this new marker of time will be a beginning of the raising of consciousness our founding fathers believed in. May we live the vision so we can know the coming of Intuitive, Spiritual Man.

CONCLUSION

I realize this book may upset the apple cart of many people's world views.

The religionist may need to revise their ideas that God created the physical body of man (the thinker) and humanity. This revision may still include the idea that God created the souls or I AM in people's bodies.

The evolutionist may need to revise their ideas about Homo sapiens arising from natural (nature) selection and by accident of mutation. Darwinism may have to be revised.

The Egyptologist will need to revise their ideas of Egyptian civilization. They will need to realize the Egyptians civilization is many thousands of years, and yes, in fact, the Egyptian civilization is many tens of thousands of years older than they thought.

The geologists will need to revise their assumptions about uniformitarianism. They will need to realize that continental drift and Earth changes do not always proceed at the same physical time rate.

The cosmologists will need to revise their assumptions about uniformitarianism for much the same reason as geologists. The solar system was not created from the beginning to be as it is now. In fact, some of the planets formed much later than others.

The anthropologists will need to change their assumptions that Homo sapiens arose from proto-Human or ape-like creatures. They will need to recognize the off-world influence.

Archeologists will need to come to see the prehistory of the Earth in a new light. They will need to gain the perspective on dinosaurs to realize from the material in this book that dinosaurs were more mineral than animal. They will also need to realize that humans or intelligent beings have been influencing this planet for hundreds of thousands of years more than thought previously.

In short, it is time for a new world view. An understanding that thought is cause and nothing happens by chance. Intelligent thought from the Creator, from other star systems and from enlightened beings of humanity have always been guiding mankind's evolution.

We are evolving into our next stage which is a more crystalline rather than carbon-based body.

Planet Earth and its inhabitants are moving into a higher dimension of consciousness.

I would like to once again thank my beautiful wife Barbara without which this work, this gift to the world, would not have been possible. The two of us working as a team combined our 50 years of experience, training, and teaching of the Mind and the power of the mind to bring this truth and Light to the world.

The vehicle of the School of Metaphysics, this not-for-profit institute of which we are a part, continues to educate millions of beings to develop their minds. This then is leading to and helping to bring about the Christing of planet Earth, the evolvement of consciousness to enlightenment.

APPENDICES

APPENDIX I

I (Daniel) thought it best to include this knowledge in an appendix. Although it is not about the Human Race or Homo sapiens specifically, in general and universally, this knowledge is very important to the future of mankind.

The dolphins are intelligent beings though they have somewhat of a different consciousness than unevolved human beings. Yet many consider them to be the most intelligent species on the planet, after the Homo sapiens. Dolphins have shown a great affinity throughout history for humans. Dolphins especially love or show a great interest in human infants sending their sonar beams through them, aiding their nervous systems to be healthy, to mature, and to evolve.

The more one evolves or grows in consciousness, the more one perceives and understands there to be greater connectedness in the universe and, in fact, in all things.

The more unevolved one is, or to put it another way, the more engrossed and entrapped in the five senses and physical body one is, the more one views everything in one's life and universe as separate and isolated. This is illusion. This is falsity. This in India is referred to as Maya.

The five senses, being limited in perception, fool the person into thinking he is no more than a physical body and only what he perceives with the five senses of sight, hearing, smell, taste, and touch is the extent of reality. This is not true. There are many rates of vibration of Light that are not visible to the five senses. Infrared and ultraviolet are but two of these.

The dolphins live in a connected consciousness. Their consciousness extends beyond themselves to each other and beyond planet Earth to their home planet, the planet of their origin.

WATER PEOPLE - Dolphins

The Dogon people, an African tribe, tell in their history of a spaceship that arrived from a dogstar and dolphin people came out and taught them. You will relate concerning this.

We see that previous to Atlantean time there was the exploration of this planet throughout the Lemurian and Mu time periods of those energy forms which could live within water, of all types and all temperatures. We see that they were quite mobile in terms of the capacity to live in any kind of environment. This is not the only group of people who encountered these ones.

Did these people stay on Earth, did they continue to reside? Are they here today?

     No with the way the Earth changed there was not the sustainability. Some of them returned to their home. Ones who stayed did not survive all the Atlantean movements that occurred.

What was their home?

     Canis. (401bgc/drc)

Canis Major and Canis Minor (Latin for "great dog" and "lesser dog") are constellations lying respectively southeast and east of Orion and separated by the Milky Way. Canis Major contains Sirius, the brightest star in the sky. Canis Minor contains Procyon, which is far less bright than Sirius, but still a first magnitude star. In midsummer, Sirius rises at dawn and many of the Egyptian temples are in alignment with this.

     Could it possibly be that the founders of the Egyptian civilization and the dolphins share a commonality, a connectedness; one group being from Canis Major and the other from Canis Minor?

The dolphins of the oceans today. Are they an evolvement of this planet or did they come from another planet?

     They are actually an evolvement from these ones who mutated enough to continue to survive. Their capacity to live at different forms was sacrificed for the mutations that needed to come about in order for it to be sustained.

What is the level of intelligence of the dolphins today?

     It is connected with the home planet. It is different than other forms that exist on Earth. It is synergistic. It is still connected although their form is not, but they maintain it within their being.

Are they aware of this connection?

     Yes.

Are the people on the other planet aware of the connection here?

     Yes.

Are dolphins sapient beings?

Yes.

Whales...Are they a development from this planet or another planet?

They are relative to the dolphin. It is not the same.

What is the difference?

There was some mutation. A kind of intermingling of forms that did discontinue the connection that the dolphin form maintains.

Connection to the home planet?

Yes. And in large part to others of like species.

Is this mutation from interbreeding with other animals forms from this planet or...

Yes. (401bgc/drc)

As each individual gains enlightenment and makes the shift into a more connected and expansive consciousness, we will experience a greater understanding, oneness, and connectedness with the dolphins. They may be our long lost cousins.

Just as Homo sapiens came from the development and changing of native species in order to give vehicles or bodies for those of the Beldane and those of Sirius, we were the dolphins.

The dolphins were developed as a way to survive and thrive on planet Earth in the oceans instead of on the land. They were developed by intelligent beings with a different kind of consciousness than Humans. They retained, and have maintained, a connected consciousness. Their technology is a mental technology unlike humans which went the physical route and developed physical technology.

APPENDIX II

This section gives a brief description of the development of the solar system. Some of the knowledge is already known or deduced. Some may be new to you, the reader.

One of the fascinating particles of knowledge is the awareness that the planet Mercury was originally a part or particle of the planet Uranus for conventional uniformistic scientific thinking believes that each planet developed on its own, in its current orbit, from condensations of early proto matter, substance or plasm in what would become our solar system. The intuitive reports tell a different story.

Another insight is that Venus and Earth were once one albeit while they were still in energetic form. In other words, this was before they coalesced into solid planets as we know them today.

Far from being a dead planet, Mars is evolving or going through its planetary cycle at a slower rate than planet Earth. This could indicate a wonderful opportunity for earthlings, or Homo sapiens to not only colonize Mars but to terraform it. Instead of trying to breathe life into a dead planet, we will be quickening and helping along a process that is already occurring much like the Xena, Centaurus, Beldane, and Siriuns did with planet Earth.

There are, however, two very large differences:

1. Mars has already been visited by the Siriuns who built the face on Mars and the pyramid and tetrahedron complex at Cydonia, Mars.

2. There is already life on Mars, and it is oxygen-based, not carbon-based.

Therefore, Earthlings who explore the planet Mars will have to be aware of that fact. Otherwise, they may destroy this wonderful form of life out of sheer ignorance.

What is the history of the solar system?

This particular segment is as a molecule with its magnetic center that does capture and include into its expression other elements and this is as the sun and its planets are.

What is the history of the planet Mercury?

Most of what are called planets have been thrown off at one time or another from the original star which is called the Sun. We see the growth of the planet themselves have been the development of, in some cases, other spatial material, space debris as it might be called, that enabled there to be a focal point upon which there could be the workings of polarity that would be strong enough to sustain itself. Mercury actually was a particle from that which is referred to as Uranus.

How long ago did this occur?

There is no measurement for time.

What is the history of the planet Venus?

At one time, the substance, the energy that forms Earth and Venus was one. There was a splitting between the two.

What caused this split?

A vibrational frequency that would be best described as a kind of sound.

What was the source of this sound?

It was moving through space, like a wave.

What is the history of the planet Mars?

This was a kind of twin planet of the combination of the Earth and Venus when it first began to form. Once the division between that which is currently known as Venus and Earth occurred, then there was a speeding of rotation for a period of time in the movement of magnetism; therefore, the Earth evolved quicker than that which is referred to as Mars. (42601bgc/drc)

Here is presented the fact that the rotation of a planet is related to its magnetic field. As the Earth slows in its rotation, and it is slowing down, so the magnetic field is reduced. The magnetic field of Earth is getting weaker and weaker at an accelerating rate. For more on this see the book Zero Point by Gregg Braden.

Why does Mars seem to be devoid of atmosphere today since Earth was evolving quicker?

Part of this is due to the lack of extraterrestrial involvement. Part of it is a different kind of life form that has not been interpreted upon this planet. Part of it is potential energy that has yet to express. It is all these factors.

As on Earth there is carbon-based life, what is life based on on Mars?

Oxygen-based. (42601bgc/drc)

The giant red spot on Jupiter is a sending and receiving station for energies. This has been figured out by Richard Hoagland scientifically. It is the basis of a new science. Refer to Hoagland's The Monuments of Mars for more.

One of the most fascinating facts about the solar system given in this book is that Pluto is a satellite and therefore a moon. Pluto is a satellite of an energetic form. Therefore, if scientists wish to discover this extra planet in the solar system that they know is out there and have been unable to find, they will need to search with different methods. Instead of using visual telescopes, they will need to use equipment that detects different types of energy radiation searching the LIGHT spectrum until it is located.

The amplified energy between the Sun and Venus could be tapped by humanity as an inexhaustible source of non-polluting energy. Science could investigate this possibility.

What is the history of the asteroid belt?

At the time when the first expansion of the star exploded, there were portions that were thrown off and trapped in a type of gravitational field of the star itself. As it compacted they were almost brought back and we see that this was part of it, that referred to as Jupiter, Saturn, Uranus and Neptune were all part of this as well. There was also another significant chunk that was captive but no longer exists.

Captive by who?

The gravitational pull of the Sun.

What is the history of Jupiter?

Its origin has just been stated.

What is the cause of the giant red spot?

It is a sending and receiving station area, for energies.

From where to where? By whom, for what?

This is not known. It is not identifiable.

What is the history of Pluto?

Pluto is a satellite.

Of what?

Not determined. It is an energetic form however that doesn't have a core.

What is its substance made of?

Enough to sustain a form. Substance itself is not known. (42601bgc/drc)

APPENDIX III

Crop circles are a means by which the Earth communicates growing awareness and consciousness to the universe. People can use these to understand the universal constants of consciousness and creation. Some of these universal constants are the Pythagorean or Platonic solids, PI, PHI and other forms and relationships that are together known as sacred geometry.

What is the relationship of crop circles to the Earth and the evolution of humanity and other intelligences?

These have become a means by which there can be communication in an energetic sense within the Earth itself. This is an expression of energy from the Earth that at times is mimicked by others who are not of the planet, but more often it springs from the planet itself.

This is a communication to human beings?

It is becoming so, the impetus is not this. It is a communication to others who are beyond the planet.

Of what?

Of development. It could be seen as an expression of consciousness, a code or reflection of the point of evolution.

What is a master key, a key to unlocking this code? Understanding it?

It is within most cultures. It is within the Mayan calendar and the texts of the Maya. It is in the Sephiroth. It is in the I Ching. It is within many of the universally sound structures that have existed within the planet for ages. (71201bgc/drc)

There are in this universe certain universal symbols or codes of creation. The Platonic solids are one. The Fibonacci series is another. Phi may be expressed as the ratio of the numbers in the Fibonacci series. To illustrate the Fibonacci series:

0, 1, 1, 2, 3, 5, 6, 13, 21, 34, 55, 89, 144

Each number is the sum of the previous two numbers. For example, $1 + 1 = 2$. $1 + 2 = 3$. $2 + 3 = 5$. $3 + 5 = 8$. $5 + 8 = 13$. And so on.

It turns out that as you divide the next higher number into the next lower number that you approach the figure .618. This number, called phi, is the Golden Ratio or Golden Mean and was the basis upon which all ancient sacred structures were built, such as the Great Pyramid of Giza.

Phi governs all life on Earth, the branching of trees and roots, lightening branches, and water movement as well as human body proportions.

Other universal codes of creation include Pi and the prime numbers sequence. These are universal symbols that indicate universal constants on this planet.

Crop circles can be and need to be investigated in this manner to discover the universal messages of awakening and progressing consciousness that our planet Earth is giving us.

Just as one person or soul inhabiting a physical body can talk with, listen to, and communicate with another soul in a physical body, so can our planet Earth communicate, listen to, speak to other intelligent planets and stars, and does so.

The I Ching is a universal message giver. It comes from China. The Mayan calendar and texts of Maya are Universal Message givers from the Mayan of Yucatan, southern Mexico and Central America.

The Sephiroth or Tree of Life is a universal message giver of the Egyptians and, through them, to the Hebrews. It explains or gives the message of the movement of LIGHT and SOUND or vibration as it manifests through the Higher Dimensions or inner levels of Mind. The LIGHT and vibration of creation needed to be slowed down to a vibrational frequency perceivable to one or more of the five senses in order to be used for learning and growth by human and reasoning man. The universal decoders of creation help us to understand our part and place in creation. There are others.

These ancient texts or secret teaching come first from the Xena, Centaurus, Beldane, and Siriuns. They are still with us today. This is why so much of the very ancient thinking process, technology, and life seem alien to us today. They came from aliens.

By understanding these gifts of Universal Truths, we can today build mental technology to quicken and accelerate our soul growth and spiritual development or we can build physical technology to take us to the stars. A book called <u>The Gift</u>: <u>Crop Circles Deciphered</u> tells the story of the author Doug Ruby. He used the pictures taken of crop circles to build a three-dimensional model of a spaceship.

He is now in the process of finding a new crop circle that will give him the means of propulsion.

For supplemental information on selected topics in this book:

Egypt
Serpent in the Sky: High Wisdom of Ancient Egypt by John Anthony West
copyright 1993, The Theosophical Publishing House, Wheaton, Illinois

Le Temple de l'Homme 3 volumes by Swaller de Lubiz
copyright 1993 by Theosophical Publishing House, Wheaton, Illinois

Atlantis
Atlantis: Antediluvian World by Ignatius Donnelly
copyright 1882, Harper & Brothers, New York, NY. copyright 1976, Dover Publications, New York, NY

Indigo Children
The Indigo Children by Lee Carroll and Jan Tober
copyright 1999 by Hay House, Carlsbad, California

History
Forbidden Archaeology by Michael Cremo and Richard Thompson
copyright 1994, Govardhan Hill Publishing, Badger, CA

America B.C. by Berry Fell
copyright 1989, Pocket Books, New York, NY

The Bible Code by Michael Drosnin
copyright 1997, Simon & Shuster, New York, NY

Sacred Architecture by A. T. Mann
copyright 1993, Barnes & Noble/Element Books, New York, NY

A Brief History of Science by John Gribbin
copyright 1998, Barnes & Noble/Ivy Press Limited, New York, NY

History of the World by Marvin Perry, Scholl, Davis, Harris, Von Laue
copyright 1993, Houghton Mifflin Company, Boston, Massachusetts

Civilizations of the World: The Human Adventure by Richard L. Greaves, Zaller, Cannistraro, and Murphey
copyright 1997, Addison-Wesley Educational Publishers Inc.

Fibonacci series
The Essence of the Cabalah by William Eisen
copyright 1984, Devorss & Company, Marina Del Rey, CA

The Ancient Secret of the Flower of Life by Drunvalo Melchizedek
copyright 1998 by Light Technology Publishing, Flagstaff, Arizona

Crop Circles
The Gift: Crop Circles Deciphered by Doug Ruby
copyright 1997, Blue Note Books, Cape Canaveral, Florida

Earth/Consciousness Changes
Awakening to Zero Point by Gregg Braden
copyright 1997, Radio Bookstore Press, Bellevue, Washington

America's Secret Destiny by Heironomus
copyright 1989, Destiny Books, Rochester, Vermont

The Monuments of Mars by Richard Hoagland
copyright 1987, North Atlantic Books

Tesla: Man out of Time by Margaret Cheney
copyright 1981, Simon & Schuster, New York, NY

Also recommended the works of: Emmanuel Swedenborg, Rudolf Steiner, Nicola Tesla, Royal Rife.

About the Authors

As mankind approaches a higher consciousness, there has arisen a need to know the truth. Daniel and Barbara Condron have devoted this life to bringing a greater truth, a more enlightened consciousness to this planet.

Individually, their paths have paralleled. They were both raised in Missouri, attended the University of Missouri then studied with the School of Metaphysics. Both have served as a teacher, director, field director, and as president of this visionary school which openly teaches the application of the secret wisdom of the ages. Over the past three decades, Daniel and Barbara have touched millions through books and radio-television appearances.

Daniel's lifelong interest and love of history was the seed for **Remembering Atlantis**. His favorite subject in high school was ancient world history. Throughout his life he has studied and researched the way in which energies move across the planet. This is why he majored in agricultural economics. As part of his Masters work he lived in Peru where he experienced vibrational history of Macchu Picchu.

Barbara's early years were rich in Biblical teachings. Her family lived with her grandfather, a Pentecostal faith healer, until the age of 12. This set her course to find the common ground of religion and science, heart and head, intuition and reasoning. Her desire to continually learn about people and life led her to leave home and major in journalism. Although she would find this education useful in the years to come, her desire would be fulfilled through studying, practicing, and teaching metaphysics – how to live within the universal laws and truths governing creation.

Daniel and Barbara trained with disciplined effort to become a conductor and reporter, respectively, for intuitive research. By 1978 they were traveling across the country offering the Intuitive Health Analyses and Past Life Profiles the School of Metaphysics has pioneered. In the 1990's their lives came together and some of what led to their current intuitive research is detailed in this book.

The Condrons have been an active part of developing an intuitive database for a quarter of a century. This database of over 100,000 intuitive reports accessed from the Akashic Records is the largest volume of intuitive research on planet Earth. Going beyond the limits encountered by physical research, the Akashic records expand our knowledge enabling us to include Atlantis and Mu (Lemuria) in our world history and offering unlimited possibilities for answers to mankind's most pressing questions.

Through intuitive research taught at the School of Metaphysics, Subconscious wisdom can be paired with Conscious reasoning giving humanity a depth and breadth of knowledge. The Intuitive investigations documented here reveal more than just an expansion of humanity's knowledge of the past. They share truths of our collective destiny. Daniel and Barbara continue to dedicate their lives to the understanding and fulfillment of this destiny.

Currently, Daniel serves as Chancellor of the College of Metaphysics in Missouri and Barbara as Governor of International Education which includes the School of Metaphysics' MultiDimensional Living programs. Their innovations as leaders and teachers have made them respected and sought-after speakers, both are recognized in Who's Who in America and Who's Who in the World, and their unparalleled intuitive research is daily forging new horizons to help us understand ourselves, our world, and the place we hold in all of Creation.

Society ᶠᵒʳ Intuitive Research

Want to learn more about Atlantis?

We are actively creating a means by which people across the planet can have this information readily available. In 2002, the School of Metaphysics is launching the Society for Intuitive Research. The Society will be a fellowship of scientists, artists, clergymen, leaders, parents, craftsmen, business people, united by a common urge to know.

The School of Metaphysics possesses the most extensive records of intuitive research on the planet. Now we are actively assimilating this vast knowledge into the most exciting science yet conceived. The new science of intuitive research has already answered individuals' most pressing questions...

What is my purpose in life? How can I regain and sustain good health? How can I fulfill my mission? What do I need to do to attract love and friendship? How can I reach deeper states of meditation? What is my creative potential? Have I lived before, when and where? Did I accomplish what I set out to? How can I disconnect self-defeating thoughts and behaviors? How can I become closer to the Creator?

Now we are exploring the universal ones.

We invite you to join us as we learn the lessons the past offers to live today in such a way as to bring about the promise of the future, the Christing of planet Earth. Every month members receive detailed accounts of School of Metaphysics research - past and present - to add to their home libraries. These are invaluable resources for professionals in every field.

Excerpts cover every area of human endeavor. Whether it's the elements of wholistic health or spiritualizing marriage and career, whether insights into the force of karma in our lives or the radiance of dharma, these excerpts and interpretations are fascinating, revelatory, and personally rewarding. Become a Spiritual Activist by learning and by helping fund this unique research. Join the Society for Intuitive Research today, write us at School of Metaphysics World Headquarters, 163 Moon Valley Road, Windyville, Missouri 65783 USA. Or go to our website at www.som.org

Additional titles available from SOM Publishing include:

Interpreting Dreams for Self Discovery
Dr. Laurel Clark & Paul Blosser ISBN: 0944386-25-3 $12.00

Karmic Healing
Dr. Laurel Clark ISBN: 0944386-26-1 $15.00

The Bible Interpreted in Dream Symbols
Drs. Condron, Condron, Matthes, Rothermel
ISBN: 0944386-23-7 $18.00

Spiritual Renaissance
Elevating Your Conciousness for the Common Good
Dr. Barbara Condron ISBN: 0944386-22-9 $15.00

Superconscious Meditation
Kundalini & the Understanding of the Whole Mind
Dr. Daniel R. Condron ISBN 0944386-21-0 $13.00

First Opinion: Wholistic Health Care in the 21st Century
Dr. Barbara Condron ISBN 0944386-18-0 $15.00

The Dreamer's Dictionary
Dr. Barbara Condron ISBN 0944386-16-4 $15.00

The Work of the Soul
Dr. Barbara Condron, ed. ISBN 0944386-17-2 $13.00

Uncommon Knowledge Past Life & Health Readings
Dr. Barbara Condron, ed. ISBN 0944386-19-9 $13.00

The Universal Language of Mind
The Book of Matthew Interpreted
Dr. Daniel R. Condron ISBN 0944386-15-6 $13.00

Permanent Healing

Dr. Daniel R. Condron   ISBN 0944386-12-1 $9.95

Dreams of the Soul - The Yogi Sutras of Patanjali

Dr. Daniel R. Condron   ISBN 0944386-11-3 $13.00

Kundalini Rising

Mastering Your Creative Energies

Dr. Barbara Condron   ISBN 0944386-13-X $13.00

Upcoming titles...

Spiritual Science of Dreaming

The Tao Te Ching in the Universal Language of Mind

How to Raise an Indigo Child

Multidimensional Living - Experiencing Cosmic Consciousness Now

To order write:

School of Metaphysics

World Headquarters

163 Moon Valley Road

Windyville, Missouri 65783   U.S.A.

Enclose a check or money order payable in U.S. funds to SOM with any order. Please include $4.00 for postage and handling of books, $8 for international orders.

A complete catalogue of all book titles, audio lectures and courses, and videos is available upon request.

Visit us on the Internet at *http://www.som.org*

e-mail: som@som.org

About the School of Metaphysics

We invite you to become a special part of our efforts to aid in enhancing and quickening the process of spiritual growth and mental evolution of the people of the world. The School of Metaphysics, a not-for-profit educational and service organization, has been in existence for three decades. During that time, we have taught tens of thousands directly through our course of study in applied metaphysics. We have elevated the awareness of millions through the many services we offer. If you would like to pursue the study of mind and the transformation of Self to a higher level of being and consciousness, you are invited to write to us at the School of Metaphysics World Headquarters in Windyville, Missouri 65783.

The heart of the School of Metaphysics is a four-tiered course of study in mastering consciousness. Lessons introduce you to the Universal Laws and Truths which guide spiritual and physical evolution. Consciousness is explored and developed through mental and spiritual disciplines which enhance your physical life and enrich your soul progression. For every concept there is a means to employ it through developing your own potential. Level One includes concentration, visualization (focused imagery), meditation, and control of life force and creative energies, all foundations for exploring the multidimensional Self.

Experts in the Universal Language of Mind, we teach how to remember and understand the inner communication received through dreams. We are the sponsors of the National Dream Hotline®, an annual educational service offered the last weekend in April. Study centers are located throughout the Midwestern United States. If there is not a center near you, you can receive the first series of lessons through correspondence with a teacher at our headquarters.

For those desiring spiritual renewal, weekends at our Moon Valley Ranch offer calmness and clarity. Full Spectrum™ training is given during these Spiritual Focus Weekends. Each weekend focuses on a ray that corresponds to a level of consciousness, an energy transformer, and a quality of thinking. More than a traditional class or seminar, these gatherings are experiences in multidimensional awareness.

The Universal Hour of Peace was initiated by the School of Metaphysics on October 24, 1995 in conjunction with the 50th anniversary of the United Nations. We believe that peace on earth is an idea whose time has come. To realize this dream, we invite you to join with others throughout the world by dedicating your thoughts and actions to peace for one hour beginning at 11:30 p.m. December 31st into the first day of January each year. Living peaceably begins by thinking peacefully. We invite SOMA members to convene Circles of Love in their cities during this hour. Please contact us about how you can become a Peace Correspondent.

There is the opportunity to aid in the growth and fulfillment of our work. Donations supporting the expansion of the School of Metaphysics' efforts are a valuable way for you to aid humanity. As a not-for-profit publishing house, SOM Publishing is dedicated to the continuing publication of research findings that promote peace, understanding and good will for all of Mankind. It is dependent upon the kindness and generosity of sponsors to do so. Authors donate their work and receive no royalties. We have many excellent manuscripts awaiting a benefactor.

One hundred percent of the donations made to the School of Metaphysics are used to expand our services. Donations are being received for Project Octagon an international center for multidimensional living. This proposed multipurpose structure will include an auditorium, classrooms, library and study areas, a cafeteria, and potential living quarters for up to 100 people. Donations to the School of Metaphysics are tax-exempt under 501(c)(3) of the Internal Revenue Code. We appreciate any contribution you are free to make. With the help of people like you, our dream of a place where anyone desiring Self awareness can receive education in mastering consciousness will become a reality.

We send you our Circle of Love.